Shifting the Balance

A BROOKINGS LATIN AMERICA INITIATIVE BOOK

Shifting the Balance

Obama and the Americas

Abraham F. Lowenthal
Theodore J. Piccone
Laurence Whitehead
editors

BROOKINGS INSTITUTION PRESS
Washington, D.C.

Library of Congress Cataloging-in-Publication data

Shifting the balance : Obama and the Americas / Abraham F. Lowenthal, Theodore J.
Piccone, and Laurence Whitehead, editors.
    p.   cm.
  Includes bibliographical references and index.
  ISBN 978-0-8157-0562-8 (pbk. : alk. paper)
  1. United States—Foreign relations—Latin America. 2. Latin America—Foreign
relations—United States. 3. United States—Foreign relations—2009– 4. Obama,
Barack. I. Lowenthal, Abraham F. II. Piccone, Theodore J. III. Whitehead, Laurence.
  JZ1480.A53S55 2010
  327.7308—dc22   2010041501

9 8 7 6 5 4 3 2 1

Printed on acid-free paper

Typeset in Minion

Composition by Cynthia Stock
Silver Spring, Maryland

Printed by R. R. Donnelley
Harrisonburg, Virginia

Contents

Foreword

The Obama administration has been in office nearly two years, long enough to determine its approach and priorities and to set them in motion. Although President Obama's approval ratings remain extraordinarily high in Latin America, there are some indications that the grace period is over. First, the pillars that the U.S. administration has set as priorities in its hemispheric agenda lack concrete and visible results. This is interpreted by many as disengagement. Second, and more important, political polarization in the United States—especially in regard to migration and trade—not only does not allow the agenda to move forward, but also has made many governments in Latin America worry about what lies ahead if Washington adopts an even more protectionist stance.

But there are also positive signs. As the authors of this book see it, while initial results are somewhat disappointing, the Obama administration has successfully shifted some policies and is using the language of collaboration and partnership rather than confrontation. Precisely because of this, the administration can build on specific opportunities for more constructive and effective relations with the diverse countries of the Americas.

Few administrations, and none in many decades, have inherited such a daunting agenda as has the Obama administration: a cascading and interconnected series of financial and economic problems; two prolonged, difficult, and unpopular wars; the continuing threat from international terrorists; the proliferation of weapons of mass destruction; global climate change and complex international negotiations to respond to this challenge; an impasse in world trade negotiations; international currency misalignments and rising protectionist measures; energy and food insecurity; crime and international trafficking of drugs, people, and arms; and the ever more complex management of relations with the Middle East, Europe, Russia, China, the South Asian subcontinent, and sub-Sahara Africa.

In this extraordinarily challenging context, few observers expected the incoming administration to devote much attention to relations with the countries of the Americas. They do not present direct and immediate challenges to U.S. security, nor are they a major source or target of international terrorism. Their economies are bouncing back well from the global recession, and poverty and inequality are decreasing.

Here at Brookings, the Latin America Initiative is focused on how U.S. relations with the region could be improved in such a complex environment. The region may not pose imminent security threats, but it is every year more important for the day-to-day welfare and longer-term interests of the United States, because these near neighbors are increasingly intertwined with their northern neighbor; they are important markets for U.S. exports; many of them can play decisive roles in confronting global challenges from energy development to climate change, global trade and governance, public health and narcotics. With these points in mind, Brookings in 2008 convened a Partnership of the Americas Commission to provide forward-looking recommendations for the incoming administration on these and related issues.

As part of that effort, we also commissioned a symposium volume of essays by leading experts from Latin America, Europe, and the United States. The resulting book, *The Obama Administration and the Americas: Agenda for Change*—coedited by Abraham F. Lowenthal, Theodore J. Piccone, and Laurence Whitehead and published on the eve of the Summit of the Americas that took place in Port of Spain, Trinidad and Tobago, in April 2009—was a timely and well-received contribution to a more balanced and constructive rethinking of U.S. policies. The summit's atmosphere was suffused with high expectations, as the new administration's leading officials, including the president himself, projected an image of openness toward a new era of mutual respect and partnership on common challenges, echoing many of the recommendations for change coming from the Partnership for the Americas Commission, the edited volume, and other reports calling for revised approaches.

Eighteen months later, in October 2010, many observers, both in Latin America and in the United States, have expressed disappointment with the follow-up to the summit and with U.S. policy on a number of issues: the coup in Honduras, the military presence in Colombia, the Copenhagen climate change negotiations, bilateral and global trade agreements, immigration reform, relations with Cuba, policy on narcotics, and the vexing issue of the Guantánamo detention center.

What accounts for the Obama administration's surprising early focus on Latin America and then for its disappointing follow-up? How are the region's problems evolving, and what challenges do or will they pose for Washington? What opportunities still exist for meaningful inter-American cooperation? What steps can and should the Obama administration undertake at this stage, both regionally and in a host of critical countries from Mexico and Haiti to Brazil and Venezuela?

These are the important questions addressed in this timely and forward-looking volume of updated and new chapters covering regional strategy and a more in-depth look at seven countries. Lowenthal, Piccone, and Whitehead, three seasoned and respected analysts, again have assembled an excellent group of experts, including some of the region's most respected observers as well as younger scholars just beginning to gain international recognition. Taken together, these essays provide a highly informed, richly nuanced, and constructive guide to the challenges and opportunities of inter-American relations today. A companion volume is currently available in Spanish published by Planeta and will be released later in Portuguese by Fundação Getúlio Vargas.

The Latin American Initiative is grateful to the ongoing and generous support of its work from Liberty Mutual. The editors are also grateful to Emily Alinikoff, Alexandra Barahona de Brito, and Carrie McCaskill for their invaluable research assistance and coordination; Janet Walker and Vicky Macintyre for their careful editorial direction and guidance; and Martin Indyk, Steven Bennett, Kemal Dervis, and Strobe Talbott for their enduring leadership and support.

Mauricio Cardenas
Senior Fellow and Director, Latin America Initiative
The Brookings Institution

one
The Obama Administration and the Americas

Abraham F. Lowenthal

Barack Obama entered the U.S. presidency with a daunting agenda. At home he faced deep economic recession, a near collapse of the country's financial institutions, rising unemployment, decaying infrastructure, a dysfunctional health insurance system, and countless other accumulated problems. Abroad he inherited two costly and unpopular wars, the continuing threat from al Qaeda, dangerous confrontations with North Korea and Iran, strained relations with Russia, multiple challenges from a rising China, the specter of implosion in Pakistan, the festering Israel-Palestine impasse, the looming dangers of climate change, pandemics, and nuclear proliferation—and much more.

Few observers predicted, therefore, that the Obama administration would devote much attention to Latin America and the Caribbean. None of the region's countries poses an imminent threat to U.S. national security. None seems likely to be a source or target of significant international terrorism.

During the campaign, moreover, Senator Obama said little about Latin America. He confined himself to one dedicated speech on the region (to a Cuban American organization in Miami), a proposal to appoint a special ambassador for the Americas, suggestions during the "Rust Belt" primary

An edited and condensed version of this essay appears in *Foreign Affairs* 4 (July–August 2010, 110–24). I appreciate helpful comments on an earlier draft from Marcel Biato, Kevin Casas-Zamora, Richard Downie, Daniel Erikson, Jorge Heine, Jane Jaquette, Carlos Malamud, Cynthia McClintock, Alister McIntyre, Jennifer McCoy, Michael O'Hanlon, Theodore Piccone, Christopher Sabatini, Thomas Shannon, Michael Shifter, and Laurence Whitehead.

campaigns that the North American Free Trade Agreement should be rene-
gotiated, and a few statements expressing reservations about the Colombia
and Panama free trade agreements pending ratification by the U.S. Senate.

After his election, however, Barack Obama and members of his administration quickly showed interest in Latin America and the Caribbean. As
president-elect, Mr. Obama met with only one foreign leader, Felipe Calderón of Mexico. His first foreign visitor to Camp David was Brazil's President
Luiz Inácio Lula da Silva. The new president also soon welcomed Chile's
President Michelle Bachelet and Colombia's Álvaro Uribe to Washington.
Secretary of State Hillary Rodham Clinton's first meeting with a foreign head
of state was with Haiti's President René Préval, and she then pushed success-
fully for expanded international assistance to Haiti. Vice President Joseph
Biden visited Chile and Costa Rica in March. Secretary Clinton, Attorney
General Eric Holder, Homeland Security Secretary Janet Napolitano, and
Michael Mullen, the chairman of the Joint Chiefs of Staff, all traveled to
Mexico by early April 2009, ahead of a trip by President Obama himself. All
were notably receptive to Mexican perspectives, and their visits were well
received.[1] The new administration also announced initiatives on Cuba, loosening restrictions on travel and remittances by Cuban Americans and opening up the possibility of U.S. investment in telecommunications networks
with the island. The president himself called for a "new beginning" in U.S.-
Cuba relations. The State Department began exploratory conversations with
Cuban officials on a potential postal service agreement and resumed long-
suspended bilateral consultations on migration.

No concrete actions were taken to approve the free trade agreements with
Colombia and Panama, but administration officials quickly backed away
from Mr. Obama's earlier skeptical posture. The president's announcement
that he would press for comprehensive immigration reform was greeted
warmly in Mexico, Central America and the Caribbean, and several South
American countries. And President Obama's participation in April 2009 at
the Fifth Summit of the Americas in Port of Spain, Trinidad and Tobago,
won praise throughout the Americas for his consultative manner and his
expressed interest in multilateral cooperation.

Why did the Obama administration take a strong initial interest in Latin
America and the Caribbean? What was the content and what were the sources
of its approaches? Are the Obama administration's policies in the Western
Hemisphere likely to take fuller shape, be implemented, and endure? Or
will they be attenuated or even abandoned, as has often happened to U.S.

policy initiatives toward Latin America in the past? What can and should the Obama administration do to improve U.S. policies toward and relations with Latin America and the Caribbean in the years ahead?

Putting Latin America on the U.S. Agenda

The main reason for the Obama administration's early engagement with Latin America was the new team's perception that even though the countries of Latin America and the Caribbean raise no urgent issues for the United States, some of them, especially Mexico, are increasingly important to America's future. This perception was driven home early by Mexico's deepening problems, marked by a surge in homicides and confrontations between the Mexican government and the narcotics cartels, some of them near the U.S. border. Mexico's abrupt economic downturn, a consequence of the U.S. crisis—exacerbated by the outbreak of the H1N1 virus—compounded a sense of urgency.[2] The Obama administration found itself faced with a choice: plan emergency efforts to quarantine the United States from troubles in Mexico, or devise a more effective partnership with Mexico in order to help deal with that country's problems and their implications for the United States.[3]

Growing concern about Mexico helped concentrate minds in Washington. The administration's commitment to attend the Trinidad and Tobago summit was a preexisting reason to pay attention to Latin America. Doing so was reinforced by a calculation that a change in U.S. attitudes and rhetoric would be welcomed in the region and could therefore produce a quick foreign policy success.

In focusing on Mexico and preparing for the summit, U.S. policymakers recognized that Latin America matters to the United States today for four main reasons:

First, the borders between the United States and its southern neighbors have blurred because of massive and sustained migration and growing economic integration. It is projected that growth in the size of the U.S. labor force from now until 2050 will be entirely due to immigrants and their descendants, mainly from Latin America and the Caribbean.[4] This demographic and economic interdependence has given rise to complex issues that have both international and domestic facets—the so-called "intermestic" questions—including narcotics, human and arms trafficking, health care, immigrants' remittances, driver's licenses, youth gangs, portable retirement pensions, drug trafficking and consumption, and bilingual education.[5] The

Obama administration knew from the start that it could not ignore these issues; the media focus on Mexico's troubles underlined their high salience for the U.S. public.

Second, Latin America matters economically to the United States as a prime source of energy and other key resources and as a major market for U.S. goods and services. The United States obtains nearly half of its energy imports from the countries of the Western Hemisphere, and more than half of these come from Latin American and Caribbean suppliers. There is great potential for expanded energy production in the Americas, from both renewable and nonrenewable sources.[6] The value of the goods and services the United States exported to Latin America in 2008 was $273 billion—20 percent of all U.S. exports, four times the value of U.S. exports to China, and about equal to U.S. exports to the European Community. U.S. firms still have a competitive advantage in Latin American markets, arising from proximity and familiarity plus demographic and cultural ties. Building upon this advantage in a region of expanding middle-class consumption is more pressing at a time of economic stress at home.

Third, Latin American nations are increasingly seen in Washington as critical for confronting such transnational issues as energy security, climate change, crime, narcotics trafficking, and public health. The new administration recognizes that these challenges cannot be managed effectively without close and sustained cooperation from several countries of the Americas— bilaterally, regionally, and in global forums.

Fourth, Latin Americans share important core values with North Americans, especially the commitment to human rights, including free political expression, effective democratic governance, and the rule of law. The broad normative commitment throughout Latin America to democratic governance and the rule of law is noteworthy, in spite of uneven practice. The Western Hemisphere remains a largely congenial neighborhood for the United States and its values in an international environment that is often hostile.[7]

The Legacy

When Obama took office, in January 2009, administration officials understood that despite Latin America's growing day-to-day significance for the United States, U.S. policies toward the region in recent years have often been ineffective and sometimes even counterproductive. The administrations of both Bill Clinton and George W. Bush emphasized showy Western Hemisphere summits to induce and demonstrate high-level governmental attention to Latin America, but these meetings typically produced little beyond photo opportunities, rhetoric, and an occasional new program or process of consultation. Both administrations continued to talk about a proposed Free Trade Area of the Americas (FTAA) long after that goal became unachievable. After the September 11, 2001, attacks, Washington came to view Latin America mainly through an international terrorism and security lens, and in these terms the region was a relatively low priority. Washington wasn't focusing on the issues Latin Americans themselves considered most important: poverty, education, income distribution, and citizen security.

Many Latin Americans resented Washington's perceived inattentiveness and felt that Washington was still following something of a cold war script. They rejected significant U.S. policies during the Bush years, including the Washington Consensus economic paradigm and especially the invasion of Iraq. Hugo Chávez of Venezuela took advantage of this sentiment by stepping up his flamboyant anti-U.S. rhetoric; he also sought favor in the region by boosting subsidized petroleum sales and other economic assistance to Central American and Caribbean nations; making a timely purchase of Argentine government bonds; cooperating closely with Cuba to furnish medical and other social services in many countries; and making bold promises to finance energy infrastructure projects in South America.

Many Latin American and Caribbean countries, meanwhile, have been strengthening subregional integration, in part through formal institutions, but even more through trade and investment, Latin America–based multinational corporations, and professional and business networks. Many South American countries engage actively in various regional and world forums. Venezuela established the Bolivarian Alliance for the Peoples of Our America (Alianza Bolivariana para los Pueblos de Nuestra América, or ALBA), with Bolivia, Ecuador, and eight Central American and Caribbean nations.[8] Brazil has taken a leading role in creating the Union of South American Nations (Unión de Naciones Suramericanas, or UNASUR) and the South American Defense Council. It is not yet clear how important these organizations will turn out to be in practice, but they clearly reflect a regional preference for intra–Latin American rather than Pan-American approaches.

Several countries—especially Brazil, Chile, Peru, Venezuela, Mexico, and Cuba—have been diversifying their international relationships beyond the Western Hemisphere, building ties with countries of the European Union, members of the Asia Pacific Economic Cooperation forum, and particularly with China, India, Russia, and Iran.[9] China has displaced the United States as the main export market for Brazil and Chile, and is expected to become Peru's main market in 2010. Brazil has developed a strategic alliance with India and South Africa, strengthened ties with the other so-called BRIC countries (BRIC stands for Brazil, Russia, India, and China), played a leading role in the G-20, the G-8, the Doha trade negotiations, and the Copenhagen talks on climate change, and offered itself as an intermediary in the Middle East and with Iran.

As the international activity and self-confidence of Latin American nations have grown, support for pan-American approaches to problem solving has waned. The Organization of American States (OAS) has often been ineffectual, and the Inter-American Democratic Charter has not produced many meaningful results. The Inter-American Development Bank has weakened in recent years, as liquidity in private international capital markets has increased, and as the Andean Development Corporation and the Brazilian National Bank for Economic and Social Development (BNDES) have gained importance. As extra-hemispheric actors have become more active and visible in Latin America, the influence of the U.S. government has been perceptibly declining. This was the state of inter-American relations that Barack Obama inherited.

Taking on U.S.-Latin American Relations

With its decisive electoral victory and evident mandate for change, the Obama administration took up Latin America policy as part of its overall efforts to "reset" U.S. foreign policy. Key advisers posited that the severe international economic crisis might make inter-American approaches more attractive once again in much of Latin America. They believed that clear signals of a strong U.S. interest in regional ties could therefore yield dividends. This initial premise undergirded the new administration's first steps in the Americas.

The administration sought to gain the confidence of the U.S. public, of Latin Americans, and of the rest of the international community through its resolve and ability to reverse the deterioration of the U.S. economy. How well it succeeds in this aim will be highly relevant in Latin America, especially to those countries in the northern tier (Mexico and the Caribbean and Central American nations) that are especially dependent on U.S. investment, remittances, tourism, and trade.

Instead of reverting to soaring rhetoric about building a partnership reaching from Alaska to Tierra del Fuego, the new administration emphasized that it would prefer to work with Latin American and Caribbean governments on a few issues that could be dealt with soon, if only partially, such as bolstering financial institutions, restoring credit and investment flows, and tackling the challenges of energy, the environment, and citizen security. The administration aimed to rebuild U.S. credibility without making promises it couldn't keep and creating unfulfillable expectations, by helping confront the underlying issues that have created space for Chávez and other radical populist movements.

Although it is a commonplace that Latin American countries always have been diverse, there has been a bipartisan tendency in Washington since 1990 to believe that convergence was occurring within the region toward democratic governance, market-oriented economics, and policies of macroeconomic balance. The U.S. policy community came to think of Latin American countries as mostly proceeding at different rates along the same path, with Chile blazing the trail. These convergent trends have been important (albeit sometimes exaggerated), but the Obama team recognizes that key differences still persist among the countries of Latin America and the Caribbean, and that some of these differences are growing. The most important differences lie primarily along five dimensions:

1. The level of demographic and economic interdependence with the United States

2. The degree and nature of openness to international economic competition

3. The strength of such key aspects of effective democratic governance as checks and balances, accountability, and the rule of law

4. The relative capacity of the state and of civil and political institutions beyond the state, such as political parties, the media, religious organizations, trade unions, and other nongovernmental entities

5. The extent to which the countries face the challenge of incorporating traditionally excluded populations, including more than 30 million marginalized, disadvantaged, and increasingly politically mobilized indigenous people, as well as Afro-Latin Americans and migrant workers.

Key U.S. officials understand that Latin American countries are moving on different trajectories and that their important structural differences need to be taken into account in U.S. policy. They recognize, therefore, that hemisphere-wide summits and broad regional initiatives are less likely to be effective than efforts that bring together smaller groups of variable composition, with comparable or complementary concerns.

Changing Washington's Mind-Sets

Within its first hundred days, the Obama administration set out to reshape five important mind-sets regarding Latin America policy.

The first was a change of focus from the "war on terrorism" to confronting broadly shared challenges more salient in Latin America: economic growth, jobs, socioeconomic equity, citizen security, energy, migration, health, democratic governance, and the rule of law.

Second was a shift in the approach to another metaphorical war—the "war on drugs": from concentrating on interdiction and eradication of supply to reducing demand and offering treatment to drug users in the United States.[10] The beginning of such a shift was suggested in the new administration's appointment as head of the U.S. Office of National Drug Policy (or "drug czar") of the former Seattle police chief Gil Kerlikowske, known for his emphasis on treating the drug problem as a public health, not a criminal, issue. The incipient new approach was reinforced by low-key steps, mainly at the state level, to decriminalize the use of marijuana for medicinal purposes, and indications that the Department of Justice would not oppose such steps. The Obama team also began to acknowledge the role the United States itself has played in fueling and facilitating both the drug trade and the associated traffic in small arms and bulk cash.[11]

Third was acceptance that some of the key issues affecting U.S.–Latin America relations—particularly immigration, narcotics, small arms trafficking, trade, and energy conservation and development—require better U.S. performance at least as much and perhaps more than they do action by Latin American and Caribbean states.

Fourth was the recognition that Latin America's realities today do not call for smaller governments, but rather for more efficient governments that concentrate on citizen security, education, infrastructure, and other needs not being adequately provided by market forces. This turn away from market fundamentalism toward pragmatic, hybrid approaches—building on gradual changes of emphasis in the latter years of the George W. Bush presidency, and aligning with dominant Latin American currents—was doubtless reinforced by some of the measures the new administration needed to take domestically in response to the financial and economic crises.[12]

Finally the new administration turned away from overarching hemisphere-wide approaches to develop policies tailored to specific issues in four high-priority target regions:

1. The closest neighbors of the United States in Mexico, Central America, and the Caribbean

2. Brazil, the region's largest and most powerful country

3. The diverse and troubled nations of the Andean ridge, each posing a different challenge

4. Cuba, long a neuralgic issue for the United States, where changes in U.S. policy are overdue

In each of these cases, the Obama administration introduced new rhetoric and took modest, concrete steps toward signaling new policy directions. This declaratory phase of the administration's Western Hemisphere policy won immediate praise throughout the Americas and among those in the United States who closely follow inter-American affairs.[13] The initial contrast between the Obama administration's posture in Latin America and that of his White House predecessor was widely acclaimed. By mid-2009, hopes were high in many Latin American circles that a new era in U.S.–Latin America relations was dawning.

The Sources of the Obama Administration's Approach to Latin America

Barack Obama came to the presidency with a life experience that was more international than that of most of his predecessors, but he was personally unfamiliar with Latin America, a region he had never visited, and his inner circle of foreign policy advisers did not include any Latin America hands.

Some elements of the Obama administration's approach to Latin America continued significant changes in U.S. policy that had been quietly introduced during the second term of George W. Bush. These changes were largely due to the work of Ambassador Thomas Shannon, a career diplomat who became assistant secretary of state for inter-American affairs in October 2005 and fashioned a carefully nuanced case-by-case approach to the various populist and potentially populist regimes: those of Venezuela, Bolivia, Ecuador, and Nicaragua, as well as Paraguay, Honduras, and El Salvador. In contrast to his predecessors in the first George W. Bush administration, who had a cold war– and Cuba-centered outlook, Shannon emphasized social and economic inequities as the root cause of many of Latin America's problems. Shannon paid special and deferential attention to Brazil, and sought multilateral cooperation. Ambassador Shannon's approach had been authorized by Secretary of State Condoleezza Rice as a means of keeping Latin American issues off the desk of the President Bush, at the time preoccupied with the Iraq War. The Obama administration, however, positively embraced many of Shannon's innovations at the presidential level.

The Obama administration's initial approach toward Latin America and the Caribbean also reflected a high degree of consensus among nongovernmental experts on the region, evident in several reports published in the electoral and post-electoral window for external policy input.[14]

These reports recommended greater emphasis on policies directed toward mitigating poverty and inequality and citizen security and developing energy and migration initiatives; new approaches to narcotics trafficking, gun traffic, and immigration; increased cooperation with Brazil; and intensified partnership with Mexico. They generally counseled restrained, nonconfrontational responses to Hugo Chávez and new initiatives toward Haiti and Cuba, more because of their broader international symbolic significance than because of pressing bilateral concerns.[15] These reports reinforced think tank studies on other international issues ranging from climate change to immigration, narcotics, human rights, the Middle East, Europe and Asia—all of them recommending more multilateral policies; greater respect for international law, institutions, and opinion; and all rejecting the neoconservative ideology and rhetoric of the prior administration.[16]

The proximate cause for the Obama administration's quick start in addressing U.S.–Latin America relations, however, was the need to deal with growing troubles in Mexico. Mexico's difficulties galvanized the new administration's attention in a way that no bureaucrat or think tank report could have done.

Obama's First Year: From Auspicious Start to Growing Disappointment

During the first months of 2009 there was consensus in Latin America that the Obama administration was off to a promising start in its approach to the Americas and in the international arena. The new administration was widely seen as being positively disposed toward multilateral approaches; given to listening rather than instructing or demanding; respectful of international law and opinion; open to dialogue, even with adversaries; willing to acknowledge U.S. co-responsibility for shared problems; explicitly committed to eschewing prior U.S. interventionist and paternalist practices; and inclined to avoid the bloated claims of many recent U.S. administrations that promised much more than they could deliver. The most applauded moves by the Obama administration to transform America's foreign policy included the president's campaign pledge, reiterated on his second day in office, to close the Guantánamo Bay detention and interrogation facility, his eloquent Cairo overture to the Muslim world, the new U.S. efforts to engage Iran and North Korea, the conciliatory approach to Russia, and the priority accorded to achieving a just and secure peace between Israel and Palestine. The concepts and tone underlying these initiatives were also seen as shaping the administration's first steps on Western Hemisphere issues.[17] The president's statement in Port of Spain, that his administration sought to develop a new relationship without "senior and junior partners," epitomized what was fresh and attractive about the Obama vision.[18]

These perceived changes were welcomed throughout the Americas. The president's background as an African descendant who grew up in modest circumstances also made a powerful positive impression. President Obama's individual popularity as well as the more general image of the United States in Latin America increased strikingly, according to various public opinion polls.[19]

By the end of the Obama administration's first year, however, the prevailing sentiment about its policies in Latin American diplomatic and political circles and among their U.S. counterparts was turning to disappointment. Critical comments were coming not only from the "usual suspects"—Fidel and Raúl Castro in Cuba, Chávez in Venezuela, Evo Morales in Bolivia, Daniel Ortega in Nicaragua, and Nestor and Cristina Kirchner in Argentina—whom one would expect to be critical of U.S. policies, but also from Brazil's Lula, and from diverse and experienced Latin American analysts.[20] In the United States, the Obama approach to Latin America came under intense attack from editorial writers in the *Wall Street Journal* and from Republican political figures, most notably Senator James DeMint of South Carolina. For different reasons the new administration was also sharply criticized by a number of think tanks on the left.[21] Even initially sympathetic centrist observers expressed disillusion with the state of the Obama administration's policies toward the Americas after the first year.[22]

Several specific issues contributed to the expressed disappointment. The president's early call for a new approach to Cuba, so broadly welcomed throughout the Americas, turned out not to go very far. Resistance emerged within the Obama administration to the growing sentiment in the Organization of American States to lift the 1962 suspension of Cuba from that organization.[23] After its first steps reversing some of the sanctions on Cuba that had been imposed by the George W. Bush administration, the Obama government indicated that any further U.S. measures toward rapprochement would require that Cuba make the next moves. Far from implementing a new beginning, the administration soon seemed to be reverting to the stance of several consecutive prior U.S. administrations: waiting for Cuba to change.

Suggestions that the United States was moving beyond earlier hegemonic attitudes soon seemed to be contradicted as well, when Secretary of State Clinton stated that China's and Iran's increasing activities in the region were a source of concern; by hints that some in the administration opposed Brazil's welcoming Iran's President Mahmoud Ahmadinejad on a state visit; and then by more overt comments by Secretary Clinton that those in the hemisphere who cooperate with Iran should "think twice about the consequences," a warning that rankled many Latin Americans, even those wary of Iran, who found it heavy-handed.[24]

President Obama's early promise that comprehensive immigration reform would be a first-year priority gave way to a more limited commitment only to begin consultations in the first year, and then to growing indications that even this modest goal would likely recede into the future. After the administration acknowledged the need to regulate the export of small weapons from the United States to Mexico, President Obama himself suggested that this goal was unrealistic because of domestic politics, a comment he punctuated by signing the economic stimulus legislation despite a provision that made it legal to bring concealed weapons into U.S. national parks.

The Obama administration's approach to trade policy during its first year was confusing at best. The president explicitly rejected protectionism soon after taking office, but then accepted a "Buy American" provision in the economic stimulus legislation. The administration signaled willingness to proceed with free trade agreements with Colombia and Panama but continued to postpone any concrete action. It talked up energy cooperation with Brazil but preserved the subsidy for U.S. corn-based ethanol producers and a high tariff on imported ethanol. And it actively promoted enhanced partnership with Mexico but allowed Congress to end funding for the experimental program that had permitted Mexican truckers to enter the United States, leaving the United States in noncompliance with an important NAFTA provision.

Perhaps the most immediately damaging developments emerged from two issues that surely were not on the administration's to-do list at the outset. One was triggered by the forcible overthrow and deportation by the Honduran armed forces on June 28 of that country's constitutionally elected president, Manuel Zelaya. The Obama administration's first response, consistent with its declaratory stance, was to reject this act, to push for a strong multilateral response from the hemisphere's nations through the OAS, and to impose some limited sanctions to give teeth to its rejection of the Honduran coup. Over time, however, Washington was reluctant to apply the harsher sanctions that some Latin Americans advocated. The administration hesitated in part because domestic critics, Senator DeMint foremost among them, were accusing it of intervening on behalf of Zelaya against Hondurans who were longtime friends of the United States. They charged that Zelaya was at best erratic and could credibly be portrayed as an acolyte and perhaps even a tool of Hugo Chávez.[25] Intense lobbying by those who had pushed the Cuba-centric and anti-Chávez agenda during the first George W. Bush administration polarized the Washington environment.

Neither the OAS diplomatic mission nor a second multilateral effort spearheaded by President Oscar Arias of Costa Rica was able to resolve the impasse in Honduras between Zelaya and the de facto regime that had replaced him, with the explicit blessings of the Honduran Congress and Supreme Court. Sentiment increased in many nations of the Americas for the United States to exercise its historic influence to restore the constitutional government—for example, by exercising its power as by far the main source of foreign exchange for the Honduran economy. The Obama administration sent Ambassador Shannon to Honduras in October 2009 to negotiate a solution, and he soon brokered an accord that was signed by both the de facto regime and Zelaya and hastily announced by Secretary Clinton. But the two Honduran parties interpreted this "agreement" differently, so no mutually acceptable solution ever actually took effect, and the de facto government, still unrecognized diplomatically by any nation, continued to organize the previously scheduled national elections. In these circumstances, Washington, while continuing to reject the de facto government, indicated its intent to recognize the eventual electoral victor as the legitimate authority in Honduras, provided that it would fulfill the commitments made in the negotiated accords to establish a "truth commission" and otherwise work to consolidate the country's deep divisions.

The U.S. government's pragmatic accommodation to Honduran realities was rejected by several of the larger South American nations because it did not restore the constitutional government and thus in effect accepted as legitimate elections that were carried out by an illegitimate regime. However, no Latin American government put forward a workable alternative approach or could exert any plausibly effective pressure to oust the coup's perpetrators and supporters. The Honduran imbroglio showed above all the limits of multilateral approaches when there is little in-depth understanding of a local situation, when there is no shared disposition to take joint concrete measures, and when intense lobbying is undertaken in Washington on an issue about which very few are well informed.[26]

The second case that provoked Latin American criticism of the Obama administration was its handling of a ten-year agreement with Colombia, announced in August 2009, allowing access by U.S. military personnel, long capped at fourteen hundred, to seven Colombian military bases. The agreement had been negotiated after Ecuador's decision, in 2008, not to renew the agreement that had allowed U.S. access to its facility at Manta, which U.S. personnel had used for the previous ten years for surveillance of narcotics trafficking in the Andean regions and Central America. Brazil, Chile, Venezuela, and several other South American governments raised questions about the Colombia-U.S. accord, with some calling for transparency regarding all the agreement's provisions and seeking formal guarantees that U.S. military activities would be restricted to Colombian territory. Most of the expressed concerns diminished as both the United States and Colombia provided additional details about the agreement, and early in 2010 Brazil and the United States signed their own mutual security agreement, the first such agreement in more than sixty years. But the commitment to consultation and transparency that the Obama administration had projected at the Port of Spain summit was somewhat undercut by this incident.

The impression created by these episodes was reinforced by widespread disappointment regarding the administration's broader international approaches. Closure of the symbolically important Guantánamo prison, originally promised within a year and strongly applauded throughout Latin America, was postponed. In time the Obama administration came to make arguments couched in security terms for loosening legal barriers to coercive interrogation and prolonged incarceration without trial. To citizens of many Latin American countries this sounded like the discredited positions of the prior administration, and reminded some of actions taken by the region's authoritarian regimes in the 1970s and 1980s. The administration's initiatives to engage Iran and North Korea appeared to be faltering, in the absence of reciprocal interest. The even-handed approach toward brokering an Israel-Palestine two-state solution seemed to be stalled as well. Questions were increasingly raised about the viability and durability of the Obama administration's initial foreign policy approaches.[27]

Assessing the Obama Policies in the Americas

One new U.S. administration after another in recent decades has announced a new policy for the Americas, usually with considerable fanfare. Often, however, these initiatives have come to naught, or little more.[28]

There is a recognizable cycle: Incoming policymakers closely associated with a newly elected president push for fresh starts. Political pressures often lead to overdramatizing these new approaches. Resistance to the initiatives emerges from the career bureaucracy of the U.S. government, from interest and pressure groups, or from both. Other domestic and international issues soon take up the time of senior officials. Uncertain, contradictory, and ineffective implementation of the new policies leads to their tacit or even explicit abandonment.

It is much too early to be sure how the Obama administration's policies toward Latin America will develop, or how U.S. relations with the diverse countries and subregions of Latin America and the Caribbean will ultimately evolve. This uncertainty arises in part because U.S. policies in the Americas are generally shaped less by international power relationships and strategic considerations than by the interacting influence of various domestic pressure groups on political and bureaucratic processes. Multiple actors enjoy access to policymaking in the extraordinarily permeable U.S. policy process. On issues short of imminent threats to national security, it is much easier to influence policy affecting Latin America than it is to coordinate or control it.

These tendencies are reinforced by the proliferation of U.S. government agencies involved in inter-American affairs. The Departments of State and Defense and the Central Intelligence Agency no longer necessarily dominate U.S.–Latin America relations, as they did practically without challenge from the 1940s through the 1980s. In many countries in Latin America today, the Treasury Department, the Commerce Department, the Federal Reserve, the U.S. Trade Representative, the Department of Homeland Security, the Department of Justice, and the Drug Enforcement Agency all have considerable influence. A bewildering number of departments and agencies have a hand in shaping U.S. relations with Mexico, for example, which makes coordination a major challenge.[29] When it comes to many specific issues in U.S.–Latin America relations, such as trade and immigration, the U.S. Congress, with its various committees and caucuses, is more relevant than the executive branch, and is much more responsive to diverse societal influences. The judiciary, and even state and local governmental authorities, also have a say. In the end, bureaucratic and interest-group politics, shaped by domestic political calculations and heightened by ideological polarization, generally have more impact on U.S. policies toward Latin America than do grand foreign policy designs. Inconsistencies and contradictions are inevitable; what is uncertain in advance is how important these various groups' influence will be, and whether such pressures will overwhelm any attempt to initiate a new approach.

All these points were abundantly illustrated during the Obama administration's first year. The administration's approach to Cuba was constrained both by the ongoing political influence of Cuban Americans and also by the procedures of the U.S. Senate, where one member's intensely held position can be decisive. The trucking dispute with Mexico and the stalled Colombia and Panama Free Trade agreements were attributable to labor union lobbying, compounded in the case of Colombia by that of human rights organizations. The administration's failure to press forward with comprehensive immigration reform results from its making this goal a lower priority than the need to get legislation passed to reform the American health-care system, which finally occurred in March 2010. It made a political calculation that an aggressive pursuit of immigration reform would seriously harm the chances of achieving a viable coalition to pass the health plan, a jobs bill, and other top-priority legislation. The chances for significant immigration reform were further complicated by Arizona's adoption of a law permitting police officers to require that persons whom they reasonably suspect of being undocumented residents produce their immigration papers.

Lobbying from Midwest agricultural interests accounts for the continuing subsidies for corn-based ethanol producers and tariffs on ethanol imported from Brazil. The clumsy handling of the Colombia bases agreement reflected, at least in part, a temporary imbalance in the Washington policymaking process between the continuity in Pentagon personnel and the lack of continuity within the State Department, which was deprived of leadership for its Western Hemisphere division for many months because of blocks in the Senate of the nominations of Arturo Valenzuela and Ambassador Shannon for top posts. The ambivalent Honduran policy was influenced by the anti-Zelaya lobby, which sought to use this issue both to weaken Chávez and to challenge Obama.

These examples underline the difficulty the Obama administration has faced in implementing its stated policies for the Americas—but the constraints need not be permanent or irreversible if the administration can set forth and pursue a strategic approach to the region. In fact, the policy community's tendency to see individual decisions as straws in the wind could have led it to miss trends of potentially greater lasting significance. The Obama administration's apparent tacit abandonment of regime change as the prime goal of U.S. policy toward Cuba may ultimately turn out to be much more important than its caution in moving toward full normalization of relations with a Cuban government that at present is, in any case, unwilling or unable to reciprocate. The administration's high-profile commitment to working out a path toward citizenship for unauthorized migrants who have worked in the United States for an extended period without incurring criminal violations could turn out to be of historic import. Washington's increasingly close day-to-day cooperation with Mexico on a variety of border, economic, social, and law enforcement issues may help positively transform a crucial bilateral relationship.

Differences of perspective between Brazil and the United States have been evident vis-à-vis Honduras, the Colombian bases, trade issues, and the preferred approach to Iran. Yet some such differences should be expected between large and complex countries with diverse interests and contradictory domestic political exigencies. Brazil and the United States during the Obama presidency could well still become much more significant partners on a variety of important international questions, including trade, climate change, environmental protection, intellectual property, and global governance reform.[30]

Looking Forward

How the Obama administration's policies toward Latin America and the Caribbean actually unfold and how U.S.-Latin American relations develop in the coming years will largely depend on factors that are still difficult to gauge. Much of the impact of the United States in the Americas is ancillary—a consequence of decisions made for other reasons. What the Obama administration does about homeland security and deficits, what the Federal Reserve Bank does about interest rates, how Washington handles trade and currency disputes with China, and the nuclear issue with Iran all will likely affect Latin America and U.S.-Latin America relations more than decisions taken directly to influence them.

On a number of issues, President Obama's ability to deliver will depend on the administration's success in cultivating domestic public support, through a combination of performance, political strategy, and communication skills. A great deal will depend on whether the U.S. economy recovers. A renewed or prolonged economic downturn and the consequent loss of public confidence in the administration would undermine its approach to trade and immigration, and would deprive it of latitude to resist interest-group pressures on many issues, from trade to border security, from energy to counternarcotics. Whether or not President Obama and his party can build on the passage of health insurance reform legislation to reverse the erosion in public and congressional support that was evident early in 2010 will determine how much persuasive authority Mr. Obama can bring to bear on a host of issues.

It is certainly possible that the initial hope for a new era of inter-American cooperation will continue to be overwhelmed by the many pressures to which the Obama administration is subject, especially if the economic downturn deepens or the administration's political capital is further depleted. A contrary case can still be made, however. The Obama administration could yet persist in carrying out the implicitly coherent but never fully articulated approach suggested in its first months: cooperating on shared transnational challenges and opportunities; concentrating most on strengthening relations with America's closest neighbors in Mexico and the Caribbean Basin and on forging a strategic relationship with Brazil on issues both within and beyond the hemisphere; responding in a carefully differentiated way to diverse populist and nationalist movements; moving cautiously toward a pragmatic working relationship with Cuba on matters of mutual interest without diluting U.S. concerns about fundamental human rights, supporting Latin America–led multilateral efforts to strengthen effective democratic governance in the region; and working with specific countries to confront other specific shared challenges, including climate change and the development of alternate energy sources.

If the administration manages to recover its political footing and if the U.S. economy stabilizes, implementation of the Obama administration's positive vision might still occur. Its approach to Latin America and the Caribbean is supported by the president's own foreign policy team, by the career government bureaucracy specializing in Western Hemisphere affairs, by most Latin American specialists outside the U.S. government, and by many major external groups. Unlike what happened in the Kennedy, Carter, and Reagan administrations, therefore, the Obama administration's Latin American policy is unlikely to be torpedoed by systematic conflict between the career bureaucracy and political appointees. Although interest groups will continue to press their views, many of the most important groups—large corporations as well as NGOs such as religious organizations, environmentalists, and human rights advocates—generally share the vision the Obama administration has projected.

The Obama administration's tenets of Latin America policy fit well with its overall internationalist approach, and with its domestic priorities and political coalitions. It is not based on special considerations or exceptions for the Americas, but is grounded in the president's own fundamental worldview.

The 2008 elections weakened some of the forces that shaped previous U.S. policies. The hard-line sector of Florida's Cuban American community has lost ground. Cuban Americans born and raised in the United States as well as the rapidly increasing number of Hispanic and Latino voters of other backgrounds have been gaining influence, and they generally support the Obama administration's proposed changes in immigration policy and in relations with their countries of origin.[31] The farm subsidies lobby has lost some clout, particularly in a period of fiscal concern. Trade union clamor for protectionism is weakened by the urgent need to expand exports in order to revive the U.S. economy.

Thus, the Obama administration may have somewhat greater room to maneuver than did recent U.S. administrations. This is suggested by the moves early in 2010 toward resolving the trucking dispute with Mexico; President Obama's emphasis on doubling U.S. exports and his specific mention in his January 2010 State of the Union Address of Colombia and Panama as important trading partners of the United States; growing efforts on Capitol Hill to repeal the U.S. tariff on Brazilian ethanol; and the intensified efforts to adopt a bipartisan approach to immigration reform.[32]

Finally, several Latin American governments, including some that differed sharply with the Obama administration over Honduras and the Colombia bases, might reach out for improved cooperation with the U.S. government. Important actors in foreign and finance ministries and in the private sector understand that the Obama administration offers greater chances of positive-sum relations with the United States than has been the case in many years, and that signals of reciprocal interest in closer cooperation might therefore be timely. Such signals may also be easier to provide in the context of Chávez's mounting internal difficulties, which could reduce pressures in several countries to keep their distance from Washington. Significant Latin American moves to work more closely with the United States, especially by Brazil, would help consolidate the Obama approach.[33]

The Obama Opportunity

The catastrophic earthquakes that struck Haiti in January 2010 and Chile in February were dramatic reminders that agendas and policies often must respond to the unexpected. They also underlined the special ties of history, geography, trade, and demography that link the United States closely to its southern neighbors, and especially to Haiti and other countries in the Caribbean Basin region. The Obama administration quickly demonstrated its solidarity, emphasizing multilateral cooperation in its response to these catastrophes rather than intervention or imposition. In Haiti, the Obama administration cooperated with Cuba and Venezuela as well as Brazil, Ecuador, the Dominican Republic, Canada, and other nations to provide rapid, substantial, and effective aid, while letting the United Nations take the lead.[34]

Early in its second year the Obama administration refocused on Latin America. Secretary of State Clinton made trips to Uruguay, Argentina, Chile, Brazil, Guatemala, and Costa Rica in late February and early March 2010 and to Mexico later that month; on the Mexico trip she was accompanied by Defense Secretary Robert Gates, Joint Chiefs of Staff Chairman Mullen, and Homeland Security Secretary Napolitano. President Obama had meetings with President Mauricio Funes of El Salvador and President René Préval of Haiti in March, and hosted Mexico's Felipe Calderón for a state visit in Washington in May.[35] Considering how many other problems, domestic and international, the administration was then facing, this spurt of high-level attention suggests that the Obama administration still seeks the opportunity to improve U.S.-Latin America relations.

To effectively grasp that opportunity, the Obama administration should consider following ten recommendations that emerge from the analysis this book presents:

First, the administration should accept as a basis for policy that Latin America and the Caribbean cannot receive much sustained high-level attention in and from the U.S. government, even one disposed to do so; there are just too many other competing and compelling issues. Even sincere promises will not change this reality. The aim, therefore, should be to devote higher-quality attention, based on better concepts, more appropriate mind-sets, and improved processes.

Second, the Obama administration should clearly articulate a positive vision and broad framework for U.S. policies and relationships in the Americas. The administration's wise decision to eschew an overly ambitious overarching program such as the Alliance for Progress and to approach the

Summit of the Americas primarily in a listening mode should not now preclude it from setting forth its strategic approach to Western Hemisphere relations. It should articulate clearly why Latin America matters to the United States, what ideals and interests the countries of the Americas share, and how the United States and its neighbors can work together to pursue common goals. The elements of such a vision have been implicit from the start, but they have not yet been articulated in a comprehensive and authoritative way. A clear policy statement, delivered with the eloquence for which President Obama is recognized, would go a long way toward building the *confianza* on which cooperation depends.

Third, the Obama administration should acknowledge that a broad pan-American partnership from Alaska to Patagonia is less relevant in today's world than a series of smaller partnerships anchored in specific issues, involving particular countries or clusters of countries willing to work together on mutual concerns. It is vital at the same time to reinvest in those broad-hemispheric institutions—especially the Organization of American States and the Inter-American Development Bank—that can take on selected challenges on which there is broad consensus in the Americas.[36]

Fourth, the administration should explicitly recognize that U.S. relations with Mexico are unique. The special issues that stem from the exceptional and accelerating functional integration between the two societies and economies require new concepts, policies, modes of interaction and governance, norms, and institutions, in the border region and more broadly.[37] Crafting them should be an explicit strategic priority for both countries for many years to come.

Fifth, President Obama should invite Mexico and Canada to join the United States in long-term positive engagement with the countries of Central America and the Caribbean, where all three North American nations have strong demographic and economic ties, as well as overlapping security, public health, environmental, and humanitarian concerns. In that context, it is important that the United States government consistently express the aim to move beyond the cold war confrontation with Cuba, and for Washington to take concrete steps in that direction—such as cooperating on shared concerns, including responding to humanitarian crises and protecting the environment and promoting student and academic exchanges, while maintaining a concern for human rights that is consistent with U.S. values and policies toward the Americas.

Sixth, the United States should work to build synergy with Brazil in order to respond effectively to climate change, prevent and contain global pandemics, curb nuclear proliferation and strengthen international governance arrangements, and strengthen global regimes of trade, finance, and investment. Cultivating mutually supportive relations with Brazil will require sustained effort in both nations.

Seventh, the Obama administration should invite all the countries of the Americas, whatever their political orientation, to join in dealing with three challenges that affect them all, and on which the United States has as much to learn as to teach:

—Narcotics: Improve research, open debate, and undertake concerted efforts to curb the violence and corruption the drug trade produces; reduce consumption by investing more in treatment, rehabilitation, and effective education programs; reduce and mitigate the harm done by the drug trade and the use of narcotics.

—Citizens' security: Improve citizens' security by focusing on what can be learned from experiences throughout the Americas and beyond on the relationships between citizen security and economic prosperity, social equity, political participation, community-based policing, and judicial and penal reform.

—Climate change: Explore and implement all feasible ways to understand and respond effectively to climate change and its consequences, by developing alternative energy sources, developing responses to hurricanes and other severe weather consequences, and protecting countries threatened by rising sea levels.

Eighth, the administration should take measures within its capacity and available resources to help strengthen Latin American economies, including passing the Free Trade Agreements with Colombia and Panama, and expanding multilateral, bilateral, and private-sector flows of investment to strengthen Latin America's infrastructure.

Ninth, the administration should keep an appropriate focus on how, working though multilateral approaches as much as possible, it can help strengthen effective democratic governance, the protection of fundamental human rights, and the consistent application of the rule of law while appreciating that the challenges of bolstering democratic governance are especially complex in countries that must incorporate large numbers of historically excluded indigenous participants with special issues of identity, ethnicity, culture, and long-standing marginalization and consequent resentment.

Tenth, the U.S. government should work with interested Latin American countries to strengthen the quality of and enhance access to education at all levels, as a basic human right, in part to facilitate the region's greater participation in the global knowledge economy.

Barack Obama came to the presidency of the United States at a critical moment for his country, the Americas, and the world. He and his administration face multiple difficult challenges, some of unprecedented magnitude and complexity. In the Americas, however, the Obama administration encounters exceptional opportunity, not grave threats. The Western Hemisphere provides the chance to make progress on many issues with feasible effort, provided that the United States develops, articulates, and pursues a proactive and integrated strategy, rather than mainly ignoring a region that is increasingly important for the future of the United States or merely reacting to issues one at a time as they emerge. That is the essence of the Obama opportunity in the Americas. It is not too late to seize it.

Notes

1. See, for example, Ken Ellingwood, "Hillary Clinton Wraps Up Mexico Visit, Calls Drug Violence 'Intolerable,'" *Los Angeles Times*, March 27, 2009; Mayolo López and Claudia Guerrero, "Ponen lupa a frontera y armas" [A closer look at the border and weapons], *Reforma.com*, April 17, 2009; and Peter Nicholas and Tracy Wilkinson, "Obama and Calderon, in Mexico, Stress Partnership," *Los Angeles Times*, April 17, 2009.

2. Various former U.S. officials began talking, albeit loosely, about the possibility that Mexico could become a "failed state," which would have dire consequences for the United States. A report by the U.S. Joint Forces Command suggested that worst-case scenarios in the medium term were most likely in Pakistan and Mexico. See United States Joint Forces Command, *Joint Operating Environment 2008* (Suffolk, Va.: November 25, 2008; see especially p. 36). Media coverage of Mexico's troubles rose abruptly in 2008 as the violence escalated.

3. See Agnes Gereben Schaefer, Benjamin Bahney, and W. Jack Riley, *Security in Mexico: Implications for U.S. Policy Options* (Santa Monica: RAND, 2009).

4. See Jeffrey S. Passel and D'Vera Cohn, *U.S. Population Projections: 2005–2050*, Pew Hispanic Center Report (Washington, D.C.: Pew Research Center, February 11, 2008) (http://pewhispanic.org/files/reports/85.pdf; accessed July 18, 2010).

5. The term "intermestic" was coined by Bayless Manning in "The Congress, the Executive and Intermestic Affairs: Three Proposals," *Foreign Affairs* 55 (2; January 1977): 306–24. Various writers who use the term frequently—including me—have been erroneously credited with coining it.

6. See "Developing Sustainable Energy Resources and Combating Climate Change," in *Rethinking U.S.–Latin American Relations: A Hemispheric Partnership for a*

Turbulent World, Report of the Partnership for the Americas Commission (Brookings Institution Press, 2008), pp. 13–16 (www.brookings.edu/~/media/Files/rc/reports/2008/1124_latin_america_partnership/1124_latin_america_partnership.pdf).

7. See Laurence Whitehead, "A Project for the Americas," in Abraham F. Lowenthal, Theodore Piccone and Laurence Whitehead, eds., *The Obama Administration and the Americas: Agenda for Change* (Brookings Institution Press, 2009), 203–24.

8. ALBA members besides Venezuela are Antigua and Barbuda, Bolivia, Cuba, Dominica, Ecuador, Nicaragua, and Saint Vincent and the Grenadines. Honduras officially withdrew from the alliance in January 2010.

9. See, for example, Riordan Roett and Guadalupe Paz, eds., *China's Expansion into the Western Hemisphere: Implications for Latin America and the United States* (Brookings Institution Press, 2008); Robert Evan Ellis, *China in Latin America: The Whats and Wherefores* (Boulder: Lynne Rienner, 2009); Javier Santiso, ed., *The Visible Hand of China in Latin America*, OECD Development Centre Report (Paris: Organization for Economic Cooperation and Development, 2007); Nicola Phillips, "Coping with China," in Andrew F. Cooper and Jorge Heine, eds., *Which Way Latin America? Hemispheric Politics Meet Globalization* (Tokyo: United Nations University Press, 2009), 100–139; Jorge Heine, "Playing the India Card," in Cooper and Heine, *Which Way Latin America?*

10. See, for example, Latin American Commission on Drugs and Democracy, "Drugs and Democracy: Toward a Paradigm Shift," declaration released February 9, 2009 (www.plataformademocratica.org/Publicacoes/declaracao_ingles_site.pdf). Among the commission's members are three former presidents: Fernando Henrique Cardoso of Brazil, Ernesto Zedillo of Mexico, and Cesar Gaviria of Colombia.

11. See Mark Landler, "Clinton Says U.S. Feeds Mexico Drug Trade," *New York Times*, March 25, 2009; Ariadna García, Mayolo López, and José Díaz Briseño, "Necesitan aliarse EU y México—Hillary" [Hillary: Mexico and the United States must work together], *Reforma.com*, March 26, 2009.

12. For an excellent statement of the prevailing Latin American view, see Alejandro Foxley, *Market versus State: Postcrisis Economics in Latin America*, report (Washington, D.C.: Carnegie Endowment for International Peace, November 2009) (http://carnegieendowment.org/files/market_versus_state.pdf).

13. The Obama administration's quick, positive start put Hugo Chávez on the defensive, at least temporarily, as was evident at the Americas summit in Port of Spain, where the Venezuelan leader felt the need to show that he, too, could be friends with Obama. See Alexei Barrionuevo, "At Americas Summit, Leaders to Press U.S.," *New York Times*, April 16, 2009; Dan Froomkin, "More Humility from Obama," *Washington Post*, April 16, 2009.

14. These reports were in a tradition of reports by independent entities that have been influential in framing policy toward Latin America. Latin Americanists are especially aware of this periodic opportunity for affecting the policy approaches of incoming administrations. Thus, the Linowitz Reports (prepared by the Commission on

U.S.–Latin American Relations, chaired by Sol Linowitz in 1974 and 1976), strongly influenced the Carter government; "A New Inter-American Policy for the Eighties" (often called the Santa Fe Document) by the Committee of Santa Fe (affiliated with the Council on Inter-American Security) and released in 1980 had an impact on Reagan's policies; and the Inter-American Dialogue reports "Consensus for Action: The Americas in 1989" and "Toward an Era of Hemispheric Cooperation" (1993) influenced the administrations of George H. W. Bush and Bill Clinton, respectively (see www.thedialogue.org/page.cfm?pageID=42 for links to both reports). I was a contributor to the Linowitz report and to the Inter-American Dialogue reports.

15. A number of influential reports have been published since 2007: Washington Office on Latin America, *Forging New Ties: A Fresh Approach to U.S. Policy in Latin America* (November 25, 2008) (link at www.wola.org/index.php?option=com_content&task=viewp&id=580); Abraham F. Lowenthal, "Toward Improved U.S. Policies for Latin America and the Caribbean," prepared for Task Force on New U.S. Policies for a Changing Latin America, Center for Hemispheric Policy, University of Miami (September–December 2007) (https://www6.miami.edu/hemispheric-policy/FinalDraftLowenthal-11-21-07.pdf); Council on Foreign Relations, *U.S.–Latin American Relations: A New Direction for a New Reality* (May 2008) (www.der.oas.org/Institutional_relations/CFR report.pdf); Partnership for the Americas Commission, Brookings Institution, *Rethinking U.S.-Latin American Relations: A Hemispheric Partnership for a Turbulent World* (November 2008) (www.brookings.edu/reports/2008/1124_latin_america_partnership.aspx); James M. Roberts and Ray Walser, "10 Points for President Elect Obama's Latin America Strategy," Heritage Foundation Web Memo (January 2009) (www.heritage.org/Research/Reports/2009/01/10-Points-for-President-Elect-Obamas-Latin-America-Strategy); Americas Society and Council of the Americas, Trade Advisory Group, *Building the Hemispheric Growth Agenda: A New Framework for Policy* (January 13, 2009) (www.as-coa.org/files/BUILDING THE HEMISPHERIC GROWTH AGENDA - FINAL.pdf); and Inter-American Dialogue, *A Second Chance: U.S. Policy in the Americas* (March 2009) (www.thedialogue.org/uploads/2008_Sol_M__Linowitz_Forum/A_Second_Chance,_FINAL_to_post.pdf).

16. Some examples of these think tank reports on other foreign policy issues are Mark Agrast, "Restoring America's Moral Authority," *Center for American Progress Action Fund* (online magazine) February 28, 2007 (www.americanprogressaction.org/issues/2007/moral_authority.html); Audrey Singer, *Reforming U.S. Immigration Policy: Open New Pathways to Integration*, Opportunity 08 position paper (Washington, D.C.: Brookings Institution, February 2007) (link at www.brookings.edu/papers/2007/0228demographics_singer_Opp08.aspx#); Council on Foreign Relations, *Confronting Climate Change: A Strategy for U.S. Foreign Policy*, Task Force Report (New York: June 2008) (link to full text at www.cfr.org/publication/16362/confronting_climate_change.html); Nina Hachigian, Michael Schiffer, and Winny Chen, *A Global Imperative: A Progressive Approach to U.S.-China Relations in the 21st*

Century, report (Washington, D.C.: Center for American Progress, August 13, 2008) (www.americanprogress.org/issues/2008/08/china_report.html); Karim Sadjadpour, *Iran: Is Productive Engagement Possible?* policy brief (Washington, D.C.: Carnegie Endowment for International Peace, October 2008) (www.carnegieendowment.org/ files/us_iran_policy.pdf); Richard N. Haass and Martin S. Indyk, *Restoring the Balance: A Middle East Strategy for the Next President* (Brookings Institution Press, 2008).

17. For a representative statement, see Felipe de la Balze, "Con Obama regresó el realismo en la política" [With Obama, a return to realism in politics], *Clarín*, February 28, 2010.

18. The official transcript of President Obama's press conference on April 19, 2009, is available online (www.whitehouse.gov/the_press_office/Press-Conference-By-The-President-In-Trinidad-And-Tobago-4/19/2009).

19. See Pew Global Attitudes Project, "Confidence in Obama Lifts U.S. Image Around the World—Most Muslim Publics Not So Easily Moved" (Washington, D.C.: Pew Research Center Publications, July 23, 2009) (http://pewresearch.org/ pubs/1289/global-attitudes-survey-2009-obama-lifts-america-image); Ian T. Brown, "U.S. Leadership, Obama Winning Favor in Latin America," Gallup website, December 1, 2009 (www.gallup.com/poll/124514/leadership-obama-winning-favor-latin-america.aspx); and Informe Latinobarómetro 2009 (www.latinobarometro.org/ documentos/LATBD_LATINOBAROMETRO_INFORME_2009.pdf).

20. See President Lula da Silva's interview with Lionel Barber and Jonathan Wheatley of the *Financial Times*, November 6, 2009; President Cristina Kirchner's interview with *CNN Español*, February 25, 2010; Jorge G. Castañeda, "Adios, Monroe Doctrine: When the Yanquis Go Home," *New Republic*, December 28, 2009; Rubens Ricupero, "Horror ao Vácuo" [Horror of a vacuum], *Folha de São Paulo*, October 25, 2009.

21. See Guy Hursthouse and Tomás Ayuso, "¿Cambio? The Obama Administration in Latin America: A Disappointing Year in Retrospective," Council on Hemispheric Affairs, January 26, 2010 (www.coha.org/cambio-the-obama-administration); Laura Carlsen, "CIP Analysts Look at Obama's First Year," Americas Program, Center for International Policy, January 27, 2010 (www.cipamericas.org/archives/2761).

22. See Peter Hakim, "Obama y Latinoamérica: Un Decepcionante Primer Año" [Obama and Latin America: A disappointing first year], *Foreign Affairs Latinoamérica* 10, no. 1, 2010 (www.thedialogue.org/page.cfm?pageID=32&pubID=2234); Michael Shifter, "Obama and Latin America: New Beginnings, Old Frictions," *Current History* 109, no. 724 (February (2010): 67–76; "Obama's Disappointing Year in Latin America," Julia Sweig, interviewed by Robert McMahon, Council on Foreign Relations website, January 12, 2010 (www.cfr.org/publication/21177/obamas_disappointing_year_in_latin_america.html).

23. Friction between the new administration and the Latin American countries was eventually smoothed over by a compromise formula that reversed the 1962

OAS exclusion of Cuba but left Havana's reentry for future consideration, subject to further conditions.

24. Hillary Rodham Clinton, "U.S.–Latin America Relations," speech delivered at the State Department, December 11, 2009; see also "Hillary Clinton Warns Latin America Off Close Iran Ties," *BBC News*, December 11, 2009 (http://news.bbc.co.uk/ 2/hi/8409081.stm).

25. Latin American perspectives on the Honduran imbroglio were far from uniform. A particularly lively debate took place in Brazil, with indications that domestic political calculations shaped both the Lula government's policies and the critique of them by opposition analysts. See, for example, Marco Aurelio Garcia, "O que está em jogo em Honduras" [What is at stake in Honduras], *Política Externa* 18, no. 3 (December–February 2009–2010): 123–29; Luiz Felipe Lampreia, "Brasil comete erro de avaliacão em Honduras" [Brazil commits an error of judgment in Honduras], *Política Externa* 18, no. 3 (December–February 2009–2010): 117–22; Marcel Fortuna Biato, "Winds of Change: From Trinidad and Tobago to Honduras," Norwegian Peacebuilding Centre, October 5, 2009; Ricupero, "Horror ao Vácuo." See also João Augusto de Castro Neves and Matias Spektor, "Obama and Brazil" (this volume, chapter 3).

26. See Kevin Casas-Zamora, "The Honduran Crisis and the Obama Administration" (this volume, chapter 8), and Christopher Sabatini and Jason Marczak, "Obama's Tango: Restoring U.S. Leadership in Latin America," *Foreign Affairs*, January 13, 2010 (www.foreignaffairs.com/articles/65923/christopher-sabatini-and-jason-marczak/ obamas-tango).

27. An interesting collection of comments from U.S. observers was published in *The American Interest* 5, no. 3 (January–February 2010): 4–31. On Latin American opinion, see, for example, "America Latina, decepcionada ante el primer año de Obama" [Disappointment about Obama's first year], Infolatam/EFE, December 22, 2009.

28. For an early discussion of this pattern, see Abraham F. Lowenthal, *Partners in Conflict: The United States and Latin America in the 1990s* (Johns Hopkins University Press, 1990).

29. See Jorge I. Dominguez and Rafael Fernandez de Castro, *Between Partnership and Conflict: The United States and Mexico*, 2nd edition (New York: Routledge, 2009), especially 80–90, 130–34.

30. Abraham F. Lowenthal, "US-Brazil Relations Are Critical," *San Diego Union Tribune*, March 5, 2010. See also Matias Spektor, "How to Read Brazil's Stance on Iran," Council on Foreign Relations website, March 4, 2010. See also João Augusto de Castro Neves and Matias Spektor, "Obama and Brazil" (this volume, chapter 3).

31. See Bendixen & Amandi (polling firm), "National Poll of Cubans and Cuban Americans on Changes to Cuba Policy," poll, April 20, 2009 (www.bendixenand associates.com/Cuba_Flash_Poll_Executive_Summary.html); Gary Segura, "The

Latino Electorate at 100 Days: Obama Popular, But Want to See Action on Immigration," *Latino Decisions* (blog), May 4, 2009 (http://latinodecisions.wordpress.com/2009/05/04/the-latino-electorate-at-100-days-obama-popular-but-want-to-see-action-on-immigration).

32. The fact that Colombia's Constitutional Court in March 2010 finally nixed the reelection of President Uribe for a third term may make it considerably easier for the administration to obtain approval for the Colombia Free Trade Act. See Michael Shifter, "The United States and Colombia: Recalibrating the Relationship" (this volume, chapter 4).

33. The recent formation by thirty-two Latin American and Caribbean nations of the Community of Latin American and Caribbean States, to include all countries of the Americas except the United States and Canada, could allow those countries disposed to try greater cooperation with the United States to hedge their bets, and to undertake pragmatic cooperation with little political risk.

34. See Daniel P. Erikson, "Obama and the Haitian Earthquake," *FocalPoint: Canada's Spotlight on the Americas* 9, no. 2 ("Focus on Haiti," March 2010): 1 (www.focal.ca/pdf/focalpoint_march2010.pdf), and Juan Gabriel Valdés, "Haiti: Life beyond Survival" (this volume, chapter 9).

35. In Brazil, too, Ambassador Shannon welcomed six U.S. cabinet members to the country between February and April.

36. The pledge made by the United States and other countries at the annual meeting of the Inter-American Development Bank in Cancún in March 2010 to a substantial expansion of capital commitments to the Bank is a step in the right direction, especially as the international financial crisis has greatly tightened private credit and has made the bank much more important again.

37. The May 19, 2010, declaration by the governments of Mexico and the United States outlining a new vision and procedures for border management was an important step in this direction. See "Declaration by the Government of the United States of America and the Government of the United Mexican States Concerning Twenty-First-Century Border Management" (www.america.gov/st/texttrans-english/2010/May/20100524151635SBlebahC0.1740032.html).

two

Mexico and the United States: The Search for a Strategic Vision

Carlos Heredia and Andrés Rozental

As usual, most Mexicans viewed the election of a new U.S. president in 2008 with high expectations. It did not much matter that Mexico had not figured prominently in Barack Obama's electoral campaign, or that he had never set foot on Mexican territory. Mexicans hoped that he would abandon the kind of unilateral exercise of power practiced by the outgoing administration of George W. Bush in violation of bilateral agreements and even international law.

Though domestically driven, three of Obama's campaign promises were in fact highly relevant for Mexico: (1) to submit to Congress a comprehensive reform bill on immigration; (2) to revise the North American Free Trade Agreement (NAFTA) between Mexico, the United States, and Canada for the benefit of workers and not just big business; and (3) to improve border cooperation. Furthermore, Obama's twenty-two-hour visit to Mexico City on April 16–17, 2009, served to reaffirm the many ties between the two countries and shifted their focus to "shared responsibility," thus inspiring hopes for a new tone in bilateral relations.

Obama's Brief Honeymoon

Getting to the White House is far different from exercising power there, however. As the recent debate over health care reform shows, promoting and implementing initiatives is an uphill struggle today because executive authority is very fragmented and American public opinion is polarized on practically every issue—as is reflected in a much divided Congress. Owing to these circumstances, the enthusiasm Mexicans felt at the start of the "Obama era" has gradually morphed into measured caution.[1]

This shift in Mexico's attitude has also been fueled by developments in two central areas of mutual concern—security and the economy. On the evening of September 15, 2008, during Independence Day festivities in the city of Morelia, eight people were killed by fragmentary grenades in what Mexico came to see as the first direct attack on a defenseless civilian population by drug gangs. This event led to growing demands for an end to the U.S.-backed "war" on drug-related crime announced by President Felipe Calderón in December 2006, and for a new emphasis on citizen security instead.

Only hours before these killings, the U.S. economy was approaching a turning point: the legendary Wall Street investment bank, Lehman Brothers, had declared bankruptcy, giving rise to America's biggest financial crisis since the Great Depression. Just as in 2001, when the United States became focused on the "war on terror" in the wake of 9/11, Mexico was relegated to the sidelines. After the autumn of 2008, the White House and the Congress had to contend with the domestic toxic loans crisis, the bailout of banks and large U.S. conglomerates, and health reform. Internationally, Washington was busy with the wars in Iraq and Afghanistan, the dangerously volatile situation in Pakistan, the complexities of the Middle East situation, nuclear-related skirmishes with Iran and North Korea, and China's challenge to U.S. leadership in international financial institutions and on climate change. Clearly, the U.S. administration had too much on its plate to pay close attention to its southern neighbor—except for two nagging problems, organized crime and border security.

Bilateral Issues and Actors: Toward Shared Responsibility?

As a result, combating crime and maintaining security have become the central axis of U.S. relations with Mexico, and the U.S. Departments of Defense and Homeland Security are playing an increasingly important role in those relations. For its part, the State Department is facilitating contacts between these agencies and their Mexican counterparts, rather than articulating a comprehensive vision of bilateral relations and a new narrative about a united North America.

On the Mexican side, it took President Calderón three years to schedule a state visit to the United States (on May 19–20, 2010), whereas Mexican presidents of the past fifty years have usually done so during their first year in office. This delay may reflect the fact that Mexico's image in the U.S. media has been deteriorating. As Jesús Silva-Herzog Márquez describes it,

> Behind the diplomatic gala of the Mexican government there is no voice, there are no ideas, there is not even any will. There are porcelain, tablecloths and glasses: this is a glass-tinkling diplomacy. Mexico's insecurity seeps across the country's borders. As he realizes Mexico's image in U.S. public opinion, President Calderón reels out the tired discourse of a "campaign against Mexico." The president's diagnosis, and what is worse his strategy, is mistaken. Mexico's is not a simple image problem. . . . Its domestic problem is real, deep and complex. At this hour, the absence of an imaginative foreign policy is particularly serious. The diplomacy of nationalist lamentation cannot replace the diplomacy of tinkling glasses. We urgently need a lucid and audacious diplomacy that commits our neighbor to resolving a shared problem. Seen from this angle, the fact that the United States worries about our violence could be seen as an encouraging sign. It could be if our foreign policy were self-possessed and lucid.[2]

At the same time, civil servants in both countries report increasing levels of interaction, not only in the frequency of high-level bilateral meetings, but also in the contacts between the respective government entities, the opportunities for shared intelligence, and the degree of proximity between the Mexican ambassador and the U.S. president. Yet none of this has led to a more fruitful bilateral relationship because Mexico has no strategic vision of what it wants from Washington, while Washington, which makes Mexico a priority only when it senses a threat to its security, has also failed to forge a shared vision of a future bilateral relationship and regional integration.

The Mérida Initiative

Mexican public opinion has gradually become more open to the possibility of bilateral cooperation to combat drug-trafficking, however. In a 2008 survey undertaken when George W. Bush was still president, 49 percent of respondents supported U.S.-Mexican cooperation in patrolling the border, ports, and airports to combat drug-trafficking (61 percent of "elite" respondents did not). The extradition of criminals to the United States was highly favored by 58 percent of all respondents and 76 percent of elite respondents. Furthermore, 55 percent of all respondents and 70 percent of elite respondents would welcome financial aid from the United States to combat drug-trafficking and organized crime.[3]

In fact, action on this front was already under way in 2007 with the launching of the Mérida Initiative, a cooperative security program to combat organized crime that includes some Central American and Caribbean countries. The U.S. Congress approved US$1.35 billion to be spent on it over three years from 2009 onward, to equip Mexico's armed and federal police forces with helicopters and high-tech equipment for port and airport security, to establish communications networks for intelligence agency cooperation, and to provide training in financial intelligence and human rights. The program does not include firearms or cash payments. U.S. forces have been assigned US$74 million to block illegal arms trafficking from the United States to Mexico, although it is not yet clear what measures this would entail.

Ideally, the Mérida Initiative should commit both neighbors to resolving a shared problem. Interestingly, the language that the U.S. side uses to describe the initiative suggests otherwise: U.S. politicians and diplomats refer to it as "aid," "help," "assistance," and "support," while Mexican civil servants characterize it as "cooperation" or a "shared initiative."

This is not merely a difference in semantics. At least three factors complicate the resolution of the problem as it pertains to the deployment of the armed forces in President Calderón's so-called war against organized crime: (1) Mexico's armed forces are not used to public scrutiny by journalists and domestic and international civil organizations; (2) its soldiers are not trained to do jobs normally carried out by the police; and (3) military officers fear they will be accused of human rights violations and even be placed under arrest by judicial authorities for supposedly taking on functions beyond those sanctioned by law for the military. The Mexican Congress has thus failed to approve reforms to the National Security Law that would provide legal backing for this sort of intervention by the armed forces.

The U.S. State Department insists that there should be a detailed report on the human rights impact of the Mérida Initiative to facilitate congressional approval of the future disbursement of funds for the Mexican government. Mexicans, in turn, argue that reciprocity is essential if the initiative is really to be a cooperative program. Moreover, Mexicans think that the United States must stop hiding behind its Constitution's Second Amendment, on the right to bear arms, and actually cooperate with Mexico in identifying the source of assault weapons bought in U.S. gun shops and weapons fairs that end up in the hands of Mexican drug gangs and organized criminals and whose firepower far exceeds that of the Mexican police.

During a meeting to evaluate the Mérida Initiative in Mexico City on March 23, 2010, both Mexico and the United States admitted they could not win the battle against organized crime on their own and broadened the program to include education and health, as well as economic and social development aid to areas most affected by drug violence. What was left unsaid, however, was that the United States has done little or nothing to reduce the demand for drugs, dismantle distribution networks, or change the laws governing these issues. Many Mexicans wonder why their country should bear the brunt of the battle and be left with the majority of its victims when the country responsible for drug demand does little more than make encouraging speeches and offer a financially paltry cooperation program.

The Necessary Immigration Reform

Another point of bilateral disagreement is the flow of Mexican workers to the United States. Mexico wants the United States to recognize that it needs Mexican labor, which makes a fundamental contribution to the prosperity and competitiveness of various sectors, including agriculture, industry, construction, and hospitality services. According to the Department of Labor's Bureau of Labor Statistics, immigrants, many of them Mexican, will account for 100 percent of the growth of the U.S. labor force between 2010 and 2030.

During his electoral campaign, Obama repeatedly complained that the U.S. immigration system was "broken" and notoriously "dysfunctional," promising Latino or Hispanic organizations that he would repair it. This promise had palpable electoral results: 67 percent of Latino voters—citizens of Latin American origin—voted for Obama in 2008, compared with only 57 percent for John Kerry in 2004. The Latino vote was decisive in the defeat of Republicans in disputed states such as Colorado, North Carolina, Florida, Indiana, New Mexico, and Virginia. However, Latinos are still waiting for Obama to fulfill his promise. Most leaders of immigrant organizations believe that U.S. society is in effect telling them, "We need you but we don't want you."[4]

According to U.S. elite opinion, any immigration reform submitted to Congress must meet at least four requirements: (1) provide measures to control borders and entry points to the United States, monitor places of work, and impose sanctions on employers who hire undocumented laborers; (2) regularize the status of undocumented workers already in the United States in accordance with the law mandating they pay a fine and get in line behind all those already waiting to acquire a visa; (3) establish a legal route for regularized workers to become permanent residents and then citizens of the United States; (4) create a scheme to regulate worker flows, using guest or temporary worker mechanisms.

In early 2010 President Obama reaffirmed his "unwavering" commitment to immigration reform, but to date no proposal has been submitted to Congress, although one is being elaborated by Charles Schumer (D-N.Y.) and Lindsey Graham (R-S.C.). In December 2009 Luis Gutiérrez, Democratic representative for the Fourth Congressional District of Illinois and of Puerto Rican descent, submitted to Congress the Comprehensive Immigration Reform for America's Security and Prosperity (CIR-ASAP), which, according to the *New York Times*, "has the right ingredients for a comprehensive reform."[5]

During a massive march on Washington on March 21, 2010, Latin American and other immigrants called on Obama and Congress to ensure that U.S. immigration laws reflect the values of migrant communities in the United States and recognize the degree of economic, political, and social integration they have achieved. Marchers also noted that in contrast to the Schumer-Graham proposal, which considers migrants a burden on the United States, the Gutiérrez bill recognizes the changes that migrant communities deserve and that the country needs.[6]

While the reform has been in the works, more than 600 miles of a physical and virtual wall have been built along the U.S.-Mexican border at a cost of more than US$2.4 billion since 2005 (its maintenance is expected to cost triple that amount). According to the U.S. Government Accountability Office (GAO), whether the wall has helped stem the tide of illegal immigration is uncertain.[7] Police raids and deportations have continued, turning immigrant workers into a shadowy underclass. As the *New York Times* has remarked, "What's been happening as the endless wait for reform drags on has been ugly . . . the Border Patrol, Immigration and Customs Enforcement and local law enforcement agencies have set loose an epidemic of misery, racial profiling and needless arrests."[8]

Although many scholars, analysts, and observers view immigration as an eminently "intermestic" issue—one that combines international and local or domestic elements—most Americans consider it a domestic affair that cannot be negotiated with the governments of other countries. Even if Washington were to issue more visas to Mexican workers, it is not clear what the Mexican government would be willing to offer in return.

Mexico's constitution guarantees freedom of movement within the national territory, but it also stipulates that "the exercise of that right is subordinated to the powers of the administrative authorities regarding the limitations imposed by emigration and immigration laws."[9] If enforced, this disposition would require overland travelers to comply with exactly the same rules that apply to air travelers, channeling them through authorized points of transit. Although most top-level civil servants and legislators do not think this idea is feasible—for it would make undocumented emigration much more difficult and thus shut a key social safety valve—the subject must be open to debate. If Mexico wants an immigration agreement with the United States, the starting point must be the consistent application of its own national law.

Shared Responsibilities at the Border

Probably no border in the world separates more contrasting societies than the 3,141-kilometer line between Mexico and the United States, running from Tijuana/San Diego in the west to Matamoros/Brownsville in the east. On one side lies a technology- and capital-rich society, on the other a country whose main export is human labor. The difficulties in managing such a border were made clear in an October 2009 report issued under the auspices of the Mexican Council on Foreign Relations (*Consejo Mexicano de Asuntos Internacionales*, COMEXI) and the California-based Pacific Council on International Policy (PCIP).[10] The only way to handle the border, concluded the report's thirty contributors, is to base all recommendations on the notion of "shared problems and solutions."

The report suggests that Mexican agencies in charge of border control be restructured to mirror U.S. border security and protection, customs, and migration agencies. To facilitate border transit and trade, it recommends the development of border infrastructure through investment in public-private associations. The North American Development Bank could be reinforced to promote economic development, in concert with support for education efforts in border communities. Since water is a precious commodity in this arid frontier zone, it could be given special attention by empowering the International Boundary and Water Commission (IBWC) to manage all surface and underground waters and educating the population about its use. In addition, the report suggests environmental regulations should be harmonized in the border region. It also calls for comprehensive migration reform in the United States to deal with the challenge of undocumented migration and for a multidimensional initiative to promote globally sustainable development in Mexico. Both governments have not only promised to assess these recommendations and the feasibility of implementing them, but have already incorporated some of them in a joint statement on the border released in Washington on May 19, 2010.[11]

Multilateral Cooperation: There Is No "M" in "BRIC"

Since the ratification of NAFTA in December 1993, the United States has lost a great deal of the hegemonic power it acquired after the fall of the Berlin Wall. This is due in large part to the emergence of powerful new geopolitical actors and a subsequent shift in the global economy's center of gravity to the Asia Pacific Basin. Nonetheless, the United States offers the greatest hope for the rapid reactivation of consumption and global economic growth, although it admittedly had a large hand in the major financial crisis of 2008–09. At the same time, Brazil, Russia, India, and China (the so-called BRIC countries) are providing daily proof of a new political independence, including a perhaps natural inclination to distance themselves from Washington's foreign policy. With its timid and unfocused foreign policy, Mexico has not yet joined this group of emerging powers.

However, Mexico has held a seat on the UN Security Council in 2002–03 and 2009–10, and in this period two opposing views have emerged regarding its position on the world stage. Some argue that Mexico should make a conscious effort to join the group of middle-range powers. Others claim that this will only foment conflicts with Washington in different world forums, as exemplified by the tensions that arose when the United States invaded Iraq.

At the time of writing, another polarizing conflict is brewing within the United Nations over sanctions against Iran, which the United States supports because it fears Teheran is developing atomic weapons through its uranium-enrichment program. Other permanent members of the Security Council disagree with the U.S. position on this matter. While Mexico voted in favor of sanctions, it must decide whether to maintain this position on an issue that could put it in conflict with Washington. The issue promises to command Mexico's attention throughout its term on the council.

Since the emergence of the G-5 (Brazil, China, India, Mexico, and South Africa), which served as an interlocutor with the G-8 at the 2007 meeting in Heiligendamm, Germany, Mexico has preferred to be an amiable mediator rather than join with the other members of its group. At the G-20 meeting in 2009, which President Obama called to broaden the debate and search for solutions to the global financial crisis, it was Brazil—not Mexico—that played a key role among the Latin American countries; the same has happened on other occasions, such as the climate summit, the crisis in Honduras, and at the Ibero-American Conference in May 2010. Mexico has also been a discreet participant in the Asia Pacific Economic Cooperation (APEC) forum. In February 2010 Mexico hosted a meeting of Latin American and Caribbean heads of state to establish a new mechanism for regional cooperation and unity among the countries of the continent, excluding the United States and Canada. This initiative seeks to mend Mexico's broken relationships with Cuba, Venezuela, and Bolivia, among other countries in the region that want to isolate Washington from regional cooperation and further debilitate the Organization of American States (OAS). Mexico should articulate its interests and strategic goals clearly and seek a flexible approach to international relations that is consistent with those interests and goals.

The North American Integration Process: No Constituency, No Future

Since the signing of NAFTA, Mexico has seen quite a significant increase in foreign direct investment and in the volume of trade with the United States and Canada. Indeed, many Mexicans regard the trade agreement as a point of arrival—a way to get into the "major leagues" and establish closer ties with and gain market access to the United States, rather than as a point of departure to increase the strengths of the Mexican economy. As various authors have pointed out, the lesson Mexico has yet to learn is that growing trade and foreign investment do not in themselves lead to dynamic economic development.[12]

In the years under NAFTA, Mexico's average annual per capita GDP has grown just over 1 percent, a rate far below that necessary to generate the employment required to absorb the growth of the workforce. This low rate is a result of structural problems such as fiscal rigidity, low levels of infrastructural investment, an outdated and inefficient education system, and strong monopolistic practices in markets for open and paid television, fixed and mobile telephones, soft drinks, land transport, cement, and banking, among others.

Paradoxically, the performance of the manufacturing sector, which should be the engine of regional integration, has deteriorated since 2001. The Mexican economy follows the U.S. manufacturing industry cycle; since the United States absorbs more than 80 percent of Mexican exports, any contraction in U.S. industrial production immediately and directly affects the Mexican economy. If anything, regional integration in key areas, including manufacturing, has regressed. Instead of consolidating productive regional chains and transforming them into a productive platform for the North American region, Mexico has become an importer of Asian goods. Although it has a trade surplus with the United States, mirroring this is a growing commercial deficit with the rest of the world, mainly with China and other countries of East Asia.

Today "North America" has no leader championing it, no enthusiastic proponent with a vision of its future. The citizenry of the three NAFTA countries believe the trade agreement has benefited the other partners more than their own country, which is not very propitious for a deepening of trilateral economic integration. Yet both Canada and Mexico have mainly sought to consolidate bilateral ties with the United States rather than push for greater integration among all three, while President Obama has not reiterated his criticism of NAFTA on the campaign trail.

However, the president's trade representative, Ron Kirk, recently announced that the administration is planning to negotiate a "new kind of trade agreement for the twenty-first century." Titled the Trans-Pacific Partnership (TPP), it is expected to strengthen environmental protection, transparency, labor rights, and development and thereby "serve as a model for the future of U.S. foreign trade."[13] By contrast, NAFTA was conceived for another era and is completely out of sync with the principles of a new-generation treaty.

Future Prospects: A North American Policy for Mexican Development

A central problem for North America is the development gap between Mexico and its trade partners. Whereas Canada and the United States have a per capita annual income of more than US$40,000, the figure for Mexico is a mere US$9,000.

In view of their respective strengths, however, Mexico and the United States could join forces to build a new manufacturing platform and regional labor market. With its relatively young population, highly qualified workforce for manufacturing production, and enviable geographical position, Mexico offers an ideal logistical platform. Meanwhile, U.S. assets—its constant technological innovation; broad range of services in finance, engineering, design, brands, and marketing; and most vigorous market in the world—are essential in a postmaterial, knowledge-based economy.

North America's three leaders—Prime Minister Stephen Harper, President Barack Obama, and President Felipe Calderón—should jointly review trends in regional economic integration, demography, and workforce education to build a shared future that takes advantage of their economic interdependences, synergies, and complementarities. They should ensure the safe and efficient circulation of people along the breadth and width of Canada, the United States, and Mexico with a view to making North America more competitive vis-à-vis other regions and other integrated markets.

A Mexican Lobby in the United States

Of the 45 million Latinos living in the United States, 31 million are Mexican or of Mexican descent: 19 million were born in the United States and 12 million in Mexico. At least 11 percent of the Mexican population lives in the United States. Theoretically, the best allies of the Mexican cause in the United States are Mexican Americans; but they rightly resist being used as a conveyor belt of the Mexican government's agenda. "It now turns out that the country that forced me to leave is making demands on me," complains Antonia Hernández, a prominent former leader of the Mexican American Legal Defense and Education Fund (MALDEF). "We feel loyalty to our families, and we are proud of the history, culture, music, food of Mexico, which is also ours; but they cannot demand our loyalty toward their government or political parties, because they have done very little to create the conditions for a dignified life for their own people."[14]

According to *The Economist,* "It is best for Mexicans to stay quiet and not get involved" in the U.S. political process.[15] In a similar vein, the Mexican government instructs its civil servants and diplomats to abstain from commenting on the legislative process of its neighbor. But high-level members of the Obama administration have claimed on various occasions that Mexicans are welcome to defend their point of view, underlining that this is not only appropriate but also necessary since Americans still know so little about Mexico. Mexicans can and must promote an intelligent, forward-looking vision of integration between both societies. Failing to do so would be tantamount to passively accepting the ideas propounded by racists and xenophobes.

Preparing for the Future

For the benefit of both parties, the United States and Mexico could translate their shared responsibility into bilateral agreements along the following lines:

1. Mexico should become a manufacturing platform and logistical distribution center connecting all parts of the hemisphere. It is ideally situated to

be the axis of an interoceanic system for the transport of containers between, say, Hong Kong and Houston. This role, already envisioned by North America's SuperCorridor Coalition, Inc., should become a strategic goal of Mexico's Communications and Transport Secretariat.[16]

2. By definition, immigration is a bilateral issue. Yet the United States is reluctant to admit it needs Mexican workers, while Mexico expels migrants and treats them as a "residual" population. Since Mexico will be involved in any solution, the Mexican Congress must call for quid pro quo measures in the reform of U.S. immigration law. But it must also change its own immigration legislation to ensure that what Mexico demands from the United States is consistent with its treatment of Central American and other migrants who are passing through Mexico en route to the United States.

3. The border should be managed in a coordinated manner by a binational authority. U.S. Homeland Security and Mexico's Secretariat must jointly define and coordinate tasks regarding border crossings, infrastructure works, and law enforcement agencies.

4. To foster a better relationship, Mexico and the United States must not only aim for mutual respect and better mutual knowledge but should also strive to identify shared interests. It is hard to believe that South Korea, which has half of Mexico's population and lies more than 9,000 kilometers away, has 60,000 students in U.S. programs of higher education compared with Mexico's 12,000. A first step should be to establish a broad, consolidated program offering student grants and exchanges. It could be launched by the Public Education Secretariat and the National Association of Universities and Institutions of Higher Education (*Asociación Nacional de Universidades e Instituciones de Educación Superior*, ANUIES) to permit U.S. candidates, particularly Mexican Americans, to study in Mexico, and to ensure that a higher number of Mexicans do so in the United States.

The United States is the only major economic power without a development policy for its less-developed neighboring countries. In contrast, the European Union has mobilized structural funds for regional development and economic and social cohesion in Spain, Greece, Ireland, and Portugal, and it is now doing the same for the countries of Eastern Europe. Japan has established similar programs for its neighbors in South and Southeast Asia.

Mexico must adopt the objective of developing a broad middle class, a goal that would be in tune with U.S. strategic interests: this would expand markets and promote economic and political stability south of the border. As President George W. Bush put it, "We must work with Mexico to develop a middle class in the long run, so people can do their duty as a parent at home."[17] The U.S., Mexican, and Canadian governments should consider creating a trilaterally funded North American Development Fund to promote convergent regional economic development.[18]

Unfortunately, increasing violence in cities near the U.S. border such as Ciudad Juárez, Reynosa, and Monterrey has led the United States to issue "travel alerts" that merely augment widespread fear of what is happening south of the border. Instead of encouraging people to think of Mexico as a business partner or a strategic ally, such measures make one wonder whether the United States will eventually try to seal the border entirely to protect itself from the growing wave of violence and crime on the Mexican side.

History teaches that citizens will forgive the mistakes of politicians and endure hard times as long as they are sure their government in on their side. If this applies to foreign governments as well, it is hard to imagine that Mexico will ever have as receptive a figure across the border as President Obama, which is all the more reason not to let this window of opportunity for improved relations close.

At the same time, Mexico must recognize that it will be relevant to the world's greatest power only to the degree that it accepts its responsibilities and understands that the key to a strong economy is a broad and vibrant middle class. Hence no international cooperation scheme can replace a national development policy that empowers state and society to build the physical, social, and institutional infrastructure required for economic growth. The three fundamental pillars of such a policy must be improved public education, economic competitiveness, and a sound strategy for industrial development.[19] This could significantly transform the way in which Mexico is perceived, not only in the United States but the world over.

Notes

1. The hope of reviving agreements such as the "Spirit of Houston" between presidents Carlos Salinas de Gortari and George H. W. Bush or the "San Cristóbal accords" between presidents Vicente Fox and George W. Bush was rapidly eclipsed by the differences and tensions in bilateral relations.

2. Jesús Silva-Herzog Márquez, "La diplomacia de brindis" (The diplomacy of toasting), *Reforma*, March 16, 2009.

3. See "México y el mundo: opinión pública y política exterior" (Mexico and the world: public opinion and foreign policy), a survey undertaken by the Centro de Investigación y Docencia Económicas (CIDE), Mexico, DF (www.mexicoyelmundo. cide.edu).

4. Oscar Chacón, leader of the National Alliance of Latin American and Caribbean Communities (NALACC), interview with Carlos Heredia, Mexico City, March 10, 2010.

5. "Reform, on Ice," *New York Times*, March 2, 2010. The bill became U.S. House Resolution 4321.

6. NALACC Press comuniqué (www.nalacc.org).

7. Daniel B. Word, "Billions for a U.S.-Mexico Border Fence, but Is It Doing Any Good?" *Christian Science Monitor*, September 19, 2009.

8. "Reform, on Ice."

9. Article 11 of the Mexican constitution.

10. *Una nueva visión de la frontera México-Estados Unidos: soluciones conjuntas a problemas comunes* (A new vision of the Mexico-U.S. border: Joint solutions to common problems), October 13, 2009 (www.consejomexicano.org).

11. See "Declaration by the Government of the United States of America and the Government of the United Mexican States Concerning Twenty-First Century Border Management," May 19, 2010 (www.america.gov).

12. Kevin P. Gallagher, Enrique Dussel Peters, and Timothy A. Wise, eds., *The Future of North American Trade Policy: Lessons from NAFTA*, Pardee Center Task Force Report 1 (Boston University, November 2009).

13. Ibid.

14. Antonia Hernández, conversation with Carlos Heredia, February 2009.

15. "Gently Does It: Mexico's Complex Relationship with America," *The Economist*, December 3, 2009.

16. The North American Transport and Trade Super Corridor should link central Northern America from the Lázaro Cárdenas Port in Michoacán (the doorway to the Asian-Pacific Basin) to the city of Winnipeg in the middle of the trans-Canadian highway, passing through Kansas City, Missouri, in the U.S. heartland (www.nasco.com).

17. Dow Jones Newswires, August 7, 2004.

18. Robert A. Pastor and others, "The Paramount Challenge for North America: Closing the Development Gap" (www.american.edu/ia/cnas/pdfs/NADBank.pdf).

19. In a February 19, 2010, report on his visit to Mexico, Vernor Muñoz Villalobos, UN special rapporteur on the right to education, noted that the Public Education Secretariat remains "subordinated" to the teachers' union headed by Elba Esther Gordillo, which "obstructs" educational advancement in Mexico. To illustrate the economic stresses, on April 5, 2010, President Calderón presented a reform bill to Congress seeking to expand the powers of the Federal Competition Commission to sanction monopolistic practices.

three
Obama and Brazil

João Augusto de Castro Neves and Matias Spektor

When Barack Obama met Brazil's Luiz Inácio Lula da Silva for the first time in March 2009, his tone was deferential. Not unlike his predecessor, Obama praised the "progressive, forward-looking leadership" qualities of his Brazilian counterpart and underlined the importance of Brazil's increasing role in global affairs.[1] However, there was not much to the meeting beyond the flattery. Except for discussing the difficulties in expanding cooperation on biofuels, the two presidents paid almost no attention to issues in which both countries play a relevant role, such as international trade, the environment, nuclear proliferation, and the global financial architecture. Since then, relations between Brazil and the United States have been marked by considerable friction and relative distance.

That is not to say that their relationship has negative undertones. Quite the opposite. Since 2000 it has been fairly positive. Nevertheless, since the end of the cold war Brazil has shown less enthusiasm toward engagement with the United States than have countries like Argentina, Chile, or Mexico. For Brazil, the moments of close alignment have been uncommon, while the overall attitude of the United States may be described as one of benign indifference.[2] Not even the good personal relationship between presidents Fernando Henrique Cardoso and Bill Clinton and between presidents Lula and George W. Bush were enough to alter that scenario. All in all, the numerous high-level meetings and memoranda of understanding between the two countries have amounted to a respectful, yet almost stale bilateral relationship. After the failed attempts to establish a Free Trade Area of the Americas

(FTAA) in the 1990s, they still have made little progress toward bilateral cooperation, even on the promising issue of biofuels.

Since 2009 the U.S.-Brazil agenda has been increasingly marked by differences in the regional sphere. President Obama's inauguration occurred only months after the creation of the South American Defense Council (2008), an arm of the Union of South American Nations (UNASUR) spearheaded by Brazil. This backdrop also includes a project to establish the Bank of the South (a financial institution of South American countries) and a proposal to strengthen other regional political mechanisms such as the Rio Group and the Latin American and Caribbean Summit (CALC). All these bodies create new spaces for Brazilian leadership at the expense of traditional U.S. influence in the region. Furthermore, Obama's arrival on the scene coincided with the emergence of China as the main market for Brazilian exports, surpassing the United States. Although the United States regained its position as Brazil's major export market in the first half of 2010, the overall effect has been to reinforce a common perception in Brazil that U.S. influence in the Americas is dwindling.

This chapter examines the relationship between Brazil and the United States in the period that coincides with the beginning of the Obama administration and the end of Lula's second term. The goal is to closely review issues that characterized the agenda and to illustrate the overall dynamics that guide the bilateral relationship.

Antecedents

Brazil watched the U.S. presidential election of 2008 with both expectation and uncertainty. Obama's surprising and fast-paced political trajectory pointed to new priorities and a new style of leadership, quite different from that of the Bush era. Lula's government, however, was used to dealing with the Republican administration rather well and found the dialogue appropriate and satisfactory, if somewhat distant. In fact, many Brazilians consider the period of the Bush and Lula presidencies to be one of the best in recent history for bilateral relations.

The relationship between Lula and Bush paved the way for a significant increase in the number of high-level visits and cooperative initiatives. In March 2003 the cabinets of both countries held a joint meeting for the first time in history. Three months later, fourteen new bilateral consultation mechanisms were in place. U.S. secretaries of state were in Brazil in 2004 (Colin Powell) and in 2005 and 2008 (Condoleezza Rice). President

Bush visited Brazil in 2005 and 2007, leaving behind agreements on biofuels, education, and science and technology. President Lula visited Washington in 2002 (as president-elect) and twice in 2003. In 2007 he met Bush at Camp David. It was no secret that in 2004 Bush was Brasilia's favored candidate for reelection against the Democratic candidate, Senator John Kerry.[3]

According to Brazil's assessment, Bush's foreign policy created an unexpected opening for Brasília on the regional stage. As the terrorist attacks of 9/11 shifted the attention of the United States away from Latin America, Brazil began to intensify its diplomacy toward the region, seeking a fresh regional consensus. New regional mechanisms were created to serve as possible alternatives to traditional institutions such as the Organization of American States (OAS), the Inter-American Development Bank (IADB), and the Inter-American Defense Board (JID). For many Brazilian strategists, the exclusion of the United States from these initiatives was not the result of a deliberate anti-American stance—although that notion may be disputed—but was a desirable outcome nonetheless. At the second meeting of CALC, held in 2010 in Mexico, the region's heads of state decided to establish a Community of Latin American and Caribbean States that excluded the United States and Canada. Lula dubbed the event historic, proclaiming "the region was finally seeking its own personality."[4]

Therefore it was no surprise that Bush's departure from office would increase Brasília's uncertainties. A sudden change in the cast of main characters that managed the bilateral relationship could bring about the reshaping of the essence and general orientation of U.S. foreign policy. Note, however, that Brasília's mild preference toward Bush did not translate into an acceptance of the Bush Doctrine. President Lula, like his predecessor, Fernando Henrique Cardoso (1995–2003), was in fact a fierce and systematic opponent of Bush's neoconservative agenda, particularly of the U.S.-led invasion of Iraq in March 2003.

Brazil also began to question America's role in the global economy, which by the end of the Bush presidency was battling one of the worst financial crises since the Great Depression. In response to the meltdown, the United States promoted the G-20 over the G-7/8 as the world's main forum for economic and financial coordination. As a result, Brazil's economic clout grew considerably, making it an important member of the G-20 along with other emerging countries. Still, Brazilians remained unsure of the future of this new mechanism of global governance under President Obama. The new Democratic administration had yet to make a gesture of goodwill toward the emerging powers, such as enhancing consultation instruments at the bilateral level (for example, the economic and strategic dialogue with China) or becoming more responsive to the demands of these countries at multilateral negotiations (such as the Doha Round or climate change talks).

Obama, Lula, and Hemispheric Relations

In its first eighteen months, the Obama administration faced several problems that ended up creating some friction between the United States and Brazil. One arose from Obama's first message to the region, addressed to Cuba. Its promise of looser restrictions on travel and remittances generated some optimism throughout the hemisphere and helped squelch somewhat the anti-American rhetoric on the rise in some countries. To many observers, the ideological polarization between Bush's unilateralism and the so-called Bolivarianism movement led by President Hugo Chávez appeared close to an end. These gestures by the United States, however, failed to reduce the pressure from Latin America to bring Cuba back to the Organization of American States (OAS). In July 2009, within a few months of an initiative spearheaded by Brazil to coordinate a common Latin American position on Cuba's status in regional forums, the OAS revoked the suspension of Cuba. (By the end of 2008, Cuba was invited to join the Rio Group, an important regional political organization.)

Despite initial signs of resistance, the U.S. government did not oppose the OAS ruling. All the same, differences between Brazil and the United States remained significant, as demonstrated in early 2010 following the death of a Cuban political dissident after a hunger strike in prison. While the Obama administration publicly condemned the incident, President Lula downplayed its seriousness and even defended the Castro regime during a visit to Havana. This was not so surprising in view of the historical links between Cuba and Lula and his Workers' Party (PT). All in all, President Obama did not have much to offer in the months following his warmly received debut address to the region in April 2009. With no major announcements or new visions for cooperation, Latin American optimism toward its relations with the United States soon became diluted.

Political events in Honduras revealed fissures between Brazil and the United States as well after the sudden ousting of President Manuel Zelaya in June 2009 by the armed forces, backed by the legislative and judiciary branches of government. Although the coup was rapidly condemned by the region, the OAS, the United Nations, and both Obama and Lula, Brazil-U.S. relations began to cool when Zelaya took refuge in the Brazilian embassy in Tegucigalpa. Brazil argued for his return to power before the November presidential election as a precondition for negotiating a solution. With the election drawing near, the United States believed the inauguration of a new president was the best way out of the impasse. By December 2009 the regional division was clear. The new government of Honduras under Porfirio Lobo was recognized by the United States but not by the Mercosur bloc (Brazil, Argentina, Paraguay, and Uruguay), Venezuela, or even Mexico. That turn of events, remarked a high-level Brazilian official, would leave the United States "isolated in its relation[s] with Latin America."[5] With the support of other countries in the region, Brazil then threatened to boycott the European-Latin American summit in Spain in May 2010 if the Honduran president were to attend. Lobo succumbed: to appease his neighbors, he attended only a small discussion at the summit.[6]

In 2009 Haiti became another litmus test for Brazil-U.S. relations. Since 2004 Brazil had been leading the United Nations Stabilization Mission in Haiti (MINUSTAH), a relatively safe task in terms of financial and military risks. Moreover, it gave Brazil an opportunity to increase its international status and strengthen its bid for a permanent seat in the UN Security Council without the common problems associated with military operations abroad. The catastrophic earthquake that hit Haiti in early 2010, however, changed those conditions. For the first time since World War II, Brazil buried soldiers killed in a military mission overseas. Furthermore, the Brazilian commanders had to deal with increasing American and European involvement in Haiti immediately after the tragedy. The enhanced U.S. operations created a dilemma for Brazilian foreign policy operators. With far less resources and experience, Brazil was likely to become a minor partner in the relief and reconstruction efforts, but a retreat amid the crisis was not a feasible option. Once viewed as a potential instrument for regional affirmation, Brazil's Haiti mission thus became a compromised strategy.

Colombia placed another complicated issue on the South American chessboard. In August 2009 it signed a deal to increase the U.S. military presence in Colombia that triggered a round of fierce criticism and suspicion in neighboring countries and underlined the distance between Colombian foreign policy and the scope of new subregional institutions such as UNASUR and the South American Defense Council (CDS). Since these institutions showed mild interest in the security threat posed by the Revolutionary Armed Forces of Colombia (FARC), Colombia saw the continuity of its engagement with the United States as the best option available to deal with the matter. The Brazilian government strongly condemned the deal, declaring that it was alert to any foreign military base in South America, and pressed Colombia for formal assurances about U.S. military operations in the region.

Brazil had mistrusted U.S. military presence in the region even in 2008, when the Bush administration decided to reestablish the Fourth Fleet of the U.S. Navy in the Southern Command area, encompassing the Caribbean and waters surrounding Central and South America. Noting that Brazil had recently discovered oil 300 kilometers offshore, President Lula remarked: "Now, obviously, we want the U.S. to explain what is the logic behind the Fourth Fleet."[7] From a Brazilian perspective, the U.S. presence in Colombia and reactivation of the Fourth Fleet are part of a coherent set of initiatives emanating from Washington. Despite its general disappointment over military issues, Brazil entered into a defense cooperation agreement with the United States in April 2010. Although the deal does not signal a major practical shift in the military relationship, it has a symbolic weight—being the first such agreement between Brazil and the United States since 1977—and may pave the way for more cooperation between the two countries in the near future.

Part of the problem hampering cooperation resided in Washington's expectation that Brazil would be keen, or at least open, to the idea of sharing the burdens and costs of maintaining the regional order. Yet the recurring message from Brazil remained a general one: that the country "can and should help build the global order, conscious of its demographic, territorial, economic and cultural weight and of the fact that it is a democracy amid a process of social transformation."[8] No explicit views emerged about Brazil's responsibility, as the largest country in South America, to contribute to regional stability and the costs of maintaining regional institutions. Brazil's stance became even clearer amid the debates on the forthcoming election of the secretary general of the OAS in March 2010. Whereas the United States backed the reelection of José Miguel Insulza, Brazil's representative argued for an open election, declaring that "the OAS is not a business corporation, it is a democracy; one country, one vote." A legislative aide to a high-ranking U.S. senator replied: "It would be great for other countries to become stakeholders and give more money to the OAS—and Brazil is a good example of an emerging country that wants a larger role in the region. It would be great if Brazil reaches into its wallet."[9]

Brazil's approach to the region may relate to three possible interpretations of its national interests. If correct, they clearly hamper attempts to achieve more active cooperation between Brazil and the United States on regional affairs.

First, being one of Brazil's main sources of external instability in the world, the countries of the region may be too close for comfort. What happens in Paraguay, Bolivia, or Ecuador increasingly affects Brazil's interests in terms of direct investments in those countries. For example, energy security became an important issue for Brazilian officials after the recent political turbulence in Bolivia and Paraguay. In 2006 Bolivia nationalized its hydrocarbon industry, directly affecting Brazil's state-owned oil company, Petrobras; and in 2008 Paraguay began pressing Brazil to renegotiate the terms of a treaty for binational use of energy derived from Itaipu Dam—an important source of electricity for Brazil's industries in the southeast and of funds for the Paraguayan government. Indeed, growing instability and increasing Brazilian interests at stake in neighboring countries may help explain why Brazil decided to forgo its conservative stance and finally agree to deepen institutions of regional governance. Perhaps it felt that more institutionalized regional architecture, such as the South American Defense Council, would help it deal with instabilities and fend off U.S. intromission in regional affairs.

Second, Brazil may believe the region works as a protective shield against negative externalities of global capitalism, particularly in the sphere of trade. After all, the long-term goal behind Brazilian regional policies is to manage globalization and to protect the national economy from external shocks. This is a well-known concern among Brazilian elites dating back to the 1960s and surviving the end of the cold war. Note that this approach to regionalism emphasizes not the sharing of goals with neighboring countries as a legitimate and desirable means to manage the world order, but the protection of Brazil's *national* potential to deal with the challenges of globalization. For Brazil, it translates into a process of adaptation (or expansion) of traditional national goals (such as autonomy) to a regional scale.

Third, Brazil might consider the region a portal to global power. As the dominant economy in the region, Brazil would mold relations in its vicinity to foster understandings and prevent conflicts, thereby increasing its leverage in global arenas. It is difficult, however, to find explicit references to this power-driven attitude in Brazilian rhetoric. As the nation's minister of foreign relations has pointed out, "Even a large country like Brazil is a small country in a world like this. . . . We do not have the capacity to stand alone. . . . I believe that Brazil does not fully exist without the union [with South America]."[10] Nevertheless, the underlying logic points to the region as a launching pad for Brazilian power, with Brazil as a natural center of political and economic gravity in the region.

Copenhagen

For both the United States and Brazil, 2009 brought a new perspective to environmental issues. Under the new Obama administration, America's approach to climate change altered significantly, with greater incentives for stricter clean energy legislation by the states and a more comprehensive interpretation of existing federal legislation such as the Clean Air Act. By the end of that year, the U.S. House of Representatives had also passed the cap-and-trade bill, establishing an emissions trading system between companies. In Brazil, the Lula administration launched a National Plan on Climate Change stipulating deforestation targets for the first time in Brazilian history. (Deforestation is the cause of more than 70 percent of Brazil's greenhouse gas emissions.)

Despite progress at the national levels and their similar interests in the climate issue, Brazil and the United States showed no movement toward an international understanding in the months preceding the United Nations Climate Change Conference in Copenhagen in December 2009. Each country remained focused on its own agenda.

The Brazilian strategy was to coordinate a common position with other developing countries in the G-77, on the assumption that the global economic crisis of 2008–09 might persuade developed states to institute protectionist measures such as those already revealed in the economic rescue plans of the U.S. and French governments. Brazil was upholding the principle of common but differentiated responsibilities, a cornerstone of sustainable development set by the Kyoto Protocol in 1997 in order to minimize developing countries' obligations to reach international greenhouse gas emissions targets. In a meeting in May 2009, Brazil also sought to articulate with the Brazil, Russia, India, and China (BRIC) coalition a somewhat accusatory strategy aimed at the developed world.

On the American side, it was clear that Obama's international negotiating leverage was constrained by the dynamics of domestic politics. Without the full support of Congress (the Senate had yet to vote on the climate change bill), the United States would have a very hard time winning the confidence of other countries. Indeed, as the Copenhagen meeting drew near, conversations between Brazil and other emerging countries were marked by criticism of the U.S. stance on climate change. At the same time, Brazil began promoting the idea of "ethanol diplomacy"—an effort to link the talks on reducing greenhouse gas emissions to the use of renewable sources of energy. The Brazilian government's international engagement focused entirely on trying to establish an alternative energy market to oil, as was evident even in the organization chart of the Ministry of Foreign Relations, the Itamaraty: most climate change negotiations were conducted by the ministry's energy division, not by the environmental sector. By the time of the Copenhagen meeting, however, the ethanol diplomacy initiative had lost most of its momentum, owing to a combination of factors. For one thing, controversy erupted over the adverse impact of biofuels on food production and prices. For another, Brazil's energy priorities began to shift after several discoveries of offshore oil reserves.

When it became clear that the Copenhagen summit was headed for a stalemate, Brazil decided to substantially alter its negotiating strategy. Instead of emphasizing emerging coalitions such as BASIC (between Brazil, South Africa, India, and China) to counterbalance the developed world (the United States and the European Union), Brazil shifted to more progressive rhetoric, announcing more ambitious voluntary targets for the reduction of greenhouse gas emissions. Moreover, during the meeting president Lula agreed to contribute to a global fund to tackle climate change, a position that had been at odds with that of the Brazilian delegation moments before.[11]

Iran

In 2010 the U.S.-Brazil relationship became even more strained. Brazil happened to be elected to a nonpermanent seat in the UN Security Council just as the United States was working to convince other permanent members of the council to support a new round of economic sanctions against Iran. With the discovery of secret nuclear facilities and further evidence that the Iranian regime was seeking to enrich uranium, the Obama administration abandoned its efforts to try to engage with Iran and pressed for harsher measures against it. Brazil rejected the proposed sanctions, however, and stressed the civil purpose of Iran's nuclear program. Amid the social unrest in June 2009 following Mahmoud Ahmadinejad's disputed reelection, Lula came out in defense of the Iranian regime. Soon after, the Iranian leader visited Brasília, and Lula was set to visit Teheran in early 2010.

In May 2010 Brazil and Turkey, also a nonpermanent member of the Security Council, clinched a deal with Iran that would resume negotiations and possibly avoid a new round of sanctions by the Security Council. The proposal restored ideas put forth by the same Security Council in October 2009, when Iran was invited to exchange uranium ore for enriched fuel from another country to allay suspicions about the goals of the Iranian nuclear program. Soon after the proposal was made, the Security Council, persuaded by the United States, passed a sanctions resolution against Iran. Although it is not clear if a deal mediated by Brazil and Turkey will succeed in the near future, Brazil's initiative was not enough to restore confidence among the permanent members of the Security Council toward Iran and vice versa.

Why was Brazil trying to become a broker with Iran? Economic interests were clearly not the reason.[12] Rather, by pursuing a prominent role in the matter, Brazil was underlining the problems surrounding power politics while trying to indicate alternative formulas for negotiation and confidence building. Moreover, it was attempting to test its influence outside its region and to reinforce the idea that it is an emerging power with global interests, as indicated by its reaction to the skeptical remarks of the permanent members of the Security Council about the Brazilian-Turkish effort: "Before it was common to ask permission to do things, a habit of being small. Brazil has finally come of age and does not need to ask permission to maintain relations with any country."[13]

Brazil's resistance to economic sanctions against Iran also appears to spring from three deeper reasons. First, it considered the sanctions a possible prelude to a military intervention in Iran. The Iraq invasion of 2003 was fresh in the memory of Brazilian officials, who argued that the last time the Security Council acted upon inconclusive evidence, the world had to deal with an illegitimate war in the Persian Gulf.

Second, Brazil did not believe that UN sanctions could bring Iran back to the negotiating table "in good faith." On the contrary, it argued, external pressures and isolation could encourage Iran to pursue nuclear weapons. Drawing support from its own recent history, Brazil noted that when the military regime of 1964–85 encountered enormous international censure in response to its efforts to develop a civilian nuclear program outside the Nuclear Non-Proliferation Treaty (NPT), it simply turned its back on the opposition and launched a secret nuclear program in the late 1970s. Although the results were limited and the cost great, the country was able to develop the technology needed to enrich uranium. As a Brazilian diplomat pointed out at a seminar on the Iranian question, "When Brazil looks at Iran, it does not see Iran alone; it also sees itself."

Third, in Brazil's view, the nuclear powers use the NPT selectively. After all, there is no pressure on Israel to acknowledge its nuclear weapons, nor was India punished when it openly defied the NPT by becoming a nuclear state. On the contrary, India was recently granted a favorable nuclear cooperation treaty with the United States. Furthermore, argue Brazilian authorities, the major nuclear powers do not have the moral authority to invoke the NPT because they failed to honor their part of the agreement, which is to progressively dismantle the existing nuclear arsenal. In fact, Brazil's official position in not ratifying the additional protocol to the NPT rests on this last argument.[14]

It would be a mistake to dismiss these three points simply as anti-Americanism, although they speak to what Brasília regards as an unfair aspect of the U.S. nonproliferation policy. This does not mean, however, that the two countries do not share common interests on the nuclear question. As one of the main beneficiaries of the collective security system established in 1945, Brazil did not challenge the conception of the existing international order. As an emerging country with a long history of vulnerability and dependence, however, Brazil sought to obstruct the use of international norms in favor of the dominant states.

The impact of the Iranian question on Brazil-U.S. relations was summed up by the U.S. ambassador to Brazil, Tom Shannon: "As Brazil becomes more assertive globally . . . , we are going to bump into Brazil on new issues and in new places such as Iran, the Middle East and Haiti." Perhaps, added Shannon, the time has come for a clear reappraisal on both sides: "It is challenging for both of us because it means we have to rethink how we understand our relationship."[15]

Brazil and the United States are arguably the two most influential countries in the Western Hemisphere today, which means the importance of each country to the other can only increase. Their current relationship, however, unveils the difficulty for both in forging a consensus on critical issues, a clear sign that more friction lies ahead in the near future. Neither their shared values—democracy, human rights, a market economy—nor common interests seem strong enough to ensure a close partnership. Rather, bilateral relations will most likely continue to suffer from mutual frustrations, with less intense cooperation on many issues.

Notes

1. The White House Blog, March 14, 2009 (www.whitehouse.gov/blog/2009/03/14/president-obama-a-wonderful-meeting-minds).

2. For Brazil, there were two clear moments of alignment with the United States: immediately after World War II and during the first years of the military regime (1964–67).

3. For an analysis of Brazil-U.S. relations, see Monica Hirst and Andrew Hurrell, *Brasil-Estados Unidos: Desencontros e afinidades* (Agreements and disagreements) (Fundação Getúlio Vargas, 2009).

4. *BBC Brasil,* February 23, 2010.

5. "EUA podem se isolar por apoio a eleição em Honduras, diz assessor de Lula" (U.S. may become isolated after recognizing the election in Honduras, says Lula's adviser), *Folha de S.Paulo,* November 25, 2009.

6. "Latin America Still Divided over Coup in Honduras," *New York Times,* June 5, 2010.

7. "Lula quer explicações dos EUA sobre Quarta Frota" (Lula wants U.S. explanation on the Fourth Fleet), *Folha de S.Paulo,* July 2, 2008.

8. Celso Amorim, minister of foreign relations, first remarks to the ministerial staff, January 1, 2003.

9. "Primeira votação na OEA deve reeleger Insulza" (First ballot at the OAS should reelect Insulza), *O Estado de S.Paulo,* March 24, 2010.

10. Celso Amorim, in a speech delivered at the Third Meeting of the Ministers of Foreign Relations of South America, Santiago, Chile, November 24, 2006.

11. "A bolha de Lula" (Lula's bubble), *Folha de S.Paulo,* December 19, 2009.

12. According to Brazil's Ministry of Development, Industry, and Trade, in 2009 Iran accounted for only 0.8 percent of Brazil's exports and 0.01 percent of its total imports.

13. Samuel Pinheiro Guimarães, secretary of strategic affairs and former deputy minister of external relations, "O Brasil não pede licença" (Brazil does not ask for permission), *Zero Hora,* November 22, 2009.

14. Brazilian National Defense Strategy (December 2008).

15. Tom Shannon, "Brazil Asserts Role on Iran," *Financial Times,* May 14, 2010.

four

The United States and Colombia: Recalibrating the Relationship

Michael Shifter

The United States and Colombia have enjoyed a long and close, yet often complicated, relationship that has gone through various stages. In light of the changed political environment both in Washington and in Bogotá under the new administration inaugurated in August 2010, the time has come to rethink that relationship. Such a rethinking might begin with the current moment.

The United States, faced with severe and competing budget pressures, is planning to wind down its decade-long anti-drug package generally known as Plan Colombia, a comprehensive program designed to reduce drug trafficking and restore security chiefly by providing military equipment and training to the Colombian government. Meanwhile Colombia is preparing to assume greater responsibility for tackling its security-related challenges. Also important to consider is Colombia's performance in improving the quality of its democratic governance. That record is decidedly mixed, marked by impressive institutional strengths and notable advances in recent years, but also by an array of pending and profound problems, including a continuing armed conflict and a serious human rights situation. All in all, the decade of Plan Colombia yields a number of lessons that should help the United States decide how best to recalibrate its relationship with such an important South American partner.

Changed Context, New Opportunity

On February 26, 2010, Colombia's respected Constitutional Court put to rest a question that had long been looming, and that created uncertainty and confusion both inside Colombia and between Bogotá and Washington. At issue was whether Álvaro Uribe, Colombia's two-term president, would be eligible to run for a third term and could proceed with a national referendum in pursuit of that aim.

In an unexpectedly categorical 7-2 ruling, the court, invoking several arguments, including procedural irregularities, found that such a referendum would be unconstitutional. Uribe respected the court's decision, expressing his "love for Colombia," and thus opened the way for a competitive campaign for the Colombian presidency.

Since his election in 2002, Uribe has dominated the political landscape in Colombia. He has been a markedly take-charge, indefatigable president, determined to pursue a "democratic security" policy that would help reassert the authority of the state in Colombian territory. Though Uribe's record and legacy will be long debated, it is beyond question that many of the key tendencies of the nation's deteriorated security situation have been reversed under his two administrations. Homicide rates are at their lowest point in more than two decades, and kidnappings have dropped sharply.

The state's capacity to protect its citizens has improved in large part because police presence throughout the country is much greater and the military is in general more professional. As a result, the public's mood and psychology have changed dramatically, as reflected in its growing trust in government institutions and confidence that they spend tax dollars wisely. That renewed optimism accounted for Uribe's record popularity and support at the end of his tenure—even though, for a variety of reasons, it had dipped somewhat in late 2009 and early 2010.

At the same time, Colombia abounds in paradoxes and contradictions, resembling its historical pattern of very positive trends coexisting with markedly worrying ones. Sweeping characterizations of Colombian democracy should therefore be greeted with some skepticism. Although the Constitutional Court reaffirmed the country's adherence to the rule of law—and thus highlighted one of its main institutional strengths—the challenges to full constitutional safeguards and democratic governance are persistent and formidable. Despite some improvements, the human rights situation remains severe, particularly in some parts of the country where violence is widespread and state protection woefully inadequate. Judicial proceedings may be more transparent, but impunity levels from criminal prosecutions are unacceptably high.

In addition, Colombia has been beset by a host of troubling scandals. One involves military personnel alleged to have killed a significant number of innocent victims extrajudicially in order to increase the count of presumed insurgents and obtain accompanying bonus payments. To add to these problems, the intelligence service continues its pervasive surveillance of political opponents, paramilitary influences have penetrated the political system, and recent security gains are backsliding with the resurgence of violence and criminal groups throughout the country. Concerns about such problems intensified when it seemed Uribe might be constitutionally able to run for a third term and, in light of his high popularity, would probably be reelected.

Had Uribe succeeded, he may very well have moved toward one-man rule and allowed the erosion of checks and constraints on executive authority to continue. Such governance would have been unprecedented for Colombia and would have imperiled the country's institutional strengths and relatively strong equilibrium. That is why the Constitutional Court's decision was overwhelmingly welcomed by those worried about the potential weakening of Colombia's democracy. Ardent Uribe supporters were no doubt disappointed and wondered whether any successor would be able to deliver positive results comparable to those registered since 2003.

The court's decision was also greeted with a measure of satisfaction by diverse quarters in Washington. The Obama administration barely concealed its relief. Secretary of State Hillary Clinton, who traveled to the region in early March 2010, personally congratulated Uribe during their meeting in Montevideo, Uruguay. And in a letter delivered to Uribe by national security adviser James Jones, Obama commended Uribe for his "invaluable example to all citizens, including presidents, in the acceptance of the law and the acceptance of the decisions of democratic institutions." While some Colombians thought the letter was condescending, others were proud that the U.S. president had explicitly recognized the country's adherence to the constitution and rule of law.

Strong-willed and resolute, Uribe had divided public opinion not only in Colombia but also in the U.S. capital. Yet supporters and detractors alike agreed that a third Uribe administration would have been costly for Colombia's democratic institutions, democratic trends in Latin America, and the U.S.-Colombia bilateral agenda. Influential U.S. and international media very keen on Uribe—such as *The Economist*, *Wall Street Journal*, and *Washington Post*—had all strongly urged him to decline a third run for the presidency. By doing so, they argued, he would not only avoid sullying a generally positive legacy but also eschew any comparisons with the Venezuelan president Hugo Chávez, who won a national referendum in February 2009 to remove term limits and pursue his barely disguised aim of perpetuating himself in power. The court's decision—and Uribe's adherence to it—enabled critics of Chávez to continue pointing to his singularly autocratic regime and to challenge claims that unlimited reelection was a region-wide trend to which presidents of all stripes were succumbing.

With the political reality in Colombia now changed, the Obama administration and the Democratic-controlled Congress have an opportunity to reassess the overall U.S. approach to Colombia and to consider which policies should be emphasized and which should be scaled back or even discontinued. An essential step would be to go beyond aid- and trade-centered thinking to vigorously pursue greater multilateral diplomacy and deeper political engagement. Major political obstacles notwithstanding, it is also important, not only for U.S. relations with Colombia and Latin America but also for its own global interests, that Washington pass the pending U.S.-Colombia free trade agreement, negotiated in 2006. Current political realities suggest that congressional approval of the pact will be contingent on Colombia's further progress on human rights and the creation of an adequate social safety net for U.S. workers.

That Uribe is stepping down as president does not, of course, guarantee a changed U.S. policy toward Colombia. U.S. domestic politics and, to some degree, conditions on the ground in Colombia, will be decisive. However, Uribe's acceptance of the court ruling could facilitate progress on the bilateral agenda. There will now likely be somewhat more margin for maneuvering and a chance to see the relationship in a different light. The "Uribe factor" was always relevant in Washington, particularly among congressional Democrats, who viewed the Colombian president's past connections with some suspicion. In a joint news conference in Washington on June 29, 2009, President Obama himself left little doubt about how he regarded the prospects for Uribe's second reelection. While stressing that this was a decision to be made by Colombians, Obama, citing the example of the first U.S. president, George Washington, affirmed his conviction in the U.S. system of a two-term limit.

Even before the court's ruling, the Obama administration issued some noteworthy signals about its posture toward Colombia on two key issues: the pending trade agreement and the substantial aid package of Plan Colombia. Obama's mention of Colombia, along with Panama and South Korea, in his State of the Union address on January 28, 2010, was a surprise. Obama was seeking to convey his intention to "strengthen trade relations" and create export jobs. Until then he had been close to silent on the trade question, instead focusing on other foreign policy priorities. (To one commentator, it sounded as if these remarks on the topic had been lifted from one of Bill

Clinton's or George Bush's speeches.) While Obama's words were meant to signal that he is prepared to work with the private sector and to demonstrate his commitment to reducing high unemployment levels, they did not commit the administration to approving the trade agreements, which remains improbable in an election year.

Furthermore, in its 2011 budget request to Congress, the Obama administration has called for some cuts in aid to Colombia. The amounts, still subject to congressional review and eventual approval, would reduce support by some $55 million, or 11 percent of the total amount of roughly $550 million. While the proposed reduction upset some Colombians, it reflects the continuation of a trend—already evident during the Bush years—to wind down U.S. assistance to Colombia and "nationalize" the effort. Indeed, it can even be viewed as an expression of confidence in the Colombian government: that in light of security gains, the same level of U.S. funding is no longer required. Yet when one considers Washington's exploding budget pressures, not only in Afghanistan and Iraq but also in Mexico and most recently Haiti, the resources proposed seem significant and suggest the continuing importance of Colombia.

The new signals in Washington and decisions made in Bogotá were unfolding in a changed regional setting, to some extent shaped by a ten-year military cooperation agreement between the two that would allow U.S. use of and access to seven Colombian military bases. News of the pact, which leaked in Colombia in August 2009 (it was signed in late October, though ultimately ruled unconstitutional in August 2010 by Colombia's Constitutional Court), helped revive South American suspicions about U.S. military motives in the region. The agreement had been championed by Uribe, who sold it as a way to ensure the country's continued security in face of potentially aggressive moves by Chávez. The deal had been in the works during the Bush administration, and the Obama administration insisted that it merely formalized the existing security relationship with Colombia and did not signify an increase in U.S. military presence in the country.

Whatever its possible merits, the agreement was not accompanied by a high-level diplomatic effort and communications strategy aimed at assuaging concerns among such Latin American friends as Brazil about the role of the U.S. military in the region. Indeed, perhaps the most costly aspect of the agreement has been the strong reaction registered by Brazil's government. The Brazilians, after all, had in 2008 launched the Union of South American Nations, which is modeled after the European Union and seeks to deal with defense issues as part of a wide-ranging regional agenda. Any agreement regarding the United States and its evolving security role in South America was bound to generate suspicion and controversy (notably inflamed by Chávez's exaggerated claims that U.S. troops would invade Venezuela). Prior consultations with senior officials of the continent's leading power should have been a top priority.

Colombia's Incomplete Democratic Agenda

Perhaps no issue better illustrates the highly complex and dynamic nature of Colombia's democracy than its so-called para-political scandal, which received considerable media attention. Ongoing revelations of the links between the illegal, brutal, paramilitary forces and sectors of the country's political establishment reveal the corruption that had become rampant in Colombia. Particularly troubling, many (though by no means all) of the accused are close associates of President Uribe, one being his cousin and confidant, former senator Mario Uribe, arrested in 2008.

Ironically, it was President Uribe's "Peace and Justice Law"—which demobilized more than 30,000 paramilitary forces between 2003 and 2005—that enabled the Attorney General's Office to investigate these para-politics cases in the first place. In the wake of its new confessions and revelations, subsequent decline in violence, and some sanctions on the paramilitaries, the process shows, as the government argues, that the judiciary is functioning, and that an attempt is under way to cleanse the system of decades-long corruption. Some sixty-eight members of Congress have been investigated and thirty-three arrested for paramilitary ties, with numerous other political figures involved as well. Still, the human rights community and others have raised legitimate concerns that the demobilization effort should have been tougher, with more severe punishments for crimes. Some recent reports even contend that the effort is responsible for the proliferation of criminal groups.

In an attempt to deal with many years of drug-fueled violence, corruption, and trauma, Colombia is undergoing a collective catharsis. Perhaps the closest parallel can be found not in Latin America but in postapartheid South Africa, which similarly sought to bring to light long-suffered abuses. Although, as already mentioned, the steps toward deeper democratic governance have helped reduce violence and insecurity, setbacks have occurred as well, notably reflected in the para-politics scandal, which revealed the considerable economic and political power accumulated by Colombia's paramilitary groups. Thus some observers acknowledge the improvement in security but emphasize the costs for political institutions and the rule of law.

Colombia's progress in ending its long-standing internal armed conflict has been similarly mixed. On one hand, the conflict continues to pose a major risk to the country's democratic governance because the Revolutionary Armed Forces of Colombia (FARC), reportedly with some cooperation from the declining National Liberation Army (ELN), has an estimated 8,000 to 10,000 combatants and stays financed through the drug trade and other criminal activity. The government, on the other hand, has considerably strengthened its military capacity and is now on the offensive, as reflected in FARC's severe setbacks, both on the battlefield and in its internal organization. Communications have broken down, and defections are on the rise. Colombia's March 2008 air strike and raid into Ecuadoran territory and July 2008 mission that freed the most high-profile hostages held by FARC were both made possible through the Colombian government's increasingly effective intelligence-gathering and communication-interception abilities. Its capabilities were further enhanced with the death of four members of FARC's seven-man secretariat, including Manuel "Tirofijo" Marulanda, the leader of FARC since its inception in 1964, and Victor Julio "Mono Jojoy" Suarez Rojas, longtime head of the FARC's expansive Eastern Bloc.

Nonetheless, it is unrealistic to expect Colombia's serious problem with violence to disappear, even in the unlikely case that a formal peace will be reached with the weakened FARC. Real negotiations are highly improbable in the short term. Even if FARC's new leader, Alfonso Cano, entered negotiations, they would not necessarily lead to immediate peace. Just as the Medellin and Cali cartels fragmented into smaller, more dispersed drug-trafficking groups in the 1990s and early 2000s, FARC is most likely to morph and fracture into new violent entities. Although the end of FARC as a national armed group would constitute an important advance, other problems are bound to emerge.

Even as demobilized paramilitary leaders confess their crimes in prison, their lieutenants are forming new mafias, sometimes in cooperation with their former enemies, the guerrillas, as both groups become less and less motivated by ideology. Fourteen of the top paramilitary leaders are in U.S. prisons, serving sentences or awaiting trial on cocaine-trafficking charges after Uribe extradited them to the United States in May 2008. Some critics have argued, however, that extradition has merely allowed paramilitary offenders to be "silenced" when imprisoned in the United States.

Overall, the Uribe government's security gains seemed to have plateaued and become less effective after 2008. Homicide rates, for example, dropped only 2 percent from 2008 to 2009. In addition, statistics show that urban violence and insecurity are now on the rise in such cities as Medellin and Bogotá, both of which had registered significant declines and had become showcases for success. The deterioration in Medellin is particularly worrying.

Of equal concern, the dynamic security conditions in Colombia have incited conflict with neighboring countries. Ideological differences between Uribe and the governments of Ecuador and particularly Venezuela already made for tense relationships. Colombia's airstrike on a FARC camp in Ecuadoran territory in March 2008 sparked a crisis that has since waned but continues to simmer under the surface. News about the U.S.-Colombia military cooperation agreement has further strained relations with Colombia's neighbors. Long-term solutions to guerrilla and drug-trafficking challenges require extensive cooperation among the Andean countries. Though it will not be easy and will call for a shift in foreign policy, Colombia needs to work through low-level diplomacy and multilateral channels to rebuild trust and restore cordial relations with its neighbors. A new administration in Bogotá in August 2010 may offer opportunities for progress on these fronts.

Another fundamental problem is that the drug trade remains essentially intact, despite significant investments from Colombia and the United States to diminish the flow of cocaine and heroin. An October 2008 report from the U.S. Government Accountability Office (GAO) found that Plan Colombia had helped improve the security situation but had failed in its goal of reducing the cultivation, processing, and distribution of illegal narcotics by 50 percent in six years. Instead, coca production levels actually increased 15 percent between 2000 and 2007. Gains in interdiction or lower levels of production in particular regions have been more than offset by the agility and sophistication of the actors involved in the illicit trade. Wherever the drug trade is flourishing there will be high levels of criminality and corruption.

The persistence of the drug problem has important implications for other fundamental aspects of democratic governance in Colombia. Journalists and others engaged in informing the public have been the target of violence and increasing threats from both paramilitaries and guerrillas, who are sustained by the drug trade. Although, happily, the number of killings of journalists has declined from previous years, threats have reportedly risen, with a corresponding increase in self-censorship. This is particularly the case outside of Bogotá and other major cities, which tend to be significantly more secure than the provincial areas. It is crucial to bear in mind when discussing the state of democratic governance that there are actually *many* Colombias. Nothing exemplifies their sharp differences as well as the contrasting conditions media face in large cities and in conflict zones.

Other vulnerable entities include union officials and human rights workers, many of whom receive threats from armed groups and require protection from the Ministry of the Interior. Although the murder of union officials has become less frequent since 2004, it remains a disturbing phenomenon and increased once again in 2008 compared with 2007. Some senior Colombian officials have leveled baseless accusations that respected human rights representatives are associated with guerrilla groups, which has complicated the work of these representatives and contributed to a tense climate.

Human rights organizations and the U.S. State Department's annual human rights review have reported a jump in recent years in the number of extrajudicial executions committed by the Colombian armed forces. Particularly disconcerting has been the increase in the so-called false positives, that is, civilians dressed as FARC guerrillas to meet unofficial army benchmarks for military success. The 1997 Leahy amendment is designed to ensure that any Colombian armed forces unit receiving aid under Plan Colombia have been certified as trained to respect human rights. That several of the units implicated in the "false-positive" scandal and other atrocities had been certified under this process reflects poorly on Plan Colombia overall, and the required vetting process in particular.

Since the peak of violence in 2001, the military have performed more professionally and in stricter accordance with human rights norms, but the recent increase in extrajudicial killings represents a disturbing reversal of a long-term positive trend. This spate of killings was indefensible, particularly as the country's security gains were being consolidated. Fortunately, the unprecedented dismissal of several top Colombian military officers in October 2008 demonstrated that the Uribe administration recognized the seriousness of these crimes and was addressing the problem.

Colombia also needs to more vigorously assist those who have the fewest resources and who are least able to defend themselves, many of whom are of African descent, indigenous, female, or all three. Sadly, these vulnerable groups are disproportionately represented among the estimated 3 million to 4 million citizens internally displaced by decades of violence in Colombia (the second highest number in the world after Sudan). The internal refugee population, which continues to grow as a result of guerrilla raids and military incursions, constitutes a serious problem of democracy.

The crisis underlines Colombia's persistent poverty and inequality, which are particularly severe in the rural sector (where poverty reaches 65 percent compared with nationwide levels of 46 percent). Any serious, long-term effort to improve democratic governance in Colombia should also focus on redressing the country's underlying social ills and injustices. Although the economic growth in recent years has been important in mitigating poverty and inequality, the recent global financial crisis took its toll in Colombia. The country's social agenda remains urgent—unemployment is among the highest levels on the continent—and must be tackled in a comprehensive way through more thorough education and health reforms.

What Can and Should Be Done Now by the United States and Other External Actors?

Despite the new opportunities that a change of national government may bring, Colombia's underlying, persistent, and severe institutional and democratic challenges need to be addressed. National actors have a primary responsibility to respond effectively, but so do other external actors, and the United States needs to be productively and wisely engaged. The new realities in Bogotá and Washington offer an excellent moment to recalibrate and adjust the bilateral relationship, to learn from past experience and build on past successes, but also to forge a more creative and effective strategy for the future.

It is important, however, to have realistic expectations about what external actors can and cannot do to assist Colombia in improving the prospects for democratic governance. Colombia is the second largest country in South America, following Brazil, and is sophisticated and highly developed in many respects. It is the continent's oldest democracy and has an enormous sense of pride and independence. Any policies and programs should be carried out with great respect and sensitivity, in close consultation and concert with key national actors.

Three principal lessons can be derived from twenty years of experience with Colombia. The first is that there are important limitations on how much can be done in pressuring Colombia to improve its democratic practices in accordance with some external standards. Lecturing Colombian officials about human rights norms through channels that are not predictable or institutionalized can prove counterproductive, with adverse effects on both communication and persuasion. Human rights should be a key part of the bilateral conversation, but the environment should be one of cooperation and mutual respect.

Second, the United States has committed a serious mistake in overemphasizing the drug question to the relative neglect of other priorities, such as security, trade and development, and the building of the democratic institutions needed for effective governance. This emphasis has been a response more to U.S. domestic politics than to Colombia's needs. And it has failed to measurably diminish the drug trade, as the 2008 GAO report previously noted makes clear. It also indicates that the purity levels of cocaine on American streets have generally increased while prices have consistently fallen, which suggests a jump in supply.

Third, even though the United States got it backwards by focusing narrowly on the drug question at the cost of other key issues, some anti-drug aid has had beneficial effects, most notably in the security and justice sectors. Compared with other U.S. policies in Latin America in recent years—and even international policies more generally—the U.S. effort in Colombia has been relatively successful. Of course, Colombians deserve the utmost credit for reasserting state authority.

The international community, including the United States, should have a sense of modesty and realism in working with Colombia in the coming years, recognizing that the effectiveness of any outside support will depend significantly on the will and commitment of democratic actors in Colombia. It is hard to know how the country's domestic politics will evolve, but fortunately such actors are not only present and active but are also determined to improve the situation and build on an existing institutional foundation. America's task here is not one of "nation-building," as it is in many other countries, but of helping a country that has been battered on many fronts and is seeking to recover from a period of deterioration.

There is ample room for constructive action by the Obama administration, the U.S. Congress, and the wider international community. The following is a menu of steps that should be considered.

Continue to Rebalance U.S. Aid toward Social Development

Too much of the public debate, particularly since Plan Colombia was adopted in 2000, has concentrated on the relative weight of different pieces of what should be a broad, coherent strategy to help bring peace and strengthen the rule of law in Colombia. Congress has moved toward greater balance between security and development aid, and it would be wise to maintain that equilibrium in future budgets—as the Obama administration proposes for 2011, with a drop in military and police assistance, from approximately $423 million in 2010 to $342 million for 2011, but only a marginal decline in economic and social assistance programs.

Unfortunately, aid decisions are too rarely geared toward larger policy purposes, in part because they fail to distinguish between policies and *instruments* of policies. In the Colombian case, one primary goal should be to further enhance the capacity of the state to carry out its basic functions more effectively, in accordance with democratic norms and the rule of law. Prevailing circumstances should determine how much assistance should be directed to social development activities or security hardware over the next several years. Moreover, realistically—as reflected in the Obama administration's budget request for 2011— overall aid amounts are likely to wind down. Nonetheless, given the importance of consolidating Colombia's gains, the United States should be prepared to maintain its support at roughly currently proposed levels for the next three or four years.

Support Diplomatic Strategies for Initiating a Peace Process in Colombia

Another option perhaps underutilized in recent years is high-level policy consultation and advice on Colombia's strategy for peace, particularly in pursuing an "end-game" directed at reaching an enduring agreement with FARC. Senior U.S. government officials should devote less time to ensuring that Colombians are meeting targets or satisfying bureaucratic requirements set in Washington and more to assisting with fundamental strategic decisions. Such a focus would take into account the opportunity presented by a new Colombian government as well as President Obama's promise to be more engaged diplomatically. The United States can and should pursue this course both bilaterally and through multilateral organizations, particularly the Organization of American States (OAS).

Support the Reintegration of Combatants into Society

The United States should work closely with other relevant actors to assist in the reintegration of former combatants into society. Despite some progress on this front, some troubling backsliding has occurred recently, with serious security implications. To ensure democratic governance in Colombia, it is essential to prevent any further retrogression in the demobilization process; otherwise it will be difficult for Colombia to achieve greater peace and security.

Pursue Opportunities for More Effective Coordination with Europe

Despite having extremely limited resources, European countries (and Canada) are showing some interest in the evolving situation in Colombia and the possibilities offered by a new government. There may also be opportunities for more productive collaboration with the United States than in the past. The traditional formula for the division of labor—the United States providing "hard" security aid and the Europeans "soft" development assistance—has led to incoherent and ineffective policymaking. More clear-sighted cooperation may now be possible, particularly if the Obama administration is flexible and forward-looking about the drug question and is willing to seriously consider alternative approaches.

Emphasize Human Rights

As already noted, the human rights situation in Colombia remains a serious problem. Helping ensure that human rights are respected should be a fundamental aspect of U.S. policy toward Colombia in coming years. International human rights organizations have helped improve the situation through their work and pressure on the U.S. government for its support. Most democratic actors in Colombia view such efforts as constructive and encourage them. The Leahy Amendment has faced some implementation difficulties but has been useful in keeping human rights on the agenda. The United States should reassess its verification process and assist in the full investigation of the extrajudicial killings related to the false-positive controversy. One welcome decision, announced by Ambassador William Brownfield in April 2010, was to discontinue financial support of the Administrative Security Department (DAS) because of alleged wiretapping of Uribe's political opponents.

Cooperation with Colombia on democratic governance and the rule-of-law questions will be more effective if the United States helps to guide work on diplomatic, security, and development levels. Only in this way can Colombia be nudged along the constructive path it wants to pursue. To this end, the law enforcement agencies of both countries should continue to solicit testimonies from the extradited paramilitaries, now in U.S. prisons, and make sure any seized assets are set aside for victim reparations. Making good on that pledge will help build greater trust between the governments and the broader Colombian population.

Support the U.S.-Colombia Free Trade Agreement

This free trade pact will deepen engagement between the two countries and enable the United States to work more constructively with Colombia on democracy and rule-of-law questions. As President Obama hinted in his State of the Union mention of Colombia, initiatives such as this are critical because removing the high tariffs on U.S. exports will help create jobs at home. Moreover, passing the agreement will make it clear to the world that the United States will not revert to protectionism, and this will enhance confidence and stability in both its bilateral relationship with Colombia and overall relationship with the region.

At present, the agreement faces enormous political obstacles in the U.S. Congress, particularly in an election year. In 2011 there may be somewhat more room to mobilize support for the pact, but this will hinge on two conditions. First, the Colombians need to show that they have taken successful steps and allocated significant resources to reducing levels of violence against union officials and to prosecuting those responsible for the abuses. Second, in an uncertain and anxious U.S. political climate, greater progress must occur in creating jobs and expanding training and placement programs, as well as in bolstering government-sponsored social protection packages. The approval of health care reform in March 2010 was an important step in this direction but may not be enough to satisfy union demands.

If approved, the free trade agreement would signal to Colombia and the rest of Latin America that the United States follows through on commitments and intends to remain engaged. Anything short of passage would not satisfy allies in Colombia, but both sides may still be open to amending the agreement or including a side letter on human rights and labor concerns, if that is what it takes to secure approval. Should the United States fail to approve the agreement, that would weaken its already diminished capacity to exercise political influence and foster constructive policies toward a critically important South American nation.

Concluding Thoughts

Over the past decade the relationship between the United States and Colombia has been in some respects quite productive but in others marked by mutual misunderstandings and some frustration. The asymmetry between the two nations has rendered the relationship particularly difficult to manage. The shifting domestic politics and heightened partisanship in Washington, along with contrasting policy priorities, have also not helped matters.

In the coming period policy differences, and some strain, will be inevitable. Still, the fresh circumstances in both Washington and Bogotá may well afford an excellent opportunity to pursue a more balanced relationship. It is important to reduce the weight of drugs and security aspects that have too often dominated and skewed the relationship. It is equally crucial to try to overcome Colombia's relative isolation by encouraging broader and more effective cooperation with its Latin American neighbors. With its emphasis on multilateralism, notably measured approach to foreign policy, and moderate and respectful tone, the Obama administration has a real chance to better align U.S. interests and values with those of a historic ally.

five

The Chávez Challenge for Obama: An Inconvenient Marriage or Frosty Separation

Jennifer McCoy

Ideology, geopolitics, and domestic political dynamics in Venezuela and the United States make for a volatile relationship between the Obama and Chávez administrations. Ever since his election in 1998, President Hugo Chávez has been trying to create a new model of politics and economics, and to challenge U.S. dominance in the region and the world. Through a strategy of intense confrontation with adversaries at home and abroad, combined with new foreign alliances globally and integrationist schemes regionally, his administration seeks to redistribute power and resources both domestically and internationally. At the same time, the mutual dependence of the United States and Venezuela on oil trade leads to a relationship full of contradictions and mixed messages. The challenge for the Obama administration is to manage this "inconvenient marriage" in such a way as to protect U.S. strategic interests in a difficult international environment while avoiding being drawn into unnecessary conflicts with a strong-willed personality.

When Barack Obama took office in January 2009, he found himself in the midst of a severe financial crisis, plummeting oil prices, and troubled relations with Venezuela and Bolivia. Venezuela had withdrawn its ambassador from Washington five months earlier in solidarity with Bolivia's expulsion of its U.S. ambassador for alleged interference in domestic affairs, and the United States had retaliated in kind. Faced with a recalcitrant but strategically important trade partner in Venezuela, the Obama administration sent signals of willingness to enter a dialogue, promising a new era of cooperation with all of Latin America. Hugo Chávez adopted a wait-and-see attitude, with prospects for conciliation when the two presidents shook hands and exchanged words of goodwill at their meeting in Trinidad and Tobago in April 2009. Two months later the two countries quietly reinstated their ambassadors. Soon, however, the contentiousness of the Bush years seemed more in evidence than any movement toward rapprochement.

Understanding Chávez's Venezuela

With the Chávez election in 1998, Venezuela became the first of several countries—Bolivia, Ecuador, and Paraguay followed in quick succession— to choose presidents to bring about radical political change through constitutional "re-founding," or rewriting, or the inclusion of previously excluded groups in the distribution of power and resources. In Venezuela's case, the demands for change arose from its political dynamics. A serious dislocation caused by the near tripling of poverty rates from the 1970s to the 1990s and subsequent rejection of the traditional political elites led to the gradual collapse of what had once been considered one of the strongest political party systems in the region. Chávez initiated a process of elite displacement, redistribution of economic and political resources, concentration of power, and experimentation with new forms of participatory democracy encoded in a new constitution written by a popularly elected constituent assembly and approved by Venezuelan voters in 1999.

The political process since then has been conflictive, with mass protests, occasional violence, an attempted coup in 2002, a two-month petroleum strike in late 2002 and early 2003, and a presidential recall referendum in 2004. Although President Chávez survived each attempt to remove him from office and subsequently consolidated his power, the country has not yet achieved a new social contract including all sectors of society, which remains polarized, albeit with less visible conflict.

Inspired by the South American liberator Simón Bolívar, Chávez's revolution is full of contradictions: it incorporates both a nationalistic and a Latin American integrationist dream, and it seeks both top-down (centralized) and bottom-up (participatory) change, with a concentration of executive power.[1] Foreign policy is a fundamental component of Chávez's vision, his goal being to counterbalance U.S. global and regional hegemony with a more multipolar world, and to use Venezuela's status as an energy exporter to enhance its influence in regional affairs.[2] Venezuela's foreign policy, like its domestic policy, is confrontational and conflictive.

The Bolivarian Revolution actually retains many of the basic traits of Punto Fijo politics, the democratic system in Venezuela from 1959 to 1998:[3] dependence on oil revenues and their distribution; highly centralized decisionmaking structures, but with a new set of privileged actors displacing the traditional elites; and poor regulatory and administrative capacities (though tax collection capability has increased under Chávez). Although still centralized, decisionmaking now rests in one person (Chávez) rather than in two hierarchical political parties, and the government helps deepen class divisions rather than encourage cross-class alliances. To achieve its goals, the Bolivarian Revolution has dismantled traditional institutions and eroded the separation of powers. Changes in economic strategy include a shift from flouting quotas of the Organization of Petroleum Exporting Countries (OPEC) and increasing market share (thus lowering prices) to helping OPEC control production in order to raise prices, as well as a shift from market capitalism to a "twenty-first-century socialism" that puts the state in control of a growing number of economic sectors.

Chávez's reelection with 63 percent of the vote in 2006 encouraged him to propose even more radical constitutional reforms in 2007. However, the populace narrowly rejected the idea, handing Chávez his first-ever electoral defeat. In response, the president reached out to dissidents within his own movement; reshuffled his cabinet to address severe problems in government services, crime, and inflation; and restored relations with neighboring Colombia while calling on the Fuerzas Armadas Revolucionarias de Colombia (FARC) to end its kidnapping and unilaterally release hostages. He campaigned heavily for his party's candidates for the November 2008 mayoral and gubernatorial elections, charging the people to vote for "the revolution" and casting the elections as a plebiscite on his rule. With a 60 percent presidential approval rate, this strategy seemed reasonable, but opposition parties united in order to field single candidates in many of the races, focusing their campaign on the problems of governance rather than the person of Hugo Chávez. This strategy won them the mayoralty of metropolitan Caracas, plus five of the twenty-two governorships—the latter in five states that represent 45 percent of the population, including oil-rich Zulia and the state encompassing the capital city.

Though not necessarily a rejection of Chávez personally, the vote reflected widespread frustration with the government's inability to solve Venezuela's pressing problems of soaring crime rates, lack of water and paved roads, unemployment, and inflation. Since dissident candidates within the government's political alliance failed to garner significant support, the results also demonstrated that it was still difficult to create "*chavismo* without Chávez," that is, to effect the radical change represented by Chávez's movement without Chávez himself.[4]

The regional elections created an opportunity for the opposition victors to deliver better government services and thus launch competitive bids for national offices during the 2010 National Assembly elections and the 2012 presidential elections. Their ability to perform, however, depends in large part on national revenue sharing and the cooperation of the federal government. The Chávez administration had already rolled back some decentralization reforms of the previous decade and decreased the autonomy of municipal and state governments. Soon after the 2008 regional elections, it took additional measures to transfer to the central government control of the ports and airports in states with opposition governors, and of a number of public spaces and buildings in the cities won by the opposition. In a more blatant move, usurping the authority of the newly elected opposition mayor of metropolitan Caracas, the government created the Capital District and displaced the elected mayor both literally and figuratively by appointing a head.

The president also asked the National Assembly to reintroduce a constitutional amendment for indefinite reelection (a proposal that had been included in the reforms defeated in 2007). Although the November 2008 elections provided a weaker mandate than he had hoped for, President Chávez indicated his desire to hold a referendum to approve such an amendment early in 2009, well in time for the 2012 presidential election. When expanded to include indefinite reelection of *all* elected officials, the proposal passed handily in February 2009, thereby opening the possibility of Chávez remaining in power indefinitely.

In recent years, the political issue drawing the most international attention has been the degree of freedom of speech and media independence from government control. Venezuelan media have long been politicized, but with the polarization and conflict that began to take hold in 2002, both private and public media, especially television, took on overt political roles. After the 2004 recall referendum, some changes occurred: the government opened several new television stations and sponsored hundreds of community radio programs, changing the balance from overwhelmingly oppositionist-controlled to a majority of official broadcast media. In addition, the National Assembly passed the Social Media Responsibility Law to regulate violence and pornography during prime-time television. Some privately owned media outlets decided to make peace with the government and take on a less political role.

Even so, the private media continue to air vigorous criticism of the government and the president, while the state-owned media are strongly politicized and pro-government. Although there is no formal censorship, legal, economic, and regulatory mechanisms create a climate of self-censorship. Owners of private media complain that they are denied equal access to government facilities and official events and are forced to interrupt regular programming to run long presidential broadcasts. Reforms to the criminal code in March 2005 increased the penalties for libel and defamation of public officials from a maximum of thirty months to four years in prison, directly counter to recent trends in Latin America and to rulings of the Inter-American Court of Human Rights.

Media restrictions are also imposed through the administration of broadcasting licenses, which at times fail to be renewed apparently because of political concerns. In the most controversial episode, in May 2007 the government declined to renew the broadcasting license of the country's oldest commercial network and most vocal critic, Radio Caracas Television (RCTV), for allegedly supporting the 2002 coup and violating broadcast norms. This suspension spawned the first student protests under the Chávez administration, a movement that was subsequently instrumental in the defeat of the 2007 constitutional reforms. Then in early 2010 the government stopped the broadcasts of RCTV's remaining cable operation, allegedly because it aired only part of Chávez's public addresses, and arrested the head of the twenty-four-hour news channel Globovisión for his critical comments about the president. Two students were killed in subsequent protests, and the U.S. government, along with many nongovernmental organizations (NGOs), condemned these actions.

U.S.-Venezuela Relations, 1999–2008

Relations between Venezuela and the United States were cool from the start of Chávez's rise to office. The strategic foreign policy goals of his Bolivarian Revolution dictated that Venezuela would challenge the United States in multiple international arenas, while Venezuela's dependence on oil exports forced it to maintain the important bilateral trade relationship. Cooperation in other areas deteriorated early, as Venezuela withdrew permission for U.S. drug overflights and rebuffed U.S. Navy assistance during devastating floods in 1999.

Since the beginning of the Bush administration, Venezuela's signals to the United States have been decidedly mixed. President Chávez sent a congratulatory letter to President-elect Bush in 2000, expressed his desire for closer relations in the event of a John Kerry victory during the 2004 presidential campaign, and reiterated the sentiment after the victory of Barack Obama in 2008. At the same time, from early on the Chávez government criticized Plan Colombia, challenged the proposed Free Trade Area of the Americas, responded weakly to the World Trade Center attacks, denounced the U.S. retaliatory airstrikes against the Taliban in Afghanistan, and increased its friendship with Cuba. Disputes over democracy also emerged early when Chávez strove unsuccessfully to privilege the concept of participatory and direct democracy in negotiations for the Inter-American Democratic Charter.

Chávez's rhetorical attacks on the U.S. "empire" were fueled in part by the Bush administration's unilateral foreign policy centered on its invasion of Iraq and "war against terror," which had alienated much of the Latin American public. The United States lost much of its moral authority in promoting democracy in the region with its welcoming of the 2002 coup against Chávez, and more broadly with its unilateral policy on Iraq, wherein "regime change" became rationalized as democracy promotion. The Chávez government alleged that the United States was funding a conspiracy against it, citing U.S. financing in the name of democracy assistance for opposition civil society organizations (NGOs, labor unions, and private sector organizations) before the 2002 uprising. Although the Office of Transition Initiatives of the U.S. Agency for International Development (USAID) continued a vigorous program of assistance to some Venezuelan NGOs, others decided to stop accepting U.S. funding in the wake of strong government criticism.[5]

The United States also supported the mediation of a tripartite group (the Organization of American States [OAS], United Nations Development Program, and Carter Center) to find a peaceful resolution to the political conflict engulfing Venezuela after Chávez's return to power in 2002. U.S. concerns about an erosion of separation of powers and civil liberties intensified after Chávez defeated the attempt to shorten his term through a recall referendum in 2004. Pressures on foreign investment and private property in Venezuela also seemed to be increasing. Then in 2005 Venezuela suspended cooperation with the U.S. Drug Enforcement Agency, and the two countries entered a destructive, high-profile "microphone diplomacy" contest, with strong recriminations and insults emanating from both sides.

The election of Barack Obama in 2008 thus presented an opportunity and a dilemma for Venezuela. The Obama administration entered office with a stated willingness to engage in dialogue and negotiation with its adversaries, including Venezuela. Moreover, the primary target of Chávez's anti-imperialist rhetoric of recent years—namely, President George W. Bush and his cabinet members—was now removed. Representing hope for millions of Americans previously discriminated against or fighting for social change, Barack Obama was not the foil that George Bush was for President Chávez. The Chávez administration had to decide whether to engage or continue confronting the United States, which in the meantime was developing an ambitious domestic policy agenda that would prevent bold steps in foreign policy beyond a revitalized Afghanistan policy. To complicate matters, Washington quickly became stymied in Iran, the Israel-Palestine conflict, North Korea, and Cuba.

The underlying conflict between the agendas of the two countries was reflected in each government's complaints about the other's policies. The Obama administration appeared to be echoing its predecessor's concerns: the reported growth in narcotics transshipments through Venezuela; Chávez's support of Cuba; the country's growing ties with Russia, China, and Iran; and increased restrictions on domestic critics and private property. In addition, the tension starting in mid-2009 between Colombia—the closest U.S. ally in the region—and Venezuela seemed a flashpoint that might turn violent.

For Venezuela's part, its preoccupation with potentially hostile U.S. intentions was deepened first by U.S. acceptance of the 2002 coup attempt and then by the 2009 formalization of U.S. access to military bases in Colombia. The one element that keeps the antagonism within bounds and has not been affected over the past decade, even when diplomatic relations have fractured, is the mutual dependence on the oil trade. In 2009 the United States bought roughly 55 percent of Venezuelan oil exports, amounting to 9 percent of U.S. imported oil (down from 16 percent in 1998).[6] If and when Venezuela gains traction in its search for alternative export markets and the United States manages to achieve greater energy independence, however, that constraint could be loosened and the antagonism could grow.

U.S. Engagement with Venezuela, 2010 and Beyond

U.S. interests in Venezuela reside in three domains. The first are strategic in nature, focusing on maintaining the supply of oil, curtailing drug transit, and countering terrorism. The second are political concerns, emanating from the desire to have stable democratic neighbors without an adverse influence in other countries. In Chávez's Venezuela, for example, the United States sees a participatory democracy experiment that overconcentrates executive power and thus risks a return to extreme polarization, destabilization, and violence. The third are regionally oriented in that defusing the rancorous standoff with Venezuela would help the Obama administration achieve its aim of establishing more cooperative relationships and resolving problems in the hemisphere.

Some U.S. strategic concerns are encapsulated in a National Intelligence Report of February 2010 noting Venezuela's growing ties with China, Russia, and Iran: "Iran has made contingency plans for dealing with future additional international sanctions by identifying potential alternative suppliers of gasoline—including China and Venezuela."[7] The report named Hugo Chávez as one of America's "foremost international detractors, denouncing liberal democracy and market capitalism and opposing U.S. policies and interests in the region." His "authoritarian populist model," it concluded, is undermining Venezuelan democratic institutions. Without supplying specific details, the report also claimed that the administration was still providing FARC with covert support.[8] In its annual Human Rights Report released soon after, the State Department highlighted Venezuela's intensifying politicization of the judiciary and recent harassment and intimidation of the political opposition and the media.[9]

Although Russia, Iran, and China have been increasing their presence in other parts of Latin America as well, Venezuela in particular has courted all three as part of its strategic effort to counterbalance U.S. influence. For Russia, Venezuela is proving to be a significant arms purchaser as it attempts to reestablish parity with Colombia, which has been receiving significant U.S. military aid for a decade. Venezuela had already purchased $4 billion of heavy equipment (jets and tanks) and small arms (100,000 AK-47 assault rifles) when Russia's prime minister Vladimir Putin announced after an April 2010 visit the possibility of a $5 billion credit line for more Venezuelan arms purchases. While analysts and policymakers question the need for heavy equipment, Venezuela responds that it is updating its military in the face of U.S. sanctions and large arms purchases by its neighbors Colombia and Brazil. The Russian Sukhoi jetfighters replaced Venezuela's aging American F-16s (purchased in the 1980s) for which the United States has refused to supply spare parts since the Chávez inauguration. In fact, the greatest U.S. concern about these arms purchases pertains to the small arms and their possible distribution to Colombia's FARC or other criminal groups. Venezuela contends that it is simply replacing aging Belgian weapons and points to the higher arms expenditures in Brazil, Colombia, and Chile.[10]

Iran and Venezuela share a long-standing relationship as cofounders of OPEC in 1960, and more recently a common foreign policy goal of curtailing U.S. influence. Iranian commercial ventures in Venezuela are increasing, with nearly 200 such projects signed by 2010; however, it is not clear how many of them have actually been implemented. The U.S. government expressed concern about the weekly Tehran-Caracas flights initiated in 2007, given the lax passport controls in Venezuela and possibility of Hezbollah entering the Western hemisphere through Caracas. The U.S. government has also noted with some concern that two joint Venezuelan-Iranian banks that allow Iran to escape international sanctions may be financing Hezbollah.[11]

On the other hand, U.S. defense secretary Robert Gates appears to downplay the threat of Venezuela's Russian arms purchases and ties to Iran. . On a tour to South America in April 2010, he said that he did not see a military threat from Venezuela and suggested its high-profile embrace of Iran was partly an attempt to distract Venezuelans from domestic woes.[12]

Drug trafficking remains a prime concern, however. State Department statistics show a marked increase in cocaine traffic, from 50 metric tons in 2004 to 300 metric tons in 2008, making Venezuela one of the principal drug-transit countries in the hemisphere.[13] Yet Venezuela argues that it is making great strides in fighting the drug trade, noting that "in 2009 Venezuelan authorities seized 60 tons of drugs, an 11 percent increase from the year prior. Additionally, 26 drug laboratories were destroyed; 8,000 individuals were arrested for drug crimes, including 14 drug kingpins; 11 maritime interdiction operations were conducted, six involving U.S. agencies; and $260 million was invested in the purchase of Chinese-made radars to track illegal drug flights."[14]

Venezuela's support to Cuba is another irritant in U.S. relations. Since 2004 Venezuela has provided subsidized oil to Cuba in exchange for the medical assistance of up to 20,000 Cuban doctors in its poor neighborhoods. The two countries have also established a joint effort to provide free cataract surgery throughout Latin America. Anti-Castro members of the U.S. Congress in particular view this support as propping up the Cuban regime. With the prevalence of Cuban advisers and security personnel in Venezuela, many of Chávez's opponents fear a "Cubanization" of Venezuela marked not only by socialism but also by a repression of dissent.[15]

Yet another aggravation is the suspected Venezuelan support to Colombia's FARC insurgency. The capture of FARC's so-called foreign minister, Rodrigo Granda, by Colombian bounty hunters in 2005 brought to light that a high-level FARC official had been living in Venezuela unrestricted for some time. Then in March 2008 Colombia bombed a FARC guerrilla camp in Ecuador and embarrassed Venezuela by subsequently leaking to the press that the computers captured in the Ecuadoran raid suggested Venezuela had provided FARC with material support. Although Venezuela denied the claim and no further evidence was made public, the 2010 U.S. intelligence report cited earlier repeated the allegations.

The State Department's concerns about the deterioration of democracy in Venezuela were echoed in the March 2010 report of the Inter-American Commission on Human Rights, an independent body of the OAS, to which Venezuela belongs. Debates about the "democratic deficits" of Venezuela continue to cloud bilateral relations.

As for Venezuela's strategic interests in the United States, they primarily revolve around reducing dependence on the U.S. export market, with a view to achieving stronger ties within the Southern Hemisphere, a multipolar world, a new model of development, and a place for Venezuela on the world stage as an energy leader. To this end, Chávez has been trying to diversify the nation's oil market by jointly developing new refineries at home and in China that can handle Venezuela's heavy crude. (Currently Venezuelan crude is refined primarily in the United States.) To date, these refineries have been slow to materialize, and oil exports to China remain small, although they will likely grow in light of a $20 billion loan-for-oil deal announced in April 2010, which includes a joint venture to develop new oil fields and refine the heavy crude to lighter fuel.

With a strong U.S. ally in neighboring Colombia and the reactivation of the Fourth Naval Fleet, Venezuela also voices fear of a U.S. invasion, especially in light of America's recognition of the coup government in 2002 and invasion of Iraq in 2003. An added threat in its view is a possible uprising of Chávez opponents in response to the 2010 U.S. intelligence report singling out Venezuela as the leader of anti-U.S. interests in the region. Public references to such a threat serve to galvanize support for the Chávez administration and justify repression of domestic criticism.

Venezuela's friendly relations and strategic and commercial alliances with U.S. adversaries such as Cuba, Iran, and Russia are part of its strategy to challenge the United States. Nevertheless, because of its continued dependence on the U.S. oil market, Venezuela cannot completely break from the United States and thus maintains a multidimensional relationship with strong commercial ties, intermittent cooperation on security and counternarcotics activities, and political competition and rhetorical conflict within the hemisphere.

Continuity in U.S.-Venezuela Relations during the First Year of the Obama Administration

For several reasons, the Obama administration made little headway in balancing this multidimensional relationship, or at least in improving communication and cooperation in some areas of mutual strategic interest during its initial year in office. First, U.S. domestic politics intervened. Despite the feel-good atmosphere of the Trinidad and Tobago Summit, the administration was consumed with its own domestic policy agenda and its review of Afghanistan and Iraq policies. Nominations for the Latin American team at the State Department were slow in coming and were then derailed by domestic politics owing to the controversy surrounding the June 28 coup in Honduras.

Thinking Venezuela might be involved in the Honduran crisis, conservative Republicans criticized the initial U.S. decision to join the rest of the hemisphere in condemning the coup. For those conservatives, the Chávez administration's visible backing of the ousted Honduran leader was proof of foreign meddling: Venezuela's foreign minister had accompanied President Mel Zelaya in his initial exile in Nicaragua and his failed attempts to reenter the country. The factor precipitating the coup—Zelaya's attempted national "survey" to gauge citizen support for a referendum to convoke a constituent assembly—involved Venezuela-provided ballot papers, which led Honduran elites to fear an influx of uncontrollable Venezuelan cash and arms that could in turn unleash a "class war." These fears increased despite the nearly unanimous congressional vote but a year earlier to join Chávez's Bolivarian Alternative for the Americas (ALBA) and receive discounted oil.[16] As the stalemate dragged on in Honduras and the United States had second thoughts about cutting off aid to the poverty-stricken nation, the Obama administration seemed to be moving to the other side of a debate within the hemisphere, away from the staunch resistance not only of Venezuela but also importantly of Brazil, Argentina, and Chile, toward recognition of the November 2009 Honduran elections without the prior reinstatement of Zelaya.

A second U.S. policy decision greatly irritated Venezuela and caused fresh friction: the negotiation of a Defense Cooperation Agreement with Colombia in August 2009, providing U.S. military personnel access to seven Colombian military bases. Most of South America expressed alarm at this development, but neighboring Venezuela was the most vociferous, accusing Colombia of providing the "imperialist" United States with a base from which to invade Venezuela. As a consequence, Venezuela "froze" relations with Colombia in mid-2009 and implied that they would not improve unless the United States guaranteed that the sovereignty of Colombia's neighbors would be respected.

Domestic politics within Venezuela also reduced the potential for a fresh start with the United States. Chávez had for several years used the Bush administration as a convenient scapegoat, citing the threat of a U.S. invasion to justify the creation of a citizen's militia in Venezuela, among other things. During the first months of the Obama administration, Chávez toned down his anti-U.S. rhetoric and instead seemed to focus on potential domestic adversaries, as his government moved to curtail the power of newly elected opposition leaders and enforce media regulations against opposition radio and television. In the wake of the U.S.-Colombian military agreement and U.S. waffling on Honduras, however, Chávez stepped up his criticism of U.S. policy, though not of Obama personally. Then, at the Copenhagen Summit on climate change in December 2009, Chávez lapsed into a personal attack on Obama. Referring to his own 2006 speech at the United Nations General Assembly characterizing George W. Bush as the devil, Chávez remarked that he still smelled sulfur after Obama left the room.

Prospects for Future U.S.-Venezuelan Rapprochement and Cooperation

Both countries have a strategic interest in achieving cooperation in specific areas. For the United States, the highest priorities are to retain access to Venezuela's oil, especially given the announced discovery of extensive reserves, and to counter the increased drug flow through Venezuela. Although Venezuela's ties to Iran and alleged support to FARC are of concern, the Obama administration does not foresee much cooperation on these security issues in the near future.[17] For Venezuela, its strategic imperatives are to balance the need for a sufficiently civil relationship with the United States to be able to continue the oil trade, with the need to defend itself against external intervention. To this end, Venezuela maintains a dual policy toward the United States, alternating between sending conciliatory messages and searching out channels of communication, on one hand, and vociferous criticism and threats to cut off oil if the U.S. intervenes in Venezuela, on the other.

Since the overarching goal of the Bolivarian Revolution is to change power balances so as to reduce U.S. influence and create more symmetry in regional and global relations, a fundamental change toward a close, cooperative relationship is highly unlikely. The Chávez administration views its role as a leading energy supplier with huge proven and potential reserves in strategic terms, striving to use that position to achieve Latin American integration and independence from the United States. Yet the anti-capitalist and anti-imperialist basis of its foreign policy has also led Venezuela to play a provocative and divisive role within the region, trying to isolate those countries that are closer to the United States and, ironically, thereby undercutting its ambitions for their integration.

At the same time, pragmatic retreats in Venezuela's ideological pursuits have occurred, especially in its volatile relationship with Washington's closest ally in the region, Colombia. Unexpectedly, immediately after the inauguration of a new president in Colombia in August 2010, Venezuela and Colombia restored diplomatic ties and Chávez called on FARC to lay down its arms and negotiate a peace accord. That same month, the Colombian Constitutional Court declared the defense cooperation agreement with the U.S. unconstitutional because it had bypassed Congress, thus potentially removing this thorn in the triangular relationship of the United States, Colombia, and Venezuela.

Another sign of pragmatism is Venezuela's willingness to leave the door slightly open for private foreign oil participation, even by major U.S. firms, in the "re-nationalization" of the Venezuelan petroleum sector. Continued economic and political vulnerabilities may produce more pragmatic retrenchments, especially with the 2010 National Assembly elections and the 2012 presidential elections taking place in the midst of unresolved electric and water shortages and declining approval ratings. Those ratings dipped to 44 percent in February 2010, the lowest since May 2004.[18] The International Monetary Fund (IMF) predicted continued inflation above 25 percent and a –2.6 percent contraction of the Venezuelan economy in 2010, in contrast to a predicted regional average of 4 percent.[19] Venezuela's dependence on oil exports (roughly 90 percent of its export revenues) and U.S. consumption of its oil render the Venezuelan economy vulnerable to both oil prices and U.S. demand. In addition, the closing of the Venezuelan-Colombian border in the wake of the 2009 U.S.-Colombian Defense Cooperation Agreement severely restricted Venezuela's trade with its second largest trade partner.

The challenge for the Obama administration, then, is to encourage and reinforce Venezuelan pragmatism as it attempts to manage this "inconvenient marriage." The first year looked like a frosty separation with little attempt to find common ground and no significant new U.S. initiatives toward Venezuela. U.S. officials have not included Venezuela in their tours of the region, and communications remain limited, though some conversations at lower levels have taken place. Indeed, the administration has adopted a strategy of working with subregional groupings of countries on strategic interests and appears to be waiting for serious signs of a commitment to cooperation before including Venezuela in these initiatives. Yet the clumsy handling of the signing of the Defense Cooperation Agreement with Colombia, incensing many countries in the hemisphere for the lack of prior consultation and explanation, and the retreats and mixed U.S. signals on the Honduran coup, made credible to some Venezuelan citizens Chávez's assertions that the United States remains imperialistic and a threat to Venezuelan security.

By allaying Venezuela's complaints that destabilizing forces are emanating from Colombia and the United States, the Obama administration can at the same time undercut the effectiveness of Chávez's criticisms of the United States in the region. Specifically, Washington should work through the Union of South American Nations (UNASUR) to reassure Venezuela that its access to Colombian military bases is not a threat to Venezuelan sovereignty. The United States should demonstrate a serious willingness to revise its approach to counternarcotics by moving away from the failed emphasis on eradication, interdiction, and militarization of the supply side of the chain. And it should take a fresh approach to trade preferences for poor countries, such as Bolivia. These last two changes would reduce the obstacles to renewed relations with a key Venezuelan ally and diminish Venezuela's ability to criticize the U.S. role in the region.

A multilateral approach is the most fruitful way to encourage the protection of individual rights and formal democratic procedures in Venezuela, given the U.S. failure to condemn the 2002 coup against President Chávez. For example, the Obama administration could build on Venezuela's strong defense of the Democratic Charter in the Honduran case and seek a consensus on ways to prevent "alterations" of constitutional order short of military coups, including executive abuse of power. Unfortunately, Washington's eventual compromise on principle for a recognition of the Honduran elections as well as Chávez's inclination against OAS interventions makes this a difficult route to cooperation.

Venezuela's neighbors are also unlikely to join in such a multilateral promotion of democracy. Constrained by Venezuelan largesse in its petrodiplomacy, their commercial interests in Venezuela, and a general desire not to interfere in each other's internal affairs (or to judge others, for fear of being judged themselves), these countries have been reluctant to comment on standards of democracy, governance, and rule of law as they apply to Venezuela, despite the growing recognition of the serious erosion of basic inter-American standards.

The Obama administration knows that the alternative approaches of seeking to isolate or confront Venezuela have been counterproductive in the past. During the Bush years the United States and Venezuela engaged in a Western Hemisphere "cold war," a competition over financial and political influence in other countries that each was attempting to lure to its side.[20] U.S. efforts to isolate Venezuela in hemispheric arenas also failed, as when it proposed and backed two candidates for secretary general of the OAS in 2005, only to find that the Venezuela-backed candidate won the vote.

By avoiding direct confrontation with Venezuela, the United States can not only defuse that destructive relationship but also work more effectively to create cooperative relationships with other Latin American countries and thereby further U.S. interests. The most important step toward changing the negative dynamic thus far has been the Obama administration's promise of a new style and attitude, with the focus on greater multilateralism, consultation, and respect. Chávez's anti-Americanism resonated at home and abroad because of general antipathy toward U.S. unilateral actions and perceived bullying, particularly during the Bush administration. Washington's new consultative style emphasizing multilateralism will go a long way toward undercutting that resentment, but it must contain real substance if it is to remain credible in the coming years.

The larger foreign policy concern for the United States may well be the uncertainty of a post-Chávez scenario. Although President Chávez has very ably resisted every domestic challenge and consolidated his own power over the past twelve years, the vulnerabilities of the 2010–12 election cycle described earlier leave the outcomes uncertain. If the United Socialist Party of Venezuela (PSUV) and President Chávez continue to win elections, there is no reason to think they will depart from the goals of deepening "twenty-first-century socialism" at home and restructuring power globally. This might ultimately put them on a collision course with the United States even if it pursues multilateral policies.

Perhaps the riskier outcome would be an electoral loss or other sudden departure of President Chávez. The deinstitutionalization of government structures and the personalization of power preventing the development of alternative leadership under Chávez's government present potentially dangerous scenarios for the transition to a post-Chávez era. If his own followers continue to fear persecution in the wake of an opposition electoral victory, they may resist with violence. If opponents to Chávez perceive no opportunity to come to power through electoral means and feel threatened and intimidated by repression of dissent, they too may resort to violence.

The most important task, then, is to encourage a peaceful process for the upcoming elections, with mutual guarantees of protection for all the players involved. The second task is to provide credible reassurances to Venezuelan citizens that the United States does not present a threat to Venezuela or its allies in the region.

Notes

1. The Bolivarian Revolution is named after Simón Bolívar (1783–1830), one of the most important leaders of South America's struggle for independence from Spain. He dreamed of a federation of South American states based on a liberal philosophy of governance, but in later years he advocated centralized power to control the internal bickering in Gran Colombia.

2. See also analyses by Carlos Romero, "The United States and Venezuela: From a Special Relationship to Wary Neighbors," in *The Unraveling of Representative Democracy in Venezuela,* edited by Jennifer McCoy and David Myers (Johns Hopkins University Press, 2004), pp. 130–50; and Ana Maria San Juan, "America Latina y el Bolivarianismo del Siglo XXI" (Latin America and Bolivarianism in the 21st century), unpublished ms., Caracas, January 2008.

3. The Punto Fijo democratic political system established in 1959 was the result of a power-sharing agreement known as the Punto Fijo Pact that ended the military dictatorship of General Pérez Jiménez.

4. When several coalition partners refused to join the United Socialist Party of Venezuela, negotiations broke down, and smaller coalition parties ran their own candidates, becoming "dissidents" in Chávez's view.

5. See Jennifer McCoy, "International Response to Democratic Crisis in Venezuela," in *Defending the Gain,* edited by Esther Brimmer (Washington: Center for Transatlantic Relations, 2007), pp. 119–32.

6. *International Petroleum Monthly,* March 2010 (U.S. Department of Energy, Energy Information Administration) (www.eia.doe.gov/ipm/imports.html).

7. Annual Threat Assessment of the U.S. Intelligence Community for the Senate Select Committee on Intelligence, February 2, 2010, p. 25. Note that Iran lacks refining capacity and is therefore dependent on imported gasoline.

8. Ibid., pp. 31–35.

9. U.S. Department of State, Bureau of Democracy, Human Rights and Labor, "2009 Human Rights Report: Venezuela," March 11.

10. Ambassador Bernardo Alvarez, "Venezuela Responds," *Armed Forces Journal,* April 2010 (www.afji.com/2010/04/4543057/).

11. Douglas Farah, "Iran in Latin America: An Overview," in *Iran in Latin America,* edited by Cynthia Arnson, Haleh Esfandiari, and Adam Stubits, Reports on the Americas 23 (Washington: Woodrow Wilson International Center, 2010).

12. *El Universal,* April 14, 2010 (http://english.eluniversal.com/2010/04/14/en_pol_art_us-defense-secretary_14A3737897.shtml).

13. Questions for the Record Submitted to Assistant Secretary-Designate Arturo Valenzuela by Senator Richard Lugar, Senate Foreign Relations Committee, July 8, 2009.

14. Alvarez, "Venezuela Responds."

15. With the arrival in Caracas in early 2010 of Cuba's minister of technology and former minister of the interior, Ramiro Valdéz, to advise on the electricity shortage, the opposition began to suspect that he was really there as a specialist in Internet control to help the government repress dissent.

16. Honduran business and political leaders, interviews with the author in Tegucigalpa, October 2009.

17. Obama administration officials, conversations with the author, April 2010.

18. Datanalisis, *Informe Escenarios Datanalisis: Marzo 2010,* Caracas.

19. International Monetary Fund, *World Economic Outlook,* April 2010 (www.imf.org/external/pubs/ft/weo/2010/01/pdf/c2.pdf).

20. Some reports estimate that Venezuela's own forms of foreign aid (discounted oil, purchase of bonds, joint energy ventures, barter trade) may well be the equivalent of total U.S. aid to the region since 1999, or perhaps even more.

six
U.S.-Bolivian Relations: Behind the Impasse

George Gray Molina

Bolivia is in the midst of rapid social and political change. Thirty years ago it was a predominantly rural society, based on Andean mining and the ever-present legacy of the 1952 national revolution—which had the close backing of the United States. Along with most of South America, it was at the end of a decade of repressive and reactionary military rule. Today Bolivia has a participatory, multi-ethnic, and left-leaning civilian government with a strong electoral mandate and a loosely "socialist" agenda. After waves of internal migration toward the eastern lowlands, it is also a predominantly urban country, with a growing mestizo and indigenous middle class. Despite these changes, it is still one of the poorest and most unequal countries of the hemisphere. In 2005, after a period of severe political polarization, the country elected Evo Morales, an indigenous and rural union leader, as president. In September 2008 the Bolivian government expelled U.S. ambassador Philip Goldberg, accusing him of meddling in internal affairs. A tit-for-tat expulsion of Bolivian ambassador Gustavo Guzman followed, as well as a diplomatic unraveling between the two countries.

As of September 2010, the diplomatic impasse continues. Despite attempts to close the rift, distances have grown—on trade, anti-narcotics policy, and democracy and human rights promotion, among other key issues. The reelection of Evo Morales in December 2009 was expected to soothe tensions as Morales affirmed that he seeks a "partner, not a *patron*," while the State Department reiterated its interest in working on "issues of mutual interest."

Two years into the impasse, it is worth revisiting the state-to-state interests that lie beyond discursive polarization—the invocation of "Andean populisms" and "Yankee imperialism"—and that threaten a longer-term divide. At the core of the diplomatic crisis lies a substantial gulf on the course of anti-narcotics policy and the realities of asymmetric power between the two countries. Although new initiatives both in the United States and in Bolivia suggest a gradual shift in drug policy, there is unlikely to be much room for overlapping interests to develop in the interim. Both countries appear to be trapped in a vicious circle of mismatched expectations on the issue.

It is time for an alternative strategy, one based on a realistic modus vivendi that is less than a full-blown "partnership" but more than a chronic impasse. How would such a modus vivendi work? First, it would demand a more nuanced view of the political process in each country: for Bolivia, this means understanding the decisive weight that the U.S. Congress—and congressional committees—have over foreign policy; for the United States, it means being more attuned to the subtext of the political discourse that sustains foreign policymaking in the current Morales-led coalition. Second, a new approach also requires moving "beyond drugs" in the substantive policy arena. This is a long-held frustration for Bolivian policymakers, but a matter of lesser importance in Washington. Third, a realistic approach would require looking into alternative diplomatic channels—both bilateral and multilateral—to gain a measure of trust and set the stage for future changes on both sides.

Before the Impasse: Fighting Words

The week that Ambassador Philip Goldberg was expelled in September 2008, social and political conflict was raging in Bolivia. In one gruesome episode of violence, at least eleven civilian lives were lost. The civic committees of Santa Cruz, Tarija, Chuquisaca, Beni, and Pando had taken over government offices and initiated hunger strikes. President Morales was not allowed to land at regional airports across the east and south, and the threat of more violence was growing. Earlier that week, he had denounced an ongoing "civic coup."[1]

Just before the expulsion, Morales declared Goldberg persona non grata for "conspiring against Bolivian democracy."[2] The action was received with dismay in Washington and led to a reciprocal expulsion of Bolivia's ambassador, Gustavo Guzman. The U.S. assistant secretary for western hemisphere affairs, Thomas Shannon, termed Morales's actions a "grave mistake." In response, in the following days and weeks the Bolivian government expelled the U.S. Peace Corps, the Drug Enforcement Agency (DEA), and lower-ranking diplomatic staff.

In December 2008 the United States decertified Bolivia for lack of progress in coca-leaf reduction. With decertification, unilateral trade preferences under the Andean Trade Promotion and Drug Eradication Act (ATPDEA) were also lost, along with Bolivia's eligibility for grants under the U.S. Millennium Challenge Account (MCA), which had been ongoing since 2005. Despite repeated attempts to "normalize" relations—the latest one between Assistant Secretary of State for Western Hemisphere Affairs Arturo Valenzuela and Foreign Minister David Choquehuanca in June 2010—they remain at a standstill.

From La Paz: Interference in Democracy, Decertification on Drugs, and Threats to Hemispheric Interests

How is the diplomatic crisis perceived in La Paz? First, the Bolivian government considers the expulsion of the U.S. ambassador a legitimate response to "meddling in its internal political affairs," allegedly through democracy promotion programs sponsored by the U.S. Agency for International Development (USAID). The first signs of discontent with USAID emerged a year earlier, when the Bolivian minister of the presidency denounced the agency for not aligning with new funding rules approved by Bolivian lawmakers: "If the U.S. cooperation program does not adjust to the policies of the Bolivian state, the doors are open for it [to leave]. We will not allow this type of cooperation to hamper our democracy, conspire against our people's rights and freedoms, and offend our national dignity, for even a single day. We are not willing to be the backyard of any foreign power."[3] Doubts about USAID programs were amplified by a *Time* magazine story citing a 2002 internal e-mail that stated democracy promotion efforts in Bolivia should "help to build moderate pro-democracy political parties that might be a counterbalance to the radicalism of the MAS [Movement for Socialism] or its successors."[4]

Second, Bolivia considers U.S. decertification of its anti-narcotics efforts another form of meddling. Given the importance of anti-narcotics policy for U.S. aid to Bolivia, decertification involved a significant downsizing of operations, although support for anti-narcotics logistical and administrative assistance continued in 2010 through Washington's Narcotics Affairs Section (NAS). Decertification meant "something more" for Evo Morales, who had dedicated most of his political life to defending the interests of coca-leaf farmers in Bolivia's Chapare region. Remarks by U.S. ambassador Manuel

Rocha in 2002 suggesting that U.S. cooperation might be suspended if a coca-leaf grower were elected president of Bolivia, actually served to boost Morales's image. In his view, the embassy had been his "best campaign manager" for the elections in 2002, 2005, and 2009.[5] For Morales, the presence of the DEA in the Chapare region is more than technical assistance; it is evidence of heavy-handed diplomacy and unacceptable foreign involvement in internal Bolivian affairs.

Third, the Bolivian government finds U.S. involvement in hemispheric political affairs polarizing, particularly in view of the July 2009 agreement giving U.S. forces access to Colombian bases and Washington's position on the 2009 Honduras coup. Echoing Hugo Chávez, Morales warned that "with foreign military bases in Latin America, there will be no peace, nor regional integration." Brazil's president Lula da Silva also questioned the presence of U.S. military advisers in the region. Hence in December 2009 Morales proposed a "consultative referendum in Latin America on whether U.S. troops should be allowed in the region."[6]

Earlier that year, Morales had met President Barack Obama at the Trinidad and Tobago Summit and come away with a favorable impression.[7] Obama had shown openness to the Bolivian agenda to an extent that was criticized back in Washington.[8] Over the next few months, however, intimations of dialogue cooled down, especially in the wake of Congress's decision not to extend trade preferences to Bolivia. On hearing the news, President Morales accused Obama of "lying to him about U.S. cooperation to Bolivia" at Trinidad and Tobago.[9] Chances for a rapprochement ended in July with the agreement on Colombian bases. Paradoxically, polls showed that 56 percent of Bolivians had a "positive or very positive" image of Barack Obama, one of the most favorable in the hemisphere.[10]

During this period, Bolivia combined confrontational and conciliatory diplomacy in its foreign policy toward the United States. The toughest positions were articulated by President Morales himself, the conciliatory ones by Minister Choquehuanca. This balancing act occurred in an electoral year in Bolivia, beginning with a constitutional referendum in January 2009 and ending with a presidential election in December.

From Washington: Decertification, ATPDEA Preferences, and Ties to Venezuela and Iran

How were these issues perceived in the United States? Its stance must be seen in the context of the expulsion of the U.S. ambassador, decertification of the drugs policy, nonextension of trade preferences, and Bolivia's cozy relations with Venezuela and Iran. Outside of the more nuanced view of the State Department and foreign policy think tanks, Washington media tend to lump Morales and Chávez together in ways that amplify the notion of "Andean populism" and often overlook the extent of the current government's popular legitimacy and democratic performance. The net effect is that Morales's words and actions tend to be questioned by much of the U.S. foreign policy community. The problem with the Andean populism narrative is that it simplifies and adds grievance to existing rifts between the U.S. and Bolivian administrations.

The starting point for U.S. relations with Bolivia is anti-narcotics policy, which has long been a key U.S. concern throughout the Andean region. Although U.S. drug policies are designed and implemented by the executive branch of government, they are checked by active congressional overview of the drug issue and the threat of gridlock. This dynamic adds bureaucratic inertia to the timeline of foreign affairs relations, stretching out the chances of normalizing them. The annual anti-narcotics reports published by the State Department feed into a regular congressional schedule, an annual "window of opportunity" for discussions on certification and decertification of anti-narcotics efforts. Besides defining "partners" and "nonpartners," the certification process illustrates the stability of policymaking, which tends to change very little from year to year, and only a little from administration to administration. Although changes to drug policy are currently under way, the certification process continues impervious to broader policy debates. For Washington, certification is a routine procedure that sets out a schedule for anti-narcotics policy discussion but does not carry nearly as much political weight as Andean countries believe.

The State Department's 2010 evaluation of anti-narcotics policy shows mounting concern over the increase in coca-leaf and potential cocaine production in Bolivia: "Despite Bolivia's success in meeting minimum eradication goals, the total effort by the GOB [government of Bolivia] fell short of its obligations as outlined in the United Nations (UN) Conventions and bilateral agreements."[11] The evaluation also notes that Bolivia's expulsion of the DEA "severely undermined Bolivian law enforcement efforts to identify and dismantle drug trafficking organizations." Moreover, both the expulsion of the DEA and Bolivia's weak response to coca cultivation and cocaine production directly affect neighboring countries: "Drug-trafficking organizations (DTOs) in the Southern Cone—Argentina, Brazil, Chile, Paraguay, and Uruguay—have taken advantage of the current situation in Bolivia to increase their drug trafficking activities in the region."[12] The report recommends that

U.S. cooperation with Bolivia should continue in agricultural development, small business development, and anti-narcotics training.

A second concern of Washington revolved around trade preferences. After the extension of preferences for Colombia, Ecuador, and Peru until December 31, 2010, President Obama "instructed his administration to work with the Government of Bolivia to improve cooperation, and if cooperation improves, to work with Congress to re-establish benefits for Bolivia."[13] However, trade preferences cannot be reestablished without the previous certification of anti-narcotics policy. Given the slow progress of bilateral and multilateral trade agreements in the region, the extension of trade preferences has become a pivotal policy issue for the U.S. Congress.

Third, Bolivia's ties with Venezuela and Iran are equally troubling. Although Washington is paying close attention to Venezuela's impact on security and economic aid in Bolivia, it finds most worrisome Bolivia's special relationship with Iran, particularly the support of the Bolivarian Alliance for the Americas (ALBA) for Teheran's nuclear program. Secretary of State Hillary Clinton, in her only explicit mention of Bolivia, warned that "if people want to flirt with Iran, they should take a look at what the consequences might well be for them. And we hope that they will think twice and we will support them if they do."[14] Mahmoud Ahmadinejad's visit to Latin America in December 2009, with its agreements for up to US$1 billion in future trade and energy investments in the region, reinforced Washington's mistrust of Venezuela and Bolivia, not to mention its concern about Iran's overtures in the region.[15]

Behind the Impasse: A Long History

Bolivia's qualms are partly rooted in its long history of relations with the United States and relate in particular to Washington's unilateral policies on international politics, security, and anti-narcotics issues.[16] In 1952 President Dwight D. Eisenhower took the unprecedented step of establishing cordial relations with Bolivia's revolutionary government, which had instituted radical agrarian reform, nationalized mining, and promoted populist politics. This "third way" approach, wedged between the political systems in the cold war communist bloc and Western liberal democracies, proved instrumental in swaying the national revolutionary leaders away from a pro-Cuban stance in the 1960s and in neutralizing pro-fascist sympathies dating to the 1940s.[17] In 1956, during the Siles Suazo presidency, a U.S. economic stabilization mission led by George Eder introduced the first modern "stabilization package."[18] By the 1960s President John F. Kennedy had launched the Alliance for Progress initiative and the Peace Corps and had provided financial support to build roads in Bolivia—which included the Chapare road between Cochabamba and Santa Cruz, the epicenter of the coca-leaf trade.[19]

At the end of the military period in the 1970s, the Carter administration played a key role in supporting pro-democracy social movements, including the hunger strike held by Domitila Chungara, which had a domino effect in the transition from authoritarian rule to democracy in the 1980s.[20] The United States also supported democratic institution building in Bolivia, most critically at the local and judicial levels of government. Since then the holding of democratic elections, incremental democratic reforms, and the expansion of civil and political rights have been the backdrop of social and political polarization. Reforms that strengthened democratic institutions, such as Popular Participation in the 1990s, also provided an arena for the collective action of social movements at the local and national levels. Many of these reforms played both a state-building and a social-mobilizing role, in part explaining the backlash to the reforms and emerging strength of nontraditional political actors in the 2000s.[21] As a result, the United States has been perceived as taking sides in the domestic debate, showing support for liberal democratic outcomes and processes, but not for multicultural politics, popular processes, and social or indigenous claims. Bolivia's score-keeping on these issues stems from its memory of Washington's long unilateral involvement in its security and anti-narcotics policy.

The Political Dimension of Anti-Narcotics Policies

Anti-narcotics policy has been the driving force in U.S.-Bolivian relations since the 1990s and, as already mentioned, helped Evo Morales gain not only local power but also the presidency because of his defiance of that policy. His stance won public support beginning in the 1980s in his home region of Chapare and even in the 2002 campaign, when the U.S. ambassador reminded the Bolivian electorate that "if they want Bolivia to return to being an important cocaine exporting country, this result would put U.S. aid in danger in the future."[22] At the same time, President Morales has been careful to broaden his political appeal beyond the narcotics issue despite his political base in the Chapare region—indeed, perhaps because of it—and in doing so he has tried to reassure the popular and middle classes that he "will not run a narco-state in Bolivia."[23] Yet during his administration coca crops and the potential for cocaine production have increased, particularly over the past three years. Bolivia has also been unsuccessful in persuading the United Nations to de-penalize the coca leaf in its narcotics substance lists.

According to most analysts, the failure to counter narcotics production can be attributed both to the weakness of supply-side controls in the Andean region and to America's inability to suppress domestic demand.[24] Patterns of coca cultivation and smuggling and the availability of low-priced cocaine in consumer markets suggest that it is time to try a different approach to the narcotics issue.[25]

Three significant trends point in this direction. First, coca-leaf production in the Andean region has been relatively stable, occupying between 200,000 and 250,000 hectares over the past two decades. This pattern has endured despite years of eradication efforts covering vast areas and a relatively aggressive policy at the ground level since 2000. If anything, UN Office of Drugs and Crime (UNODC) statistics indicate that Bolivian coca-leaf production has increased, from about 26,000 hectares in 2004 to about 35,000 hectares in 2009. Furthermore, potential cocaine production increased from about 115 to 195 metric tons in the same period. However, the relative share of Bolivia in the hemispheric drug trade has not increased, as most additional crops and potential drug production are emerging in Colombia, which in 2007 accounted for 167,000 hectares of coca-leaf and 535 tons of potential cocaine production.[26]

Second, Bolivia's patterns of production and smuggling have shifted over the past decade. On the producer side, new crop cultivation has moved from the Chapare to the Yungas region, with a higher rate of net eradication in the Chapare. A significant feature of Bolivia's coca production is that President Morales himself presides over the coca union system and is formally responsible for negotiating quota and alternative development compensation agreements. In addition, Bolivian cocaine is being smuggled increasingly through European trading routes via Brazil and western Africa. Although UN data are imprecise on the degree of movement from the United States to the European route, Brazil is clearly concerned with promoting greater joint action to reverse this trend.

Third, on the demand side, the easy availability and low price of cocaine suggest that the current policy is not having a significant impact on consumer markets. Contrary to the hoped-for effects of supply-reduction policies, the street price of cocaine has fallen substantially over the past thirty years.

For the Bolivian government, the evaluation of anti-narcotics policy goes beyond the technical aspects of interdiction or crop reduction to the political sphere: it sees U.S. engagement in anti-narcotics policy in the Andean region itself as evidence of intromission in domestic affairs. This perception is impermeable to subtle shifts in drug policy back in Washington and is based on a track record of largely unsuccessful supply-control initiatives and the very personal recollections of the Bolivian president on these matters.

Overlapping Interests

However, signs of change are evident on both sides of the narcotics issue, with implications for bilateral and multilateral relations in the region.

Bilateral Relations: Changes in the "War on Drugs"

In October 2009 the U.S. Congress passed a bill, with bipartisan support, that established a commission to rethink drug policy in the hemisphere.[27] The initiative, led by Representative Eliot Engel (D-N.Y.), will evaluate the scope and limitations of past policies, such as Plan Colombia and the Mérida Initiative, and will outline new guidelines for future anti-narcotics policy. The commission has been hailed by all sides in the anti-narcotics community, as well as by human rights organizations focusing on security issues in Latin America—including the Inter-American Dialogue and Brookings Institution in the center of the political spectrum and the Washington Office on Latin America and the Center for Economic and Policy Research on the left.

At the same time, the "drug tsar" appointed by President Obama, Gil Kerlikowske, has moved swiftly on the domestic drug policy front.[28] The Bush administration's "War on Drugs" had been gradually moving toward preventive care in public health and post-addiction treatment and away from legal-criminal action, the hallmark of past policymaking. The new chief anti-narcotics officer is a former police reformer in Seattle, where nonpunitive policies were tested successfully in recent years. Changes to drug policy are likely to have a moderating effect over demand- and supply-side policies and show political will to seek alternatives to an unsuccessful track record. This is clearly a striking opportunity for the United States and Andean countries to take joint action, which although gradual and incremental, promises to address some of the key issues in the anti-narcotics policy debate.

Multilateral Relations: Filling the Void

The DEA's absence from Bolivia has implied a de facto shift in anti-narcotics policy on the ground since 2009. Key functions of drug policy—information sharing, drug interdiction, crop substitution, and alternative development initiatives—have gradually led to a more multilateral but ad hoc approach to the drug problem in Bolivia. For example, Brazil's federal police are sharing information with and providing technical assistance to Bolivia's police forces, the U.S. Narcotics Section (NAS) continues to provide logistical and administrative support to ministry officers, the UNODC publishes its report on crops and drugs production potential, and the European Union shares a more prominent role with USAID on alternative development programs in coca-producing regions.

Although this multilateral effort is still fraught with difficulties, it signals a turning point with respect to past practice. The fact that U.S. involvement continues—now with many partners—is a positive sign for future anti-narcotics policy in the region, as well as in Bolivia.

Conclusions

U.S.-Bolivian relations are at their lowest point since the transition from authoritarian rule in the 1980s. Beyond the visible unease between the two countries—that vents mostly on the multilateral scene—substantial disagreements on anti-narcotics policy and asymmetries of power are hindering progress. Diplomatic officials talk about a "normalization" of relations based on shared values and common goals. However, the normalization strategy is unnecessarily demanding for both countries. In the short run, it makes national interest–based negotiations less likely, and in the long run, it fails to address the core problems that fester beneath the bilateral relationship. An alternative approach based on gradual interest-based approximations might be a better path to a more solid and evenhanded relationship.

Such an approach would first have to address the question of anti-narcotics policy. For the Bolivian government, as mentioned earlier, the central issues are not primarily of a *technical* nature, nor constrained by interdiction, alternative development, or security initiatives. Rather, drug policy in itself is perceived as a form of meddling into domestic Bolivian affairs. For the U.S. government, on the other hand, the current impasse is not particularly significant and merely delays the implementation of gradual changes that are under way in its own legislative process. Policy analysts on both sides agree that the U.S. shifts in anti-narcotics policy will provide an opportunity for a less heavy-handed approach to cocaine interdiction and coca-crop substitution. Meanwhile changes on the ground in Bolivia are setting the stage for a multilateral approach to anti-narcotics policy, with a larger role played by Brazilian, European Union, and UN agencies.

Second, as for relations "beyond drugs," the diplomatic freeze and mutual distrust tend to perpetuate a lose/lose scenario. Bolivia is perceived to be a minor ally of Chávez's foreign policy, while the Obama administration is considered as antagonistic to Evo Morales as the Bush administration was. Both readings are wrong and delay chances for diplomatic progress. They also suggest that this is not the best of times for a full-fledged "partnership" based on shared values. How, then, can the two sides break the ice on the impasse? Why not settle for a modus vivendi based on mutual interest and attainable goals?

Three actions could help Bolivia and the United States move forward in this direction. First, both sides need to "unpack" their view of the other side. U.S. foreign policy is highly decentralized and follows congressional and bureaucratic routines that are not well understood by the Bolivian government. For certain issues, a congressional committee or subcommittee can be as or more powerful than a secretary of state. Furthermore, there are moderate and militant allies of the Bolivian agenda in the U.S. Congress and in friendly think tanks and lobbies. Bolivian foreign policy is hardly monolithic either. Bolivia conducts pragmatic and nonideological bilateral relations with Brazil, Chile, and Argentina on trade and energy issues but maintains a sharp ideological line on ALBA, security issues, and free trade. It is important for both sides to distinguish the rhetoric from the substance, issue by issue.

Second, agendas can diversify. The Latin American regional political environment has changed in the past couple of years, a period of mounting tensions between the United States and Bolivia. A de facto multilateralization of the anti-narcotics agenda is under way, along with a decoupling of drug policy from trade and aid policies in both countries. This, in itself, is good news but is probably not enough to improve bilateral relations. A "beyond drugs" agenda is needed for more substantial progress on both sides. Such an agenda would have several dimensions, including trade, democracy and human rights, and energy and climate change.

Trade. The ATPDEA was one of the most successful policy initiatives of the past decade. Small and medium businesses in Bolivia constrained by high transportation and business costs were still able to expand into a number of niche markets in the United States, including textiles, jewelry, leather goods, certified tropical woods, and organic foods. A new trade initiative could build upon the ATPDEA experience, this time decoupling drug conditionality from market access. Explicit targets for the development of small business and the export market would align market access incentives with self-sustainability over time.

Democracy and human rights. This agenda should be redrawn to fit the current reform needs. For example, third parties clearly need to be involved in democratic strengthening and there should be a more multilateral approach to the protection of civil and political rights in the region. Multilateral organizations like the Organization of American States (OAS) and its Inter-American Commission on Human Rights can play a more prominent role in this respect. The Obama administration has greater credibility than past administrations on these issues, and the Morales administration also has incentives to match rhetoric to actions on human rights protection in Bolivia.

Climate change and energy. Bolivia is among the countries with the highest biodiversity in the hemisphere and has been an innovator of mechanisms for avoiding deforestation, including certified forestry, fair trade, and organic agricultural certification. Until now, U.S. strategy on climate change adaptation has focused mainly on major global players. Why not open channels with smaller countries that can deliver innovative and small-scale approaches to the adoption of low-carbon technology? The summit on climate change hosted in Bolivia in April 2010 showed both the need for a common approach and the degrees of separation between large and small countries regarding the climate change agenda.

Third, both countries can begin to close the divide in multilateral settings. Bilateral negotiations have not prospered in the past year and a half, but there is ample policy space for engagement in regional and hemispheric forums. Changes in regional politics—such as the elections in Chile and Brazil—will create incentives for broader cooperation based less on political affinity and more on common interests. More engagement with the OAS, the Inter-American Development Bank, and Inter-American Commission on Human Rights may help build a common agenda in the future.

With a less demanding approach to U.S.-Bolivian relations, the electoral timeline would become less important for political rapprochement. It is wrong to assume that once Bolivia completes its presidential elections there will be less incentive for political polarization with the United States. Until incentives for cooperation outweigh the gains from U.S. involvement in domestic problems, La Paz will continue to contest that involvement. In this pessimistic scenario, a wait-and-see attitude tends to sustain the impasse. On the other hand, gradual engagement on issues of mutual interest and on routine procedures might help mend fences. Paradoxically, the remaining U.S. anti-narcotics program in Bolivia is showing how the two countries might forge a new type of relationship—less spectacular but more respectful than in the past.

Notes

1. "Morales denuncia un golpe de estado de gobernadores 'rebeldes,'" Agencia EFE (Spain), September 15, 2008.

2. "Bolivia Tells U.S. Envoy to Leave," *BBC News,* September 11, 2008.

3. "Declaracion del Ministro de la Presidencia sobre la ayuda de EEUU" (Declaration of Ministry of the Presidency about U.S. assistance), Agencia Boliviana de Información, August 30, 2007.

4. Jean Friedman-Rudovsky, "Is Bolivia Cozying up to Iran?" *Time* Magazine, October 9, 2007. The article also points out that "in June 2006, half a year into Morales' term, the assistant administrator in USAID's Bureau for Latin America and the Caribbean, Adolfo A. Franco, told the U.S. House of Representatives' Committee on International Relations that his agency was still financing anti-MAS elements. 'USAID is focusing assistance to Bolivia on programs that strengthen vibrant and effective democracies,' Franco stated, 'including the support of counterweights to one-party control.'"

5. "Evo Morales dice que Bolivia está mejor sin Embajador de EEUU" (Evo Morales says Bolivia is better without a U.S. Ambassador), Agencia EFE, December 6, 2009.

6. "Discurso de Evo Morales Ayma, presidente de Bolivia, en la clausura de la VIII Cumbre del ALBA" (Speech of Evo Morales Ayma, president of Bolivia, in the closing of the VIII Summit of ALBA), Agencia Boliviana de Información, December 14, 2009.

7. "Evo ataca a la administracion de Bush y saluda a Barack Obama" (Evo attacks the Bush administration and welcomes Barack Obama), Fides News Service, January 22, 2009; "Bolivia's Evo Morales Hails Obama's Triumph as 'Historic,'" German Press Agency, November 5, 2008.

8. "Obama Offers Olive Branch to Bolivia," Associated Press, April 19, 2009.

9. "Evo Morales: Obama 'Lied' about Cooperation," Associated Press, July 1, 2009.

10. In the same survey, 33 percent of Bolivians had a "favorable or very favorable" opinion of Hugo Chávez. See Latinobarómetro survey, 2009.

11. U.S. Department of State, *International Narcotics Control Strategy Report,* vol. 1: *Drug and Chemical Control* (Washington, March 2010).

12. Ibid.

13. "Barack Obama quiere ATPDEA para Bolivia," *Los Tiempos,* December 30, 2009.

14. "Hillary Clinton Warns Latin America of Close Iran Ties," *BBC News,* December 11, 2009.

15. Friedman-Rudovsky, "Is Bolivia Cozying up to Iran?"

16. See James Dunkerley, *Rebellion in the Veins: Political Struggle in Bolivia, 1952–1982* (London: Verso, 1984).

17. See Laurence Whitehead, *The United States and Bolivia: A Case of Neo-Colonialism* (Oxford, U.K.: Haslemere Group, 1969), p. 11.

18. George Eder, *Inflation and Development in Latin America: A Case History of Inflation and Stabilization in Bolivia* (University of Michigan, Graduate School of Business Administration, 1960), p. 479.

19. See James Malloy, *Bolivia: The Uncompleted Revolution* (University of Pennsylvania Press, 1970).

20. See Laurence Whitehead, "Bolivia's Failed Democratization, 1977–1980," in *Transitions from Authoritarian Rule,* vol. 2: *Latin America,* edited by Guillermo O'Donnell, Philippe C. Schmitter, and Laurence Whitehead (Johns Hopkins University Press, 1986), pp. 68–69, 71.

21. George Gray Molina, "The Politics of Popular Participation in Bolivia, 1994–1999," D. phil. thesis, Nuffield College, University of Oxford, 2003.

22. Fernando Mayorga, "Elecciones en Bolivia: lo Nuevo y lo Viejo" (Elections in Bolivia: The new and the old), *Anuario Social y Político de América Latina y el Caribe* 6 (Caracas: Flacso/Unesco/Nueva Sociedad, 2003), pp. 9–17.

23. "Evo hizo un llamamiento a hacer un pacto contra el narcotráfico" (Evo calls for a pact against narcotrafficking), *Europress,* March 11, 2006.

24. UN Office of Drugs and Crime (UNODC), *Coca Cultivation in the Andean Region: A Survey of Bolivia, Colombia, and Peru* (New York, 2008).

25. Peter Reuter, "The Limits of Supply-Side Drug Control," *Milken Institute Review,* First Quarter, 2001, pp. 14–23.

26. UNODC, *World Drug Report 2009* (New York, 2009).

27. Washington Office on Latin America, "Congress to Take Up New Drug Policy Commission: Time to Re-Examine Decades-Old Drug Control Policies," September 15, 2009.

28. Gary Fields, "White House Czar Calls for End of 'War on Drugs,'" *Wall Street Journal,* May 14, 2009.

seven

Obama's Cuba Policy: The End of the "New Beginning"

Daniel P. Erikson

When Barack Obama was elected the forty-fourth president of the United States in November 2008, his victory raised hopes in many quarters that Washington and Havana would begin at last to overcome decades of antagonism. Even Fidel Castro, the ailing eighty-two-year-old former president of Cuba, praised the new American president as "intelligent, educated and level-headed." More broadly, a vast cross section of Cuban society—including government officials, intellectuals, cultural leaders, and dissident and civic opposition groups—appeared to welcome Obama's election to the White House. At the same time, the Cuban government was cautious about the possibilities for change that Obama had embodied during his campaign. Shortly after the January 1, 2009, celebration of the fiftieth anniversary of the Cuban Revolution, and just a few weeks before Obama's inauguration, Raúl Castro, the long-standing defense minister and younger brother of Fidel who had succeeded him as president nearly a year earlier, declared on Cuban state television that the new U.S. president had raised "excessive hopes." Raúl signaled that when it came to a possible rapprochement between Cuba and the new administration, "we are in no rush, we are not desperate."[1]

During the first year of the Obama administration, U.S.-Cuba policy consisted of a tug-of-war between hope and caution, and caution ultimately

This essay was written in the author's capacity as senior associate for U.S. policy at the Inter-American Dialogue, before accepting a position at the State Department's Bureau of Western Hemisphere Affairs. It is based on independent analysis and does not reflect the views of the U.S. government.

prevailed on both sides of the Straits of Florida. This outcome, while not wholly unexpected, is nevertheless striking, considering that this continuity immediately followed a period when both the United States and Cuba experienced major leadership transitions. In February 2008 Fidel Castro handed the reins over to Raúl, who was thought to be more pragmatic and open to dialogue with the United States. In January 2009 Obama succeeded President George W. Bush, whose Cuba policies were almost wholly developed to appeal to hard-line anti-Castro exiles in South Florida. While these leadership shifts have been accompanied by slight improvements in tone and rhetoric and several policy adjustments have taken place, the overall landscape of the U.S-Cuban relationship remains largely unchanged.

The key point to remember amid these new developments, then, is that the foremost element of Obama's Cuba policy thus far has been continuity with previous administrations. Similarly, Raúl Castro—by continuing many hard-line policies on issues related to democracy and human rights in Cuba and provoking occasional confrontations with the United States—has not deviated significantly from the path established by his brother Fidel.

Although the Obama administration came to power with broad public support and substantial room to act in new ways on the Cuba question, it chose to implement only several small policy changes. These measures, such as allowing greater Cuban American travel and opening bilateral dialogues on migration issues, did not substantially recalibrate the U.S. policy framework. Despite the changed circumstances since the cold war era, events to date have shown that when it comes to U.S. policy toward Cuba, old habits are hard to change. This has been equally true in the case of Cuba, as the Cuban government's punitive stance toward noted blogger Yoani Sánchez, callous mistreatment of the dissident Orlando Zapata Tamayo, who died on a hunger strike, and detention without charge of U.S. Agency for International Development (USAID) subcontractor Alan Gross all point to the recurrence of hard-edged tactics that will make any rapprochement with the United States all the more difficult.

To some degree, the Obama administration's approach to Cuba stems from the mixed results that the 2008 elections delivered on the trends within Miami's Cuban American community. Obama won Florida's 27 electoral votes by a comfortable margin of more than 200,000 votes, receiving 50.9 percent to John McCain's 48.4 percent. But McCain defeated Obama in one closely watched demographic: Cuban Americans voted overwhelmingly for the Republican candidate, who received an estimated 65 percent of the vote compared with 35 percent for Obama. This result still put Obama in the top tier of Democratic presidential candidates in terms of attracting Cuban American voters, but it nevertheless represented a thirty-point victory for McCain from this segment of the population in an election where Obama won virtually every other demographic. An exit poll conducted by Bendixen & Associates, a Miami polling firm, revealed a stark generational divide. Obama won 55 percent support from Cuban Americans under the age of thirty, while John McCain captured 84 percent of the votes of those sixty-five and older. In three closely watched congressional races featuring prominent Cuban American Republicans, the incumbents handily beat back Democratic challengers.

The 2008 election demonstrated that although shifts in Cuban American public opinion did not yet favor a decisive break with the historic policies of confrontation (even the Democratic candidates supported the embargo), the once monolithic support for isolating Cuba was splintering further. Moreover, Obama was the first presidential candidate to win Florida since the end of the cold war while campaigning on a platform that moved even gingerly toward greater engagement with Cuba. He did so without the support of the hard-line Cuban American community. His margin in the Electoral College was so substantial that he did not need Florida's twenty-seven electoral votes to win the White House. In short, Obama had significant domestic political scope of action to break through the traditional animosity guiding U.S. relations with Cuba. The question was whether he would choose to use it and whether the Castro regime would respond favorably.

Turning Campaign Strategy into Policy

During his presidential campaign, Obama had hewed to a carefully calibrated line on Cuba policy that rested on three central pillars: support for allowing Cuban Americans to visit and send money to relatives in Cuba, openness to greater dialogue with the Cuban government, and adherence to the U.S. embargo. At the time, he won plaudits from diverse constituencies, ranging from critics of the embargo who were anxious to see any slight opening toward Cuba to more moderate Cuban American groups who were pleased to win special travel rights for their community but supported the wider travel ban on ordinary Americans, as well as the restrictions on U.S. trade and investment with the island.

At first, new leadership in both countries, changing attitudes in the Cuban American community, and increasing international pressure on the United States to adopt a different policy toward Cuba all paved the way for a series of small changes in U.S.-Cuba relations. During his inaugural address, Obama had pledged to "extend a hand" to the world's authoritarian regimes "if you are willing to unclench your fist." This was followed by an early tsunami of calls for the United States to shift course and engage with Cuba, including reports from such influential think tanks as the Brookings Institution, the Council on Foreign Relations, and the Inter-American Dialogue, and statements from retired U.S. generals, church leaders, moderate Cuban American groups, and prominent human rights organizations. Richard Lugar, the Indiana senator who is the lead Republican on the Senate Foreign Relations Committee, circulated a staff report that strongly criticized current U.S. policy and suggested opening greater trade and diplomatic and cultural contacts, although it stopped short of calling for the full repeal of U.S. sanctions. Lugar's own criticism of the current U.S. approach was clear: "The unilateral embargo on Cuba has failed to achieve its stated purpose of 'bringing democracy to the Cuban people.' . . . We must recognize the ineffectiveness of our current policy and deal with the Cuban regime in a way that enhances U.S. interests."[2]

Indeed, it was initially the U.S. Congress—not the Obama administration—that set the pace of change. Soon the halls of Congress were once again flooded with legislative proposals to introduce new loopholes into the embargo or scrap it entirely, proposals such as the Free Trade with Cuba Act, the Cuba Reconciliation Act, the Export Freedom to Cuba Act, and the United States-Cuba Normalization Act. In particular, critical mass had appeared to gather around the Freedom to Travel to Cuba Act. The bill, introduced by Senator Byron Dorgan (D-N.D.), called for the complete repeal of the travel ban and was supported by 24 cosponsors. Representative Bill Delahunt (D-Mass.) introduced a partner bill in the House of Representatives cosponsored by more than 160 members.

The Obama administration by and large stayed out of the early back-and-forth in Congress, but the Cuba issue kept dogging top officials in the weeks leading up to the Summit of the Americas, a major gathering of the thirty-four elected leaders in the Western Hemisphere, scheduled to take place in Trinidad and Tobago in mid-April 2009. Just days before Obama's planned arrival at the summit, his administration moved to fulfill a key campaign promise by lifting all travel and remittance restrictions on Cuban Americans with families in Cuba. It also authorized U.S. companies to offer telecommunications services to Cuba, thereby implementing a measure that had been considered by the Bush administration before leaving office, under the premise that freer communications would serve to mobilize grass-roots democracy on an island where only one out of ten residents has access to a landline telephone, and cell phone usage hovered at 3 percent in 2008. While congressional advocates for lifting the embargo praised the decision, opponents like Representatives Lincoln Diaz-Balart (R-Fla.) and Mario Diaz-Balart (R-Fla.) argued that the move was a "serious mistake" because "unilateral concessions to the dictatorship embolden it to further isolate, imprison, and brutalize pro-democracy activists."[3]

Navigating the Regional Context

When President Obama arrived at the summit in Trinidad and Tobago, anticipation ran high as he would be meeting many of his counterparts in Latin America and the Caribbean for the first time. His visit had been preceded by a flurry of activity related to Cuba. A group of legislators from the Congressional Black Caucus became the first U.S. politicians to meet with Fidel Castro since the aging Cuban leader fell ill three years earlier. The Obama administration had repealed restrictions on the ability of Cuban Americans to travel back to Cuba and send money to their families living on the island, prompting Raúl Castro to declare, "We have sent word to the U.S. government in private and in public that we are willing to discuss everything, human rights, freedom of the press, political prisoners, everything." At a press conference en route to the summit, Secretary of State Hillary Clinton announced, "We are continuing to look for productive ways forward because we view the present policy as having failed. . . . We welcome his comments and the overture they represent, and we are taking a very serious look at how to respond." Evoking a "new beginning," Obama told the other leaders at the summit, "Over the past two years, I've indicated, and I repeat today, that I'm prepared to have my administration engage with the Cuban government on a wide range of issues—from drugs, migration, and economic issues, to human rights, free speech, and democratic reform. Now, let me be clear, I'm not interested in talking just for the sake of talking. But I do believe that we can move U.S.-Cuban relations in a new direction."

During a press conference at the conclusion of the summit, Obama made concrete suggestions as to how the Castro government should respond: "They could release political prisoners. They could reduce charges on remittances. . . . That would be an example of cooperation where both governments are working to help Cuban families and raise standards of living in Cuba."[4] Obama also stated that freedom for the Cuban people remained the top U.S. objective for engagement with the island: "That's our lodestone.

That's our North Star."[5] Within days, however, Fidel Castro wrote, "There is no doubt that the President misinterpreted Raúl's statements. When the President of Cuba said he was ready to discuss any topic with the U.S. president, he meant he was not afraid of addressing any issue. That shows his courage and confidence in the principles of the Revolution."[6]

In June 2009 the Obama administration confronted the regional disapproval of U.S. efforts to isolate Cuba when the General Assembly of the Organization of American States (OAS) considered a resolution calling for Cuba's readmission to the group. Ever since Cuba was suspended from the OAS in 1962, the Castro government and the inter-American system had been like two estranged partners reeling from a bitter divorce. Fidel Castro consistently denounced the OAS as a tool of imperialism and focused on new multilateral partners, like the Non-Aligned Movement or the Bolivarian Alternative for the Americas (ALBA). The OAS, for its part, kept Cuba at arm's length for fear that letting Cuba back in the door would unleash a huge family squabble, particularly with the United States. Once the OAS moved toward reincorporating Cuba, even this presumably constructive gesture revealed that Cuba and the inter-American system were still deeply estranged.

Although Cuba was a founding member of the OAS in 1948, the Castro government was excluded from participation in 1962, a move that was supported by the United States as well as a majority of Latin American countries, several of which were concerned that Cuba was supporting revolutionary movements in the hemisphere. This led to the peculiar situation in which the Castro government was excluded from OAS activities, but Cuba was still considered one of the thirty-five member states (the Cuban flag continues to fly in the OAS Hall of the Americas along with the flags of the thirty-four other member states). Following the end of the cold war and the transitions to democracy in the rest of Latin America, the rationale for excluding Cuba shifted from cold war imperatives to the establishment of democratic government as a strict requirement for OAS membership. This marked a sharp break from the institution's practices during the cold war, when many countries were ruled by dictatorships but continued to enjoy full rights as OAS members. In 2001 the OAS member states ratified the Inter-American Democratic Charter, which codified democracy as a requirement for joining the OAS, and thereby erected a new barrier to Cuban membership in the absence of substantial political change.

The OAS General Assembly took up the question of Cuba and, after a lengthy negotiation, repealed Cuba's suspension and approved guidelines for a future dialogue between the OAS and Cuba. This decision was a watershed moment, even if its short-term implications are hard to define. Faced with the fact that every Latin American country has agreed that Cuba should be incorporated into hemispheric institutions and discussions, the United States had little choice but to go along with the measure that lifted Cuba's suspension. Still, Washington, working with several other member states, won the important concession that Cuba would need to adhere to the "practices, purposes, and principles of the OAS," such as democratic standards, free and fair elections, and an open press. Secretary General José Miguel Insulza, a major advocate of reincorporating Cuba into the OAS, praised the decision as "historic" and avowed that "the lock is off the door."

As the hemisphere's leading multilateral institution, the OAS could play a significant role in bringing Cuba into the hemispheric community. But its decision to lift Cuba's suspension has not eased the bitter feelings caused by forty-seven years of divorce. From the Obama administration's perspective, however, the OAS decision to revoke Cuba's suspension played an important role in easing U.S. tensions with Latin America over Cuba policy and reducing calls from hemispheric leaders to lift the U.S. embargo of Cuba.

Cold War Legacies and Controversial Cases

In the first year of the Obama administration, the Central Intelligence Agency (CIA) continued to keep close tabs on the state of Fidel Castro's health, and its special medical intelligence unit pored over the photographs and snippets of videotape of the Cuban leader that were periodically released by the government in Havana. While the pace of Fidel's written "reflections" waxed and waned, the Cuban leader was clearly not ready to renounce the spotlight entirely and leave Raúl as the sole voice of the Cuban government. One CIA analyst confidently told NBC News that there was little doubt the elder Castro was dying: "We just don't know when."[7]

Meanwhile, new legal troubles emerged for the man who spent much of his life trying to hasten Fidel's date with the grave. In April Luis Posada Carriles, the anti-Castro militant, was indicted on eleven counts related to his alleged involvement in the 1997 bombings in Cuba that damaged a series of hotels and claimed the life of an Italian tourist. The charges against Posada Carriles, which included perjury and obstruction of a federal proceeding, marked the first time that the United States had brought legal action against him directly connected to the terrorist attacks in Cuba. The new indictment claimed that he had lied about his role in "soliciting other individuals to carry out . . . bombings in Cuba," and that he falsely denied that he "arranged to send and sent an individual named Raúl Cruz Leon to Cuba to transport and carry explosives into Cuba to carry out said bombings in 1997." A new trial was initially set for August but subsequently pushed back until 2010, and may be subject to further delays as his lawyers wrangle with U.S. authorities over the "handling of sensitive but unclassified discovery material," and whether Posada Carriles's "long-term association with U.S. intelligence and law enforcement agencies" can be entered into evidence.[8] As the legal twists and turns continued, Posada Carriles remained free in Miami.

Even as the United States breathed new life into the case against Posada Carriles, another high-profile legal battle, involving five Cuban agents convicted of spying in the United States in 2001, ran out of steam. In January lawyers for the Cuban Five filed a petition to the U.S. Supreme Court arguing that Miami's charged political climate had made a fair trial impossible and asked the justices to toss out the verdicts and grant a new trial.[9] The Supreme Court, led by Chief Justice John Roberts, was unmoved. In June 2009 it rejected the petition without comment and ended the legal odyssey of the five men that began over a decade earlier.

Still, the Cuban government continued to press for the release of its "five heroic prisoners of the empire." Raúl Castro repeatedly intimated a willingness to negotiate a prisoner swap, whereby Cuba would release its 200 political prisoners in exchange for the spies. In December 2008 Castro said of the incoming Obama administration, "If they want the dissidents, we'll send them tomorrow, with their families and all, but let them return our five heroes to us." According to human rights advocate Elizardo Sánchez, Cuban dissidents were aghast at the prospects of being exchanged in such a deal. "It's nearly unanimous among the prisoners that they not be exchanged for military men arrested red-handed in espionage activities in the United States," Sánchez averred. "They would rather stay in prison."[10] But the dissidents had little reason to be concerned about being used for that purpose.

On June 4, 2009, Washington was jolted by a new espionage case when a former State Department official, Walter Kendall Myers, and his wife, Gwendolyn, were indicted on charges related to spying for Fidel Castro's Cuba. Their arrest exploded onto the front pages shortly after the discussions about Cuba at the Summit of the Americas. In November Kendall Myers pleaded guilty to conspiracy to commit espionage and two counts of wire fraud and was sentenced to life in prison, while his wife Gwendolyn was sentenced to six to seven years in prison on related charges.

On December 4 the Cuban government arrested sixty-year-old Alan P. Gross, a subcontractor for USAID, contending that he was acting as an unregistered agent of destabilization and subversion. U.S. officials have called on Cuba to release Gross, who still awaited charges months into his detention, and claim he was simply distributing electronic goods in order to better connect the Cuban people to global communication networks. At the time of his arrest, Gross was under contract with Development Alternatives Inc., a company based in Bethesda, Maryland, that contracts out development work across the globe. The company's Cuba portfolio was funded by the U.S. government, which in the past decade has spent millions on promoting democracy in Cuba.[11]

Opening the Door to Dialogue

Beginning in April 2009, the Obama administration implemented several changes in the rules governing legal travel and financial engagement with Cuba. On April 13, the White House announced that it would work to remove restrictions on family travel and remittances to Cuba and expand the definition of family for such purposes, allow telecommunication companies to provide increased access to networks within Cuba, and broaden the definition of goods that may be legally donated to persons in Cuba.[12] The main goal of these changes was a dramatic increase in travel to Cuba by Cuban Americans, whom Obama characterized as the best ambassadors for democracy.[13] While the regulations on family travel and remittances did not take effect until September 3, Obama's early statements sent a signal that the Office of Foreign Assets Control (OFAC) would be more lenient with requests for engagement with Cuba than under his predecessor.

Within the Treasury Department, these announcements had two effects. The first was an expansion of specific licenses granted for travel to Cuba within the ten categories provided for such travel in OFAC regulations.[14] By August 2009 OFAC had authorized twenty-one public performance licenses to U.S. groups for performances or athletic events in Cuba, equal to the total number approved in 2008. In 2007 OFAC approved only seven such licenses.[15] The expectation of a more lenient regulatory framework for travel to Cuba encouraged an increase in applications, but it was too early to tell whether this would translate into a sustained policy change.

Of the groups that received special permission to travel to Cuba under the more flexible OFAC guidelines, Colombian rock star Juanes drew considerable attention. The seventeen-time Latin Grammy winner proposed to headline a multi-artist concert titled "Peace without Borders" in Havana's famous Plaza de la Revolución. This would not be the first major pop music concert to take place in Havana (predecessors included the 1979 "Havana Jam" featuring Steven Stills, Kris Kristofferson, Rita Coolidge, and Billy Joel, and the 1999 "Bridge to Havana" with Mick Fleetwood, Bonnie Raitt, Jimmy Buffet, and the Police), but it proved to be the best attended. The reaction within the Miami Cuban American community was mixed. The Colombian rocker, who owns a house in Key Biscayne, received death threats, and a group of anti-Castro revelers crushed dozens of his CDs with a steamroller in a symbolic protest. But many Cuban Americans, especially among the younger generation, approved of the Juanes concert, and hundreds if not thousands of exiles returned to Cuba to attend.

While the Obama administration had no say about the travel plans of Juanes (a Colombian citizen), a special OFAC license was required for his staff and equipment to make the 90-mile trip across the Straits of Florida. In his interview on Univision, President Obama was asked about the impact of the Juanes concert in Cuba. "My understanding is that he's a terrific musician," the president said. "He puts on a very good concert. I certainly don't think it hurts U.S.-Cuban relations." Still, he urged onlookers not to "overstate the degree that it helps."[16] Juanes had complimentary remarks for the president: "This is the right moment to start something. In the last administration, for sure we weren't talking about this. But with this administration, with Obama as president, I believe it's different."[17]

While the Juanes concert was acceptable to both the U.S. and Cuban governments, friction has arisen in other areas of cultural exchange. Guatemalan singer Ricardo Arjona abandoned his plans for a concert in Cuba after witnessing the war of words that Juanes fought with Miami over the "Peace without Borders" show. The New York Philharmonic, which had received a travel license to perform at the Amadeo Roldan Theater in Havana in October 2009, was forced to cancel its plans after the Treasury Department prohibited the trip's funders from accompanying the musicians to Havana. By contrast, in February 2008 the New York Philharmonic performed in Pyongyang, North Korea.

As a presidential candidate, Obama strongly stated and defended his willingness to engage in dialogue with America's adversaries as a central plank of his foreign policy platform. However, his preference for dialogue was more restrained with respect to Cuba, although he did say that he would encourage direct diplomacy without preconditions, "but only when we have an opportunity to advance the interests of the United States, and to advance the cause of freedom for the Cuban people."[18] Since his election, the president has encouraged lower-ranking administration officials to expand conversations with their Cuban counterparts. Under the Bush administration, there was little direct communication between the U.S. government and Cuban officials, aside from the discussions between military officers at monthly fence-line meetings at the Guantánamo Bay Naval Base. In addition, officials of both countries have communicated on issues related to weather, as well as air and sea travel. Obama has added a few more issues to this short list of talking points, including immigration, the resumption of mail service, and coordinating relief efforts in response to the Haitian earthquake of January 2010. In November 2009 Obama answered several questions posed by the noted Cuban blogger Yoani Sánchez and again underscored the importance of positive actions from the Cuban government in expanding the bilateral dialogue: "We have already initiated a dialogue on issues of mutual concern—safe, orderly, and legal migration, and re-establishing direct mail service. These are small steps, but an important part of a process to move U.S.-Cuban relations in a new and more positive direction. Achieving a more normal relationship, however, will require action by the Cuban government."[19]

In July 2009 principal deputy assistant secretary of state for Western Hemisphere affairs Craig A. Kelly met with Cuban counterparts in New York to discuss the U.S.-Cuba Migration Accords for the first time since 2003. In September Bisa Williams, deputy assistant secretary of state for Western Hemisphere affairs, traveled to Havana for special talks with the Cuban government. Williams was called to Cuba to discuss the resumption of direct mail service between the two countries—since 1963 mail has traveled through a third country—and she was also given a tour of Pinar del Rio Province. In February 2010 U.S. officials again traveled to Cuba to take part in a second iteration of migration talks. The stated purpose of both talks is successful implementation of the U.S.-Cuba Migration Accords, but these conversations may also provide the opportunity for the two governments to discuss other issues of mutual importance.

There have been some symbolic changes in the U.S. approach as well. In July 2009 the U.S. interest section in Havana turned off the large electronic billboard that had displayed quotations from notable U.S. and Cuban figures on democracy and freedom in news-ticker fashion. When it was erected in 2006, the Cuban government responded by blocking the messages with an array of 138 large black flags—a memorial to what it described as "the victims of U.S. imperialism." Likewise, when Obama made the decision to stop running messages on the electronic news ticker, the Cuban government lowered the flags. Despite these positive signals from both Washington and Havana, the U.S.-Cuba relationship still fell short of achieving the "new beginning" promised by Obama in the first months of his administration.

Cuba's Future in the Balance

Barack Obama is the eleventh U.S. president to face the Castro regime, and his administration remains caught between conflicting impulses in shaping its Cuba policy. The goal of the U.S. embargo is to deprive the Cuban government of resources, yet congressional exemptions for agricultural trade have transformed the United States into Cuba's fifth largest trading partner, while Cuban Americans send hundreds of millions of dollars back to their families on the island each year. Successive U.S. governments have set aside millions of dollars to build up domestic opposition groups within Cuba, but current immigration law grants residency rights to every Cuban who makes it onto American soil, which has allowed the Castro government to systematically export those who would otherwise be its most likely opposition. Tens of millions of dollars have been spent on Radio and Television Martí broadcasts intended to break through the Castro regime's "information blockade," but the average American citizen is still banned from traveling to the island, despite the fact that people-to-people contacts have the potential to provide important information about the outside world. The Obama administration has not changed the designation purporting that Cuba is a "state sponsor of terrorism," even though the accompanying State Department report describes Cuba as a country that "no longer actively supports armed struggle in Latin America and other parts of the world."[20] And despite its special emphasis on multilateral diplomacy, the administration has been faced with the awkward fact that virtually no U.S. ally supports the continuation of the U.S. embargo of Cuba.

Navigating a path out of this labyrinth will not be easy. Obama has begun to nudge U.S.-Cuba policy in the direction of engagement in small but potentially important ways, such as allowing greater contact and travel between Cuban Americans and their family members who still live on the island. The Obama administration supported a resolution backed by Latin American countries to lift Cuba's suspension from the Organization of American States, albeit with important conditions for its return. The two countries restarted semiannual migration talks that had broken down under the Bush administration, which may pave the way for a wider process of dialogue that includes the core political and economic issues that still divide them.

Despite its early potential, the Obama administration has not brought about a "new beginning" in the U.S.-Cuba relationship. To be sure, some of the Cuban government's actions have made it harder for those in the United States pushing for engagement to find new common ground. Moreover, while the changing politics of the Cuban American community have substantially reduced the political barriers to engaging with Cuba, there is not a clear political benefit to moving decisively away from efforts to punish Cuba through isolation and economic sanctions. Most important, the Obama administration has accepted the notion that the U.S. embargo represents a form of leverage over Cuba that should be used to extract concessions in the areas of democracy and human rights.

The forces for continuity remain very strong on both sides of the Straits of Florida. Changes in U.S. domestic politics and renewed interest by the U.S. private sector could pave the way for further congressional or executive branch modifications of the embargo. If the Cuban government demonstrates substantial economic reform, then that may lead to positive political changes that would produce a favorable response from the United States. The eventual death of Fidel Castro could consequently open the possibility for a process of reconciliation. But without a major exogenous event, U.S.-Cuban relations do not appear likely to move far beyond the political impasse that has defined the bilateral relationship for the past half century.

Notes

1. William Booth, "In Cuba, Pinning Hopes on Obama," *Washington Post*, January 7, 2009.

2. Richard Lugar, "Letter of Transmittal," in *Changing Cuba Policy—In the United States National Interest* (Washington: U.S. Government Printing Office, February 23, 2009).

3. Michael D. Shear and Cecilia King, "Obama Lifts Broad Set of Sanctions against Cuba," *Washington Post*, April 14, 2009.

4. Frances Robles, "Obama Encourages Cuba to Take Concrete Steps," *Miami Herald*, April 19, 2009.

5. Alexei Barrionuevo and Sheryl Gay Stolberg, "Hemisphere's Leaders Signal a Fresh Start with U.S.," *New York Times*, April 20, 2009.

6. Morgan Neill, "Obama Misreads Cuban Offer, Fidel Castro Says," CNN.com, April 22, 2009.

7. Robert Windrem, "CIA Analyzes Video of Fidel Castro for Clues," MSNBC, June 18, 2008.

8. Jay Weaver, "Posada Gets More Time for Perjury Defense," *Miami Herald*, June 16, 2009.

9. The Cuban Five were members of a Miami-based spy ring arrested in 1998 for monitoring Cuban exile groups and U.S. military installations. They were convicted and sentenced to long prison terms in the United States, and their return to Cuba has become a top agenda item for the Cuban government.

10. Anita Snow, "Cuban Prisoners Don't Want to Be Traded for Spies," Associated Press, April 21, 2009.

11. The budget for democracy programs in Cuba grew from $3.5 million in 2000 to over $45 million by the end of the Bush administration. President Obama has continued to support democracy promotion in Cuba, though he did cut the budget to $20 million annually.

12. "Fact Sheet: Reaching Out to the Cuban People," White House press release, Office of the Press Secretary, April 13, 2009 (www.whitehouse.gov/the_press_office/Fact-Sheet-Reaching-out-to-the-Cuban-people/).

13. Ibid.

14. These categories are listed at www.ustreas.gov/offices/enforcement/ofac/programs/cuba/cuba.pdf.

15. David Adams, "Cracks Open in U.S. Cultural Wall around Cuba," *St. Petersburg Times*, August 14, 2009.

16. Paul Haven, "Juanes' Cuba Concert Draws Huge Crowd in Havana," Associated Press, September 21, 2009.

17. "Rock Star Sees Concert Helping Thaw U.S.-Cuba Relations; Juanes Gig Set for Sept. 20 in Havana," Reuters, August 27, 2010.

18. "Remarks of Senator Barack Obama: Renewing U.S. Leadership in the Americas," Miami, Florida, May 23, 2008.

19. Yoani Sanchez, "President Obama's Answers to My Questions" (http://desdecuba.com/generationy/ [November 19, 2009]).

20. U.S. State Department, *Country Reports on Terrorism 2008* (Washington, April 30, 2009).

eight
The Honduran Crisis and the Obama Administration

Kevin Casas-Zamora

In the early hours of June 28, 2009, military personnel arrested Honduras's president Manuel Zelaya at his home in Tegucigalpa. Clad in his pajamas, he was led at gunpoint and put on a plane bound for Costa Rica. His ousting capped months of torrid conflict between Zelaya and nearly every other political actor and institution in Honduras, ranging from the Supreme Court to the Catholic Church.

Zelaya's defenestration sparked a complex political battle with hemisphere-wide implications. The episode threw in the open very significant questions about the geopolitical disputes that are raging in Latin America, the roots of populist authoritarianism in the region, the effectiveness of the Organization of American States (OAS) as guarantor of the Inter-American Democratic Charter, and the limits of U.S. influence in Latin America. For the Obama administration, the episode was a stark reminder that it can only ignore the region's complexities at its peril.

In taking stock of the Honduran crisis, one cannot escape the fact that its consequences linger on, despite the swearing in of a new democratically elected government in January 2010, led by President Porfirio Lobo. To this day, Honduras remains suspended from the OAS, and eight Latin American countries, as well as many from other regions, still refuse to grant the new government diplomatic recognition. Simply put, what has taken place is little more than the restoration of a political system with a doubtful allegiance to democratic institutions and whose considerable weaknesses are yet to be addressed. Protecting democracy in Honduras demands substantive reforms that only the Hondurans can formulate and implement, but that the United States, as the most important foreign actor in the country, can certainly promote. All in all, the Honduran story, as it has unfolded, is not encouraging for either Honduras or U.S diplomacy.

What Happened?

To understand what happened in Honduras, it is important to explore three fundamental questions. Was it a coup d'état? What were the causes of the meltdown? Why could Zelaya's overthrow not be reversed?

Coup or Constitutional Interruption?

Although the events that led to the ousting remain engulfed in controversy, the immediate cause was Zelaya's attempt to organize a nonbinding referendum (an "opinion poll," in Zelaya's words) to decide whether to include an additional ballot in the November 2009 presidential election concerning a proposal to convene a Constituent Assembly to rewrite the country's 1982 constitution. Zelaya's critics read this as a thinly veiled attempt to change the absolute ban on reelection imposed by the constitution.

Zelaya's confusing statements about his intentions and, above all, his perceived closeness to Venezuela's strongman Hugo Chávez—whose own consolidation of power started with the enactment of a new constitution in 1999—made plausible the notion that the Honduran leader simply wanted to stay in the presidency beyond the end of his term in January 2010. The real story was probably more subtle. While it is almost certain that Zelaya was trying to tamper with term limits, he was probably less concerned about prolonging his term than about controlling the levers of power of the next government via the Constituent Assembly and paving the way for his *future* return to the presidency. In a charged political environment, these subtleties were of little consequence. Through their unrelenting use of the media, the most conservative sectors of the Honduran elite, extremely alarmed by Chávez's influence and Zelaya's brash populist style, created a compelling narrative of an authoritarian power grab in the making.

This narrative had some objective facts to support it. Neither Zelaya's nonbinding consultation nor the eventual binding referendum to convene a Constituent Assembly had any clear constitutional or legal backing. In time, all the relevant political and judicial institutions in the country came to publicly oppose Zelaya's bid. On more than one occasion, the Supreme Court—a notoriously politicized body—deemed the whole enterprise illegal. In what had already become a habit of his administration, Zelaya disregarded these rulings and proceeded to organize the nonbinding referendum. Predictably, a conflict between branches of power ensued. It was a conflict, moreover, in which both sides tried to enlist the support of the armed forces, an institution with a troubling history of political intervention.

If the president's erratic behavior merited legal proceedings against him, as authorized by the constitution (Article 205.15), this was not really the way Zelaya's adversaries handled the situation. On the day scheduled for the referendum, soldiers arrested Zelaya and forcefully sent him into exile. While the military would later claim to have followed a judicial order, it was obvious from the outset that Zelaya's arrest and particularly his expulsion from the country had been carried out with very little regard for his constitutional rights. In a matter of a few days, he was formally removed by the Congress and duly replaced with its ultraconservative speaker, Roberto Micheletti.

To this day, Micheletti and his supporters claim that the sudden interruption of Zelaya's term was merely a constitutional transfer of power away from a president unfit to govern. They point foremost to Article 239 of the constitution, a peculiar provision that makes suggesting or supporting the amendment of term limits an offense, punishable with *immediate* dismissal from any public office. In one of the constitution's several inconsistencies, this measure fails to specify which authority has the power to enforce this draconian principle. In addition, the Honduran Congress circumvented the glaring absence of an impeachment process in the constitution by invoking the congressional right to "approve or disapprove the administrative conduct of the Executive branch" (Article 205.20). This was interpreted to include the power to dismiss the president and replace him.

While accepted and celebrated in conservative circles in both Tegucigalpa and Washington, these arguments are questionable at best and not surprisingly were given short shrift by the international community, including the U.S. government.[1] With remarkable unanimity, actors outside Honduras deemed the action of June 28 an unacceptable overthrow of a legitimate president. For Latin America, the sight of a president arrested and exiled at gunpoint by soldiers sparked memories of a dark age of military rule that easily trumped Micheletti's legal reasoning.

As the international reaction, not to mention history, makes clear, legal strictures, even when tidy, are not enough to redeem a coup. A coup is not merely a legal event, but a political one. From Hitler to Augusto Pinochet, perpetrators have long justified democratic breakdowns and human rights violations in the name of the prevailing legal order. As the international community rightly concluded, the legal arguments employed by Zelaya's foes to oust him were simply post factum rationalizations of a political decision to unseat, by any means available, a legitimate president.

The means in this instance was a civil-military coup d'état. This is not to condone Zelaya's own reckless and illegal behavior in the run-up to the coup. It is simply to say that when confronted with a bad political problem, Zelaya's adversaries opted for the worst possible solution. As a result, no one can take the moral high ground here. The Honduran political elite on both the left and the right collectively pushed the country to the brink.

Why Did the Coup Happen?

Zelaya's irresponsible attempt to tamper with term limits may have been the immediate cause of the meltdown, but deeper forces were also at play: most notably the chronic weakness of the country's democratic institutions, the anxieties generated by Hugo Chávez's rhetoric throughout the region, and the limited effectiveness of preventive diplomacy in the Western Hemisphere.

Honduras's political pathologies are too obvious to ignore. Both Zelaya and his political foes are the products of a rotten political system. And that is why it takes a rather large stretch of the imagination to hail the outcome of this crisis as a triumph for democracy. Let me state the obvious: in a country where 70 percent of the population lives below the poverty line and the wealthiest 10 percent of the population earns six times more income than the bottom 40 percent, populism is, at the very least, a tempting option for any politician.[2] And this temptation may become irresistible when coupled with pervasive distrust of political institutions. According to a 2008 regional survey by Latinobarómetro, trust in Congress (26 percent), the judiciary (28 percent), and political parties (20 parties) in Honduras was below the already low averages for Latin America.[3] These levels are heavily influenced by massive corruption in the country. Alongside Nicaragua, Honduras stands at the bottom of Central America in the Corruption Perception Index elaborated by Transparency International with a score of 2.5 out of a possible 10.[4] This combination of ills would entice almost any president to bash political parties and other branches of the state for their corruption and antipathy to social progress. The seeds of authoritarianism that lurk in most strands of populism have been falling on very fertile ground in Honduras.[5]

The country's constitutional architecture is of little help when these authoritarian inklings manifest themselves. Certain aspects of the nation's 1982 constitution are deeply problematic. The lack of an explicit process of political impeachment against the president introduces a dangerous element of rigidity that exacerbates presidentialism's well-known inflexibility to deal with grave political upheavals. Even more troubling, certain constitutional norms—including, remarkably, presidential term limits—have been rendered unchangeable by any means. In other cases, the rules leave crucial questions unanswered, as already pointed out in connection with Article 239. Particularly confusing are the clauses defining the mechanics of civil-military relations. The chief of the armed forces is apparently subordinate to the president, yet Congress alone retains the power to discharge this officer. The myriad confusions created by these rules and the wildly contradictory interpretations they allow played a decisive role in pushing the country to the brink of chaos.

As serious as these structural faults may be, they may produce only slight tremors until activated by other forces, which is what happened when Zelaya unexpectedly decided to join Hugo Chávez's regional alliance, the Bolivarian Alternative for the Americas (Alianza Bolivariana para los Pueblos de Nuestra América, ALBA), and adopted some of the Venezuelan president's radical rhetoric. In all likelihood, Zelaya became close to Chávez less because of ideology than because of the lure of subsidized oil. Whatever the case, his decision elicited a ferocious reaction from the country's most conservative forces, which began to view Zelaya's every move as the result of Chávez's devious machinations aimed at taking over Honduras. Although perhaps overblown, these fears were not concocted out of thin air. Chávez's record of meddling in the internal affairs of other Latin American countries—ranging from Mexico to Colombia and Argentina—was serious enough to merit concern. While Che Guevara may now be merely a T-shirt icon and Fidel Castro languishes in a tracksuit in Havana, the "red scare," thanks to Commander Chávez, is back in business in Latin America. And one should never underestimate the power of fear among the region's elites.

The Honduran crisis was fueled not only by structural weaknesses and the Zelaya-Chávez alliance, however. The shortcomings of the region's diplomatic instruments for protecting democracy also played a role. By coincidence, the OAS, the guarantor of the Inter-American Democratic Charter, held its yearly general assembly in Honduras four weeks before Zelaya's removal from office. Despite the already obvious risk of a democratic breakdown in Honduras, a studied silence was all the OAS could muster in addressing the situation. Its preventive intervention was both belated and ineffectual. Ten days before the coup, OAS secretary general José Miguel Insulza sent a special envoy to Honduras who issued counterproductive statements suggesting the OAS would "accompany" Zelaya's nonbinding poll, already deemed illegal by the country's Supreme Court.[6] A few days later, the OAS Permanent Council issued a resolution calling on all parties to the crisis to "avoid a disruption of the constitutional order" and directing a Special Commission to visit Honduras (Resolution 952). The commission failed to arrive in time to prevent the coup.

If this was unfortunate, it was not unexpected. Like other political crises in Latin America in recent years (Venezuela's 2002 coup or the ousting of Ecuador's president Lucio Gutiérrez in 2005), the Honduran episode revealed a crucial problem with the charter. On one hand, it gives the OAS the power to intervene if the democratic political institutional process or the legitimate exercise of power is at risk in any one of the member states, *but only at the request of the government concerned* (Articles 17–18). On the other hand, such intervention can only be requested by the country's executive branch. This greatly diminishes the usefulness of this resource in situations in which democratic stability is threatened by a conflict between the executive and other branches of power, a common occurrence in Latin America's presidential systems. In other words, the levers of preventive diplomacy in the hemisphere were simply too weak to ward off Honduras's widely foreseen descent into a democratic breakdown.

Why Couldn't It Be Reversed?

While diplomacy's failure to prevent the coup in Honduras was fairly predictable, its inability to effect a reversal was perhaps surprising. Honduras is, after all, a small, poor, and vulnerable country in which development assistance from foreign countries makes up nearly one-tenth of the economy.

The international community condemned the coup in a swift, uncompromising, and unanimous fashion. No foreign government recognized the de facto Honduran authorities as legitimate. The United States, the most significant foreign actor in Honduras by far, censured Zelaya's ousting immediately, as did the European Union and the UN General Assembly. The OAS took a particularly hard line, issuing an ultimatum for Zelaya's unconditional return to office and unanimously suspending Honduras's membership under Article 21 of the Inter-American Democratic Charter one week after the coup. Good or bad, these early decisions left the organization—the obvious channel for a political negotiation to reverse the coup—on the sidelines of the feverish diplomatic search for a solution to the conflict.

Despite the robust international reaction, the mediating efforts of then Costa Rican president, Oscar Arias, successive rounds of talks between representatives of the deposed government and the de facto authorities, and the signing of two agreements between the parties in San José and Tegucigalpa, Zelaya never made it back to power. Why?

The answer lies in large part with Zelaya himself. Even after his stealthy return to Honduras in September 2009, he was never able to mobilize his domestic supporters in great numbers. While selective repression by the de facto government played a part in this, much had to do with the fact that he was a highly unpopular president when the coup occurred.[7] Moreover, after the coup Zelaya's unsurpassed ability to ramble on in his discussions confirmed all the prejudices against him, particularly in Washington. Above all, he understood far too late that flying from capital to capital chalking up air miles in Hugo Chávez's plane was not the shortest route back to the presidency. This is a crucial point that neither Zelaya nor probably President Arias, the mediator of choice, understood at the time. As long as Zelaya was unwilling to put some distance between himself and Chávez, his conservative foes were prepared to go to any lengths to prevent his return. When he finally did so, for example, by seeking shelter in the Brazilian Embassy in Tegucigalpa, the damage had been done.

A second factor behind the failed reversal was the election coming up in less than five months. Zelaya's opponents made the cynical calculation that no matter how intense the international pressure, they could hang on to power until a new election absolved them of their antidemocratic sins. Moreover, several key political actors—including the Obama administration—realized that a free and fair election offered the best chance to normalize the political situation in Honduras. Thus the recognition of the election became a crucial point of contention.

For Micheletti and Honduras's business elite, securing the international legitimacy of the election was the *only* option to make the coup's economic and diplomatic costs affordable. And they had fair arguments on their side, particularly the fact that the coup had not affected the electoral process, which by June 28 was already under way as the presidential candidates had been selected according to the law. Although some troubling repression of activists, journalists, and media outlets supportive of Zelaya had arisen, it fell short of a systematic onslaught that would have been incompatible with a reasonably free and fair election.

On November 29, 2009, the election took place as scheduled, and despite the absence of reputable international observers such as the OAS and the European Union, it was generally considered free and fair.[8] Conservative cattle rancher Porfirio Lobo, from the opposition National Party, won handily with 56 percent of the votes. Although barely half of the electorate turned out, this was merely the continuation of a downward trend. Back in 2005, when the Honduran political system appeared to be in good health, the turnout had not gone beyond 55 percent.

Despite international doubts about the election, political expediency won the day. A critical mass of countries, including the United States, ended up accepting the results and the new government as legitimate. They argued, probably correctly, that refusing to do so was the surest way to prolong the effects of the crisis permanently.[9] That judgment was pointedly rejected by another group of countries, including Brazil and the ALBA member states, which as of this writing continue to reject President Lobo's government. This repudiation continues to cause Lobo grief, insofar as it has implied that Honduras remains excluded from several international meetings and forums, such as the OAS, the Latin America-European Union summit in Madrid in May 2010, and the Rio Group–CARICOM summit in Cancun in August 2010. This pressure is bearable, however. Both politically and economically, the key to the survival of the new Honduran administration lies in the endorsement granted by the United States and its Central American neighbors (except Nicaragua), as well as in the normalization of relations with the international financial institutions. Anything else is a dispensable luxury.

Thus the validation of the election by the United States put an end to the first and most acute phase of the crisis, yielding, in essence, a victory for the coup perpetrators. However, the fact that it has ended does not imply a return to democratic normalcy in Honduras or that the U.S. role was particularly constructive.

What about the U.S. Role?

For Washington, the onset of the Honduran crisis was the first opportunity to give content to President Barack Obama's vague promises of a new dawn in hemispheric relations at the Summit of the Americas in Trinidad and Tobago merely two months earlier. The coup in Tegucigalpa posed in poignant terms a question laden with historical sensitivities in Latin America. After a long history of support for dictatorships and all kinds of authoritarian exploits, including Hugo Chávez's brief ousting in 2002, would Washington at last be willing to lend unequivocal support to democratic institutions in the region?

The Obama administration's answer to this question was decidedly unclear. Its first attempts, before the coup, appeared quite promising. While conspiracy theories identifying the hand of Washington behind the events in Honduras abound, all available evidence suggests that right up to the moment of the coup, U.S. ambassador Hugo Llorens tried to stop Zelaya's ouster by deploying American influence over the Honduran military and holding talks with the conflicting parties.[10] The ambassador's actions had no discernible effect. At that point, Zelaya's recklessness and his foes' anti-Chávez paranoia were impregnable to the arguments of even the most influential external actor. These attempts were followed by President Obama's vigorous initial reaction against the coup.[11]

However, a few days into the crisis it was already clear that American diplomats sought to carefully circumscribe their intervention. The most evident sign of this was their reluctance to refer to the events of June 28 as a coup d'état. There was more at stake in these diplomatic discussions than the democratic legitimacy of Micheletti's government. Under U.S. law, any pronouncement labeling the interruption of Zelaya's term as a coup, particularly a *military* coup, would have serious legal, diplomatic, and financial implications.[12] Despite Washington's initial negative reaction to the events in Tegucigalpa, the White House and State Department spent the next two months employing verbal contortions to avoid an automatic imposition of sanctions against Micheletti's government. It was not until the beginning of September 2009 that the State Department actually labeled the situation a coup, thereby canceling all nonhumanitarian aid to Honduras and revoking U.S. visas to several individuals linked to the de facto government.[13] While significant, these sanctions were still relatively benign when compared with those genuinely feared in Tegucigalpa: the freezing of Honduran bank accounts in the United States and the imposition of commercial sanctions against the country.

In resisting the use of the term "coup," Washington hoped to keep the lines of communication with the Honduran authorities open, which would have become impossible under full-fledged sanctions. But then there was also Washington's uneasiness with the idea of having a close ally of Hugo Chávez, such as Zelaya, as the direct beneficiary of U.S. sanctions on Tegucigalpa. Consequently, the Obama administration's solution of choice was to put forward a carefully calibrated and essentially rhetorical committment to democracy.

From that moment onward, U.S. diplomacy traveled down a route marked, above all, by inconsistency: it went from indignation with the coup to indifference, confusion, and, finally, acquiescense, all in less than five months. Throughout this period, it was never clear whether the United States wanted to be an actor or a spectator in the solution to the impasse.

Thus after initially supporting OAS intervention, Washington endorsed President Arias's mediation once it became clear that the organization had painted itself into a corner. Then when Arias stumbled over the unbridgeable differences between the parties concerning Zelaya's return to power, the United States felt compelled to step in. It did so by crafting a very confusing agreement that should have led to Zelaya's restitution and hence to the coup's reversal. This agreement was anounced from Pakistan at the end of October of 2009 by Secretary of State Hillary Clinton, who hailed it as a diplomatic triumph for the United States.[14] The victory was short-lived, however, for it soon became evident that the Honduran Congress—the authority entrusted with returning Zelaya to office—had not even the faintest intention of attempting a reversal.[15] Upon learning this news, the U.S. government announced that it would recognize the results of the November 2009 presidential election, thus contradicting previous statements indicating that it would not do so unless Zelaya were reinstalled before the polls opened.[16]

The Obama administration's cumbersome handling of the affair cannot simply be attributed to the incompetence of its diplomats. The coup's perpetrators understood early on that they could tap into Washington's unease about Zelaya, and that the porosity of the American political process would give them ample opportunity to mobilize support for their cause in Washington. Hence they set in motion a very effective lobbying effort that turned the crisis into a domestic political battle within the U.S. Congress.[17] By stirring up the fears born out of Zelaya's close relationship with Chávez, this faction managed to mobilize the most conservative members of Congress—most notably Senator Jim DeMint (R-S.C.)—into forestalling any attempt by the Obama administration to drastically punish the de facto government in Honduras. In the thick of the crisis, DeMint single-handedly blocked for several months the confirmation of two crucial appointments for the administration's policy toward Latin America: the new assistant secretary for Western Hemisphere Affairs, Arturo Valenzuela, and the new U.S. ambassador to Brazil, Thomas Shannon, who was Valenzuela's predecessor.[18] Not only did this pressure deprive U.S. diplomacy of muscle during the crisis, but it also hindered any attempt by the Obama administration to move beyond its cautious position toward the de facto government.

The Obama administration wound up doing something as appropriate in one way as it was misguided in another. If it was advisable to recognize the Honduran presidential election so as to facilitate a return to political, albeit precarious, normalcy in the country, it was gravely erroneous to do so without demanding anything in return from Micheletti's government. This omission, the consequences of which remain all too evident, was U.S. diplomacy's most serious blunder in the handling of the crisis.

One would have hoped the elusive prize of international legitimacy for the new Honduran government would have set a meaningful national dialogue in motion, a process in which the *zelayistas*—and probably Zelaya himself—ought to take part. One would have also hoped to see an effort to rethink and amend a surreal constitution that leaves the country vulnerable to future democratic breakdowns—and to see serious introspection among the Honduran elite accompanied by a willingness to introduce some social reforms, desperately needed in a country afflicted by the pervasive poverty and inequalities that make populism an irresistible temptation. Despite President Lobo's best intentions, once the threat of international isolation by the United States was removed, any such hopes faded from view. A unique opportunity to introduce lasting transformations in Honduras in the wake of this unfortunate episode was simply wasted.

Hence it is not clear that the Obama administration's meandering approach to this crisis reflected any underlying rationale. Perhaps it is too much to ask for clarity from the chaotic process by which U.S. foreign policy is formulated. Even though the U.S. Constitution bestows on the president a central role in the definition of foreign policy, Washington's international policymaking never consists of the rational weighing of options by a single actor. On the contrary, it is the consequence of pressures, frictions, and compromises between several political and bureaucratic actors that provide entry points for multiple voices. It was astute of Honduras's de facto authorities to have understood from the outset that the inherent pluralism of the U.S. political process could be used to their advantage with such effectiveness.

Nevertheless, insofar as a message from Obama might be detected amid Washington's usual cacophony, it may be that this administration's words and actions with regard to democracy in Latin America will be infused with a pragmatism that will override any declaration of principles. Every intervention in favor of democracy will be gauged on its own merits, on a case-by-case rather than a normative basis, and there will be no more intervention than what is strictly necessary to further U.S. interests. When compared with Washington's long tradition of support for authoritarian ruptures in the region, the essentially rhetorical committment to democracy displayed in Honduras, limited though it is, can be seen as an improvement. Even so, when compared with the new beginning in U.S.-Latin America relations promised by the Obama administration, it is, to some extent, a disappointment.

What Was the Outcome of This Episode?

Many voices have waxed lyrical about the supposedly happy ending that the November 2009 election brought to the crisis. But there should be no room for confusion here: the move to acept the election on the part of some countries was nothing more than a necessary evil. The election was, at most, a moment of sanity that prevented Honduras's democratic institutions from collapsing entirely owing to the failings of its political elite. The structural faults that lie beneath the country's democratic edifice are not easily corrected by one barely adequate election.

The problem is not that the United States has recognized the election and the new government. The real problem is the way in which this outcome came to be and how the winners have interpreted it. It is one thing to persuade a part of the international community to turn a blind eye to a crass deposition of a legitimate president; it is quite another to achieve that end without paying any price whatsoever for it.

Clearly, the majority of the Honduran political elite treats this outcome as an unconditional victory and, above all, as a license to return to politics as usual, as though nothing had happened. That is, they feel free to return to the usual system of a well-heeled oligarchy—cheered on by an impoverished populace—fighting tooth and nail for the spoils of a weak state: a dysfunctional creature able to enrich a few but utterly incapable of addressing the dismal reality of underdevelopment.

If this was a victory for Micheletti and the ultraconservative sectors he represents, it was a defeat for almost everybody else. Zelaya will surely go down in history as the biggest culprit in triggering the crisis, and as a man who was right about something (revising the Honduran constitution) but for the wrong reasons (a desire to tamper with term limits and reelection clauses). Doomed to exile for the time being, he has no political future other than being exhibited as a cause célèbre at all the future jamborees organized by Chávez and his ALBA colleagues.[19] It was certainly a defeat for Chávez, who was left out of the picture by all the relevant actors—including Zelaya— well before the election, and who does not have a friend in Tegucigalpa now that Lobo is in office. It was also a defeat of sorts for Brazil, which after being thrown in the eye of the hurricane by Zelaya's decision to seek shelter at the Brazilian embassy, missed a chance to use its regional influence to craft an adequate political settlement. It is now clear that Central America—too close geographically and historically to the United States—is, at most, a marginal concern in Brazil's strategic outlook.

It was, in addition, a resounding defeat for the OAS, which was left in tatters, incapable of protecting the lofty goals of the Inter-American Democratic Charter and unable to bridge not just the traditional divide between the hemisphere's North and South, but now also the ideological rift that is driving Latin America apart. In particular, the fact that the United States and Brazil are publicly at odds over the validation of the Honduran election will very likely accelerate a process in which Brazil, as well as other countries, seems increasingly interested: namely, abandoning the OAS and replacing it with other regional institutions, such as the South American Union (UNASUR), where Brazil can wield its power more comfortably.

Finally, it was, at best, a mediocre outcome for U.S. diplomacy. The inconsistency with which the Obama administration approached the Honduras debacle has damaged the credibility of American diplomacy as an instrument of helpful intervention in future political crises in Latin America. Maybe that is exactly what Washington wants, to steer clear of disputes in the region, which are probably perceived as minor headaches in the big scheme of U.S. foreign policy. However, many people in Latin America and beyond will take note of Washington's overall response. Although there seems to be no imminent risk that the Honduran coup will be easily replicated elsewhere in Latin America, Micheletti's ability to make the United States dance to his tune will be remembered by other oligarchies in the region, whenever a president starts displaying dangerous signs of heterodoxy in the future. Moreover, the U.S. inability to articulate an adequate political solution to a petty power struggle in a tiny Central American country raises legitimate questions about U.S. prowess in dealing with the world's truly vexing diplomatic challenges. If the United States was unable to handle Honduras, will it rise to the ocassion in the Middle East?

In sum, there is little to gloat about in the outcome of the Honduran crisis. The celebration of a reasonably adequate election and the swearing in of a new government were certainly essential steps in pulling Honduras back from the abyss. But the path to reconciling the country and, above all, to building a healthy democracy is long and steep.

The most important steps to this end are, of course, in the hands of Honduran political actors. However, the international community, particularly the United States, can do a great deal to nudge this effort in the right direction, even though its leverage over the new authorities in Honduras is more limited today than it was before the November 2009 election.

The first endeavor should be to work toward the reconciliation of a severely polarized population, as laid out in part in the San José and Tegucigalpa accords of July and October 2009, signed by negotiators appointed by former president Zelaya and Roberto Micheletti.[20] The key to bringing back into the political system the groups that felt aggrieved by the interruption of Zelaya's term, and to normalizing Tegucigalpa's relations with the international community, is to implement in good faith both the text and spirit of these agreements.

So far, President Lobo's record in this regard is mixed. He made a commendable effort to appoint a national unity government and played a decisive role in pressing for a controversial but necessary amnesty for political offenses.[21] Another key clause of the agreements, appointing a Truth Commission to inquire into the events before and after June 28, has proved more difficult to implement. Although President Lobo signed an executive decree in May 2010 installing the commission, under the chairmanship of Guatemala's former vice president, Eduardo Stein, this body has met with considerable resistance regarding two crucial aspects of its mandate: its ability to make recommendations for institutional changes, and its powers to investigate the human rights abuses that took place in the country after the coup. These abuses have been documented and denounced by the Inter-American Commission on Human Rights (IACHR), as well as by many other organizations.[22] While the Truth Commission expects to publish its findings in early 2011, there is as yet no guarantee that it will receive the necessary assistance from the Honduran authorities, or even the cooperation of the sectors closest to former president Zelaya and Roberto Micheletti, which for very different reasons are opposed to the commission's role.[23]

The leverage that the international community still commands in Honduras must be mobilized to support the work of the Truth Commission as an essential step toward national reconciliation. At a minimum, the Honduran state needs to make an explicit commitment to fully cooperate with the commission and to seriously consider its recommendations before being readmitted to the OAS or allowed to sign any future standby agreement with the International Monetary Fund. When it comes to the latter agreement, the position of the Obama administration can truly make a difference.

The future stability of democracy in Honduras depends not only on an immediate national reconciliation but also on the willingness of its political elite to tackle substantive development challenges, a primary one being the country's fiscal base. The current level of social exclusion can hardly be expected to drop when the state is faced with a precarious fiscal base and its fundamental public goods—such as education, health care, and security—are grossly underprovided. The country's current tax burden stands at 18 percent of gross domestic product (GDP), which is below the average for Latin America and less than half the mean for industrialized countries.[24] Honduras needs to negotiate a "fiscal pact" that allows for a significant increase in taxation and a fairer distribution of the tax burden.

Similarly, if low levels of trust in democratic institutions are to be improved, the country needs to depoliticize some of the institutions entrusted with the task of controlling the exercise of power, from the Supreme Court to the general comptroller, the national ombudsman, and the Supreme Electoral Tribunal—which in Honduras enjoy very little autonomy from political parties and routinely do their bidding.

Finally, political actors must engage in a serious conversation about the country's constitutional architecture. Their current reluctance to do so is an odd reaction to a major political crisis in which the shortcomings of that design were rendered all too apparent.

These issues can only be resolved through broadly based agreements. Hence Honduras ultimately needs an inclusive process of national dialogue. While President Lobo should take the lead in convening this process, the international community can promote it and, in some cases, facilitate the discussion. Rather than regional organizations—such as the OAS, Central American Integration System (SICA), or UNASUR, which were, and continue to be, affected in different ways by the diplomatic fallout from the crisis—the United Nations, perhaps under the leadership of the United Nations Development Program (UNDP), could play a constructive role in shaping an inclusive dialogue geared toward dealing with the underlying causes of the crisis. This was done in the 1990s in neighboring Guatemala and El Salvador, under far more taxing conditions, but with profound effects. The role of such organizations could be buttressed by the appointment of a commission of international guarantors chosen by the Honduran negotiating parties, perhaps recruited from former Latin American statesmen and women.

These are merely some ideas about the most urgent steps that could help Honduras move beyond this crisis. Perhaps most important, all the parties involved in this episode—including the Obama administration—would do well to understand that it is by no means certain that Manuel Zelaya's departure has made Honduras once again safe ground for democracy. If things were only this simple. President Lobo should be commended for grasping the complexity of the crisis and its legacy and for making valuable gestures toward national reconciliation. But a great deal remains to be done. Proclaiming that the debacle of 2009 is over would be a disservice to the Honduran people and an invitation to future democratic breakdowns.

Notes

1. See, for instance, Guillermo Pérez Cadalso, "Prepared Statement before the U.S. House of Representatives Committee on International Affairs, Subcommittee on the Western Hemisphere," July 10, 2009 (www.webcitation.org/5m4YMWbeE). Also William Ratliff, "Understanding the Mess in Honduras," *Forbes* (forbes.com/2009/09/28/honduras-zelaya-insulza-opinions-contributors-william-ratliff.html). The most articulated legal opinion in favor of the constitutionality of Zelaya's over-throw is Library of Congress, "Honduras: Constitutional Law Issues" (Library of Congress, Directorate of Legal Research for Foreign, Comparative, and International Law, August 2009) (http://schock.house.gov/UploadedFiles/Schock_CRS_Report_Honduras_FINAL.pdf). This report was the subject of controversy in the U.S. Congress, where Senator John Kerry (D-Mass.) and Representative Howard Berman (D-Calif.) denounced it as factually wrong. A convincing refutation of this report can be found in Rosemary Joyce, "Library of Congress Report on Honduran Coup Filled with Flaws," Axis of Logic (http://axisoflogic.com/artman/publish/Article_57015.shtml [September 25, 2009]). See also Doug Cassel, "Honduras: Coup d'Etat in Constitutional Clothing?" *American Society of International Law—Insight* 13, no. 9 (2009). On the reaction of the U.S. government, see note 12.

2. Comisión Económica para América Latina y el Caribe (CEPAL), *Panorama social de América Latina* (Social panorama of Latin America) (Santiago, 2007).

3. Corporación Latinobarómetro, *Informe 2008* (www.latinobarometro.org/docs/INFORME_LATINOBAROMETRO_2008.pdf).

4. Transparency International, Corruption Perception Index 2009 (www.transparency.org/policy_research/surveys_indices/cpi/2009).

5. For an interesting recent discussion, see Mitchell Seligson and John Booth, "Crime, Hard Times and Discontent," *Journal of Democracy* 21 (April 2010).

6. "Cuarta urna es potestad del CN," *La Prensa* (Honduras), June 19, 2009.

7. According to the polling firm Consulta Mitofsky, as of March 2009 only 25 percent of the population approved of Zelaya's performance (http://e-lecciones.net/archivos/loultimo/MitofskyEvaMan.pdf).

8. See, for instance, National Democratic Institute, *2009 Honduran General Elec-tions—Final Report International Election Assessment Mission* (Washington, 2010).

9. As of August 2010, among Latin American countries Mexico, Guatemala, El Salvador, Costa Rica, Panama, Colombia, Peru, Chile, and the Dominican Republic had recognized Lobo's government.

10. "Coup Rocks Honduras," *Wall Street Journal*, June 29, 2009; "In a Coup in Honduras, Ghosts of Past U.S. Policies," *New York Times*, June 29, 2009. For a radical and radically different version, see Eva Golinger, "Washington behind the Honduras Coup: Here Is the Evidence" (Montreal, Quebec: Center for Research on Globaliza-tion, July 15, 2009) (www.globalresearch.ca/index.php?context=va&aid=14390).

11. "Obama Says Honduras Coup Illegal," *BBC News*, June 29, 2009 (http://news.bbc.co.uk/2/hi/americas/8125292.stm.)

12. "Why Obama Won't Use the M-Word for Honduras' Coup," *Time Magazine*, September 5, 2009; Howard Berman, "Honduras: Make It Official—It's a Coup," *Los Angeles Times*, September 3, 2009.

13. State Department, press release regarding Honduras, September 3, 2009 (www.state.gov/r/pa/prs/ps/2009/sept/128608.htm).

14. U.S. Secretary of State Hillary Clinton, press release regarding Honduras, October 30, 2009 (www.state.gov/secretary/rm/2009a/10/131078.htm).

15. "Piden informes a CSJ, Procuraduría, Ministerio Público y DDHH," *La Prensa* (Honduras), November 2, 2009. In fact, the vote to reinstate Zelaya did not take place until after the presidential election and yielded a lopsided rejection to his return. See "Congreso de Honduras resuelve no restituir a Manuel Zelaya," *El Heraldo* (Honduras), December 2, 2009.

16. Thomas Shannon, then assistant secretary of state for Western Hemisphere affairs, interview on *CNN*, in Spanish, November 4, 2009 (www.youtube.com/watch?v=asbYkOMvbj8).

17. "Leader Ousted, Honduras Hires U.S. Lobbyists," *New York Times*, October 7, 2009.

18. "DeMint Puts Nominees on Hold over Obama's Honduras Policy," *McClatchy Newspapers*, July 21, 2009. See also Senator DeMint's opinion piece, "What I Heard in Honduras," *Wall Street Journal*, October 10, 2009.

19. Following a domestic and international negotiation, former President Zelaya left Honduras for the Dominican Republic on the same day that Porfirio Lobo took office.

20. For the text of the San José Agreement of July 22, 2009, see www.elheraldo.hn/var/elheraldo_site/storage/original/application/205307a26c541f7af1d173c22454bd5a.pdf. For the text of the Tegucigalpa/San José Agreement of October 30, 2009, see www.laprensa.hn/var/laprensa_site/storage/original/application/b97a02bc3619d-207d7ea89ed6d00b394.pdf.

21. Lobo's administration includes members of the ruling National Party, as well as members of the Christian Democratic Party, Social Democratic Innovation and Unity Party, and Democratic Unification Party. The latter had a visible participation in the National Front against the coup. Note, however, that cabinet members belonging to parties other than the president's serve in government in their *personal* capacity, rather than as representatives of their political organizations. The Honduran Congress voted for the amnesty for political offenses on January 27, 2010, the day Lobo took office. It covered not just those involved in perpetrating the coup, but also former president Zelaya. The former president's inclusion in the amnesty meant that the Liberal Party, the main opposition force, refused to support the bill and chose to abstain. The amnesty does not include common offenses.

22. Comisión Interamericana de Derechos Humanos, *Honduras: Derechos humanos y golpe de estado; Informe Anual 2009,* chap. 4; and *Informe Anual de la Relatoría para la Libertad de Expresión 2009,* pp. 99–123—all available at http://cidh.org. These violations continue to be a matter of serious concern. According to the Inter-American Commission, in the month of February 2010 alone, that is, *after* the new government was sworn in, at least fifty unlawful arrests, eight cases of torture, two kidnappings, and two rapes were perpetrated against journalists, trade union leaders, and activists from sectors supportive of former president Zelaya.

23. "Honduras Launches Truth Commission with U.S. Support but Repudiation from Coup Opponents," *Los Angeles Times,* May 4, 2010; "Q&A: Guatemalan Seeks Answers in Honduran Coup," *Los Angeles Times,* May 9, 2010. See also Center for Justice and International Law (CEJIL), press release, May 4, 2010 (http://cejil.org/comunicados/comision-de-la-verdad-de-honduras-nace-con-graves-carencias-juridicas).

24. Alicia Bárcena, "Política fiscal en América Latina: Creando oportunidades para la juventud," paper presented at the Eighteenth Ibero-American Summit, San Salvador, October 28, 2008 (www.slideshare.net/Cepal/poltica-fiscal-en-amrica-latina-creando-oportunidades-para-la-juventud).

nine
Haiti: Life beyond Survival

Juan Gabriel Valdés

The catastrophic earthquake of January 12, 2010, has had a devastating impact on all aspects of Haitian society: social, economic, political, and cultural. No aspect of Haitian life was unaffected. The quake will long remain a horrific calamity in the collective memory of Haitians, clearly marked by a "before" and an "after."

Most painful has been the loss of life, estimated to be between 230,000 and 300,000. Very few Haitian families have escaped tragedy, and those hardest hit—in the capital, Port-au-Prince, or in Léogâne and Petit Goâve—are convinced that since its very foundation Haiti has been en route to a deadly and inexorable fate. At the same time, it is in the extraordinary nature of Haitians not to be bowed by disaster. They have been neither defeated nor crushed by the quake; if anything, they have developed an aura of tragic greatness and profound dignity.

The quake also brought tragedy to the United Nations Stabilization Mission in Haiti (MINUSTAH) with the deaths of more than 100 staff members, including the mission chief and representative of the secretary general, Hedi Anabi, and his entire managing team, known for their integrity and dedication to the Haitian cause.[1] This loss clearly made the work of the mission very difficult in the immediate aftermath of the quake, a situation that only began to change after the arrival of the new UN representative, Edmond Mulet. But the initial absence of MINUSTAH military forces on the ground served to highlight the dignified behavior of the Haitian people, who did not engage in looting and other excesses but instead bravely tried to save people and retrieve the dead from the ruins.

Months after the earthquake, the physical destruction of the capital remains evident everywhere and seems almost insuperable. It is traumatic to live in a city in which 105,000 homes were almost completely destroyed and 200,000 seriously damaged; in which 1,300 schools and 50 hospitals collapsed; where the Presidential Palace, the glory of Port-au-Prince, was irreparably damaged and destroyed, and the great majority of Haiti's ministries and its parliament building were demolished. The devastation is akin to that following a great war, except in Haiti's case, the frontal attack was perpetrated by nature.

More than 600,000 of the capital's 3 million residents who chose to abandon the city are finding only the most fragile of havens in the rural areas, once the original home for many of them. These territories have been devastated by erosion, and their meager agricultural returns, hard fought for, offer little guarantee of subsistence. Migration to other towns is equally uncertain and difficult, but also impossible without urgent state assistance to the already poverty-stricken settlements that would receive the new inhabitants. Moreover, this is not something that can be achieved in the short run.

After retrieving and burying the dead, survivors found refuge in large tented camps or in simple plastic-covered structures in the most accessible locations: the public squares of Pétionville, the gardens of the prime minister's mansion, the Champs de Mars, in front of the ruins of the Presidential Palace, on the vast tracts of empty lands bordering the road to Toussaint-L'Ouverture airport, and elsewhere. All this temporary resettling has been peaceful. The fears voiced by some media outlets that bandits might pillage the city, as they had done before and during the first period of the MINUS-TAH mission in 2004 and 2005, or that social unrest might break out during food distribution or with the relocation of survivors, have turned out to be unfounded. As noted in a report recently presented to the UN Security Council by Secretary General Ban Ki Moon, "The Haitian people have reacted to the disaster with admirable dignity and resilience."[2]

But the possibility of discontent is beginning to emerge, particularly with the onset of the rainy season, which is often accompanied by hurricanes and floods. It is clearly urgent to transfer refugees to safer places, but this will not be easy without an accelerated home construction program. To complicate matters, some refugees living in tents in the city center or on higher ground may resist giving up these shelters because they have never had the police protection or access to electricity, potable water, and public baths available here. Furthermore, a variety of international actors as well as the Haitian government have provided free food and, in some instances, medical attention. Although refugees would clearly be wise to move to safer places, many also resist moving away from locations close to their demolished homes, or leaving urban areas that they consider "abandoned" and to which they may have become accustomed.

A Period of Optimism

The earthquake hit Haitian society after three years of constitutional government, just as the first signs of development were becoming visible. President René Préval had stabilized the political process—albeit slowly and in a context of great institutional fragilities—and had nominated a broadly based government involving all the political parties. He had regained the trust of international economic agents and had presented a series of constitutional reforms to Haiti's Parliament that sought to dissolve the classic interbranch conflicts that had paralyzed the government. In spite of the failed government of his prime minister, Jacques Edouard Alexis, brought down in 2008 by a huge rise in oil and food prices, or that of his short-lived successor, Michèle Pierre-Louis, Préval avoided destabilization and managed to build a parliamentary majority. The nomination in November 2009 of Jean Max Bellerive, an experienced and authoritative politician, helped to generate a climate of political tranquility. Bellerive has been a key element in formulating the post-quake reconstruction plan and in generating trust within the international community.

At the same time, institutional development has been complicated by the inevitable postponement of legislative elections, which had been scheduled for February 2010. The nomination of the prime minister has yet to be confirmed, and the period for the ratification of the constitutional reform proposed by Préval, already approved by the legislature in September 2009, will be extended. Among other proposed changes, this reform provides for dual nationality, so as to facilitate the participation of the Haitian diaspora in the country's political and economic process; reduces the frequency of elections, which have placed too much of a financial burden on the international community (it gave Haiti more than $85 million between 2005 and 2009 for that purpose); establishes new rules for the nomination of the Electoral Council, thus resolving an eternal source of political disputes; modifies the awkward and often arbitrary process used to ratify the nomination of the prime minister; and establishes a new military force that can be trained to provide an efficient response to public order requirements once MINUSTAH leaves the country.[3]

Until the earthquake, the Haitian economy had been growing modestly, and international organizations supported what was considered a well-administered economic course that was showing incipient signs of development. The return to Haiti of the United States, the hemisphere's most important international actor, signaled the international community's interest in supporting an administration that seemed focused on greater accountability and that showed a better sense of good government. Although it was never completely absent from Haiti, Washington had kept a low profile after the fall of President Jean-Bertrand Aristide, not only because of its involvement in his downfall, but mainly because its engagement in Iraq prevented it from addressing other priorities. America's new commitment to its poorest hemispheric neighbor became apparent with the election of President Barack Obama, but also with President Bill Clinton's appointment in 2009 as UN special envoy in charge of establishing a development plan for Haiti.

With the UN's support, the institutional life of the country also seemed to be improving. Although beset by fragilities and poverty, Haiti had begun to experience some semblance of normality. The electoral calendar was being followed, and municipal elections were taking place in a climate of peace after a history of heated controversy surrounding the nomination of new electoral authorities.

None of this means that President Préval had managed to overcome the great precariousness of the Haitian state, or that MNUSTAH had completed its task of coordinating the international agencies to promote a coherent development program in accordance with its mandate. Haiti had not yet managed to overcome institutional fragilities, the state still lacked the means to extend its control over the entire territory, and international assistance never seemed to get past the initial task of stabilization. It was taking years to approve road projects undertaken by international organizations, and even longer to get them built. Even when roads were built or repaired, they quickly deteriorated again owing to further lack of maintenance. The training of the police force, which was also under the aegis of international organizations, was taking much longer than initially predicted. The force was hampered by dysfunctional organizational mechanisms and the taint of corruption and was still underequipped and understaffed. The country also had a dangerously overpopulated prison system, with more than 90 percent of its inmates never yet brought to trial. Above all, Haiti remained extremely poor: 70 percent of the population had no access to running water and lived on less than $2 a day.

Given the magnitude of the task, it is hardly surprising that many observers feel skeptical about the prospects for state reform. It involves much more than reorganizing functions and promoting decentralization. It requires a fully financed and internationally backed development plan that is authoritatively imposed by a strong state.

For many, the key issue is the reform of the judiciary, which is in large part responsible for the country's institutional fragility. As the International Crisis Group correctly notes, "The dysfunctional state of the Haitian judicial system has impeded the implementation of democratic reforms since the collapse of the Duvalier dictatorship." To reform the judiciary, Haiti would have to address an array of problems: "the incompetence of judges; weak legislative administration; the absence of criminal archives; prolonged periods of pre-trial detention; underpaid judges; inadequate infrastructure and lack of logistical support; lack of judicial independence; outdated codes and lack of defense attorneys."[4] Clearly, problems such as these cannot be resolved without an integral national development policy.

It was against this very shaky backdrop that natural catastrophes hit Haiti: first came the hurricanes and floods of 2008, then the larger calamity of the earthquake. In less than three minutes, the quake destroyed 65 percent of the country's economic activity—equivalent to 120 percent of Haiti's 2009 gross domestic product (GDP).[5] In an extraordinary global expression of solidarity and mobilization of resources, governments, international organizations, and nongovernmental organizations (NGOs) have tried to coordinate a response to the emergency and to help the victims—by providing shelter to hundreds of thousands of people, protecting their health and basic rights, and providing food and security. The deeply worrying question now is how to carry out the enormous reconstruction task in an environment of institutional fragility. How is institutional reform to be combined with the monumental job of physically rebuilding the country so as to generate the trust that is indispensable to attracting investment and consolidating international support? How can Haiti ensure that it is capable of exerting the considerable social discipline required to reconstruct the country?

Refounding Haiti

Three months after the earthquake and the outpouring of global solidarity, leaders of the international community met in New York to discuss a fifty-three-page Plan of Action for the Reconstruction and National Development in which the Haitian government, with the support of internationally staffed technical teams, laid out its proposals for the future.[6] The catastrophe, noted the report, made plain the absolutely precarious nature of the country's physical infrastructure. It also attributed the dimensions of the disaster to the high population density of the capital and its environs, the complete lack of construction standards, and the catastrophic environmental situation compounded by the unregulated use of land. For these reasons, the report recommended that "reconstruction should focus on tackling these areas of vulnerability, so as to avoid paying this price again." Under the heading, "We Share a Dream," the report assesses Haiti's predicament and outlines an ambitious goal:

> The situation that the country faces is difficult but not desperate. In many ways it even creates an opportunity to unite Haitians of all classes and origins in the shared task of re-founding the country on another basis. Nobody has escaped this tragedy, so nobody has the authority to act individually. We must build this new solidarity, which we hope will lead to a change of behavior and attitudes.[7]

Under the proposal, tragedy would be turned into an opportunity to "refound the country." This suggests that the government has high ambitions and the political will to face the challenges ahead, whatever critics may say about President Préval's absence during the first days of the earthquake, or about the "nonexistence" of the government in the chaotic aftermath of the quake. The refoundation proposal is not just a rhetorical statement. The policy of "devolution and decentralization" it puts forth would give the population of Port-au-Prince incentives to relocate from the capital to new "axes of development"—small decentralized urban centers—and thus would "decongest the urban area." The plan also refers to a goal long pursued by the Haitian elite: to recover the countryside and agriculture in a way that prevents further soil erosion, restores the environment, and gives the majority of extremely poor Haitians living in rural areas a chance for a productive livelihood.

Although the report portrays reconstruction as an opportunity to rebuild a country whose historical foundation has always been problematic, it is difficult not to be skeptical about the real chances of making this happen. Haiti is not just a fragile state: to institutional weakness must be added the great political difficulties in building consensus among Haitians, as well as the individualism and endemic resistance to authority typical of the country's culture. How prepared are Haitians to tackle a goal as ambitious as national refoundation? A society split by an abyss between a small elite and a poverty-stricken mass will be hard-pressed to exercise the discipline required for the social engineering tasks of population relocation, agricultural reform, and overhaul of "behaviors and attitudes." Has the earthquake created the psychological climate for a national effort of this magnitude?

The plan envisions two phases of reconstruction. The first lasts a year—a period that is clearly far too short for the proposed goal—and is to be managed by a transitional administration "until the machinery of the state is operational." The second lasts ten years and includes a three-cycle growth strategy to overcome poverty. The Haitian government made a highly significant political decision to attain these goals: it would create an Interim Commission for the Reconstruction of Haiti, a Development Agency, and a Multi-Donor Trust Fund with a view to preparing a "portfolio of interventions, programs and projects" for national reconstruction with sufficient financing and proper execution to carry the projects through.

The most critical step—the establishment of an Interim Commission for Reconstruction—would be presided over by the prime minister and a "prominent foreigner" (Bill Clinton has been nominated for the task), along with a representative group of Haitians and international technical teams. This would not only give the Haitian state the political and technical backing to guarantee the necessary financing but would also establish some external control over the returns and efficiency of investment decisions. The commission would include, with a right to vote, members of both chambers of Parliament, representatives of civil society, entrepreneurs, and workers, as well as donors and the foreign states directly involved in the process. It thereby establishes the domestic legitimacy of international participation in the Haitian decisionmaking process.

Although the reason given for establishing such a commission is that the foreign funds and resources needed for recovery from the earthquake far exceed the assistance Haiti usually receives from abroad—which is undoubtedly the case—the commission's stated functions emphasize that reconstruction must "respond to concerns regarding administrative accountability and transparency, so as to maximize the support from international donors."[8] The legislature has already approved the commission's constitution, and various private and public actors have been consulted in the context of the state of emergency, "which establishes the legal and regulatory framework for the launching of a genuine Reconstruction and Development Plan."[9] Although the government document states that the commission will hand over power to the Haitian Development Agency after its eighteen-month mandate has expired, the transfer is not likely to be speedy. It will take a huge effort to support the Haitian state if reconstruction is to proceed as hoped.

What is truly surprising about the document is the proposed flexibility in the relationship between foreign development assistance and Haitian sovereignty—a frequent source of controversy and sharp political battles. The general attitude in Haiti has been that foreign involvement in national decisionmaking concerning social and economic development damages Haitian sovereignty. By contrast, the current proposal suggests that national reconstruction cannot happen without institutionalizing the association between Haitian and external actors.

How feasible will it be to implement this plan, and how might Haitians react to the idea of "refounding" the country? It is too early to tell, but preliminary answers can be found in the Project for Political Analysis and Prospective Scenarios (PAPEP), a study carried out in March 2010 under the United Nations Development Program (UNDP) in association with Haiti's prestigious social research institute, the Center for Research and Economic and Social Development Training (Centre de Recherche et de Formation Économique et Sociale pour le Développement, CRESFED).

Post-Earthquake Politics in Haiti

The aim of this UNDP-led study was to propose possible political scenarios for the immediate development of the country.[10] A first step was to assess the population's view of the country's institutions before and after the quake. Predictably, many respondents and focus group participants stated that Haiti's institutions and services were all but decimated by the quake—the authorities had disappeared, institutions and services had ceased to exist, and despair ruled the day—whereas beforehand some institutions had been of assistance and offered hope for the future, despite their precarious nature.

The study also notes that the population's characteristic mistrust of the government and the international community has been perpetuated and augmented in recent years. It found that Haitians considered the government of President Préval to be "nonexistent" both before and after the quake and suspected the international community of harboring secret aims, of being "partisan," and of failing to coordinate the distribution of food. At the same time, many recognized that the international community had mobilized its resources in response to the earthquake, and that Haiti could not manage without this outside help. Others emphasized that Haiti's development was not the business of the international community but up to Haitians themselves. Once again, Haitians had very mixed feelings about foreign assistance—defending national sovereignty, on one hand, and recognizing that the participation of outsiders in their national development is indispensable, on the other.

Many interviewed for the study rejected the political class and parties altogether and believed that a "citizenry" mobilized by grass-roots organizations, town halls, neighborhood associations, and youth groups is the only force capable of rebuilding the country. Recognizing their weakness and lack of means, they conclude these are the organizations with the admirable qualities that the Haitian people demonstrated during the tragedy. Haitians seem to think that "a new kind of state" and a "new mentality" could be forged from the base up, and that social forces could be regrouped to establish a political pact for unity. Thus it is not surprising that elections are not considered urgent. As the report states, there is "indecision about the next elections, people are ready to participate but they do not feel that the electoral process is a short-term priority." As a whole, the population seems to be in a state of profound political and social unease.

Yet people also seem far from being mobilized around a national refoundation project. As the report points out, an extraordinary magnitude of governability effort will be required to rebuild the country. It will take more than a technical program and well-structured investments to overcome the population's skepticism and mistrust. What Haiti most needs is legitimate and authoritative leadership based on an appeal to the historical foundations of the country. Without a high-quality political process in place, reconstruction will either simply not occur or will be derailed when the first obstacles emerge, with unpredictable results.

The authors of the study envision four possible scenarios emerging from the current situation: three are clearly negative, consisting of chaos, paralysis, and authoritarianism; the fourth is a positive democratic outcome, based on hoped-for political agreement between Haitians.

Paralysis (*enlisement*) could occur if political forces either fail to act or obstruct one another, Parliament's mandate is not renewed and constitutional reform is abandoned, a weakened president governs by decree, the presidential elections at the end of 2010 or early in 2011 fail to mobilize people, and a new president is elected without great support. In such circumstances, the population will become frustrated by the absence of solutions and resigned to deteriorating conditions, while the reconstruction process drags on without progress.

"Political chaos (in the short term) and loss of sovereignty (in the long term)" is an even more negative scenario. In this case, if political entities should fail to reach agreement, decisionmaking would again be paralyzed, except that now the population would be enraged by the lack of food, rising prices, and the government's failure to arrive at solutions. Here the report's authors foresee "violent uprisings against a backdrop of political fragmentation and the absence of a collective horizon." The international community would then be forced to intervene to call elections, the result of which would be predetermined by outside interests, and Haiti would lose any semblance of sovereignty.

In the third negative scenario, involving "a phoenix (in the short term) and authoritarian populism (in the long term)," the president might gain support by fulfilling immediate basic needs and win the trust of a majority that is willing to be patient. However, Parliament might be discarded, with the president governing by decree, and a much weakened opposition would be standing by as the president establishes an alternative, presidentially dominated institutional system. With the new scheme guaranteeing stability and the first steps taken toward reconstruction, elections would be considered superfluous or untimely, and the doors opened to an extension of the presidential mandate and to a nondemocratic political order.

The only positive scenario involves "compromise (in the short term) and democratic refoundation (in the long term)." Here the main actors would gradually agree on pending constitutional issues (the renovation or extension of Parliament's mandate and other constitutional reforms), presidential elections would be set, and measures adopted to reconstitute the electoral register:

> The basic political agreement about procedures establishes a context of stability that prevents the worst from happening, but is insufficient to build the political base necessary to push forward reconstruction. To achieve the latter, all the forces of the nation (political forces, civil society and the private sector) with the support of the international community forge a socio-political pact to commit to the "re-foundation of Haiti," which prioritizes long-term development. The earthquake thus has a long-term effect on the population, which recovers its hope and participates in debates on the future of the country. A Haitian society arises based on solidarity and inclusion, and the emergence of a new democratic order.[11]

Reality Is Tougher

One can safely predict that what unfolds in reality will combine elements from all four of the scenarios just discussed. The main failing of that exercise, however, is that it assumes the international community will play only a negative role: by intervening when chaos erupts and thus contributing to the loss of sovereignty. But international actors can actually play a hugely positive role, not only by preventing negative scenarios but also by promoting a scenario based on political negotiation and democratic accords. The international community must prove it is capable of doing this, which means respecting domestic processes and, above all, demonstrating patience.

Recently the government made some key decisions regarding the reconstruction plan and the political process. In March 2010 it chose a vast tract of land in Corail Cesselesse, to the north of Port-au-Prince, for the relocation of 50,000 families, starting with those most vulnerable to possible hurricanes and floods.[12] This transfer has only just begun, and the obstacles to evicting and relocating refugees are formidable. In addition, the president has announced that presidential elections will be held in accordance with the constitutional time frame and has called on the population to participate. This decision, which is not supported by the entire political class, calls for a consensus-building effort.

The mandate of the Chamber of Deputies was set to expire in the first week of May 2010, and the provisions for extending it had not yet been formulated. The chamber's last decision, made with the Senate, was to prolong President Préval's mandate until May 2011, the goal being to ensure there is institutional leadership in case the presidential election is delayed. Clearly, it is essential to maintain Parliament's legitimacy in order to ensure that the executive is not accused of making illegitimate decisions, particularly when its mandate has been extended.

The opposition seems weak at the moment, but Haiti is known for its swift and sometimes unpredictable political shifts. In any case, it is not good politics to underestimate one's opponents. Some intellectuals and a group of former government ministers are opposed to the prolongation of the State of Emergency and the ratification of the Interim Commission for Reconstruction on the grounds that they constitute a threat to national sovereignty. Although this view does not seem to have much support at present, it may easily broaden in the present atmosphere of open social malaise. The situation is clearly tenuous and calls for the greatest seriousness in managing agreements, a higher degree of political participation, and the forging of pacts that will ensure the core decisions about reconstruction are implemented.

These are the very areas in which the international community and the United States in particular can be of assistance. The Obama administration seems to understand the scope of the challenge. Supported by the vigorous media campaign demonstrating solidarity with the Haitian people, Obama has indicated unconditional support for the Préval government, notably through the visits of Secretary of State Hillary Clinton and Assistant Secretary of State Arturo Valenzuela. Washington has also recognized the Haitian people's ownership of the process of reconstruction and has called on foreign governments and international organizations to mobilize both time and resources to help with that task.

There are few instances in the history of the hemisphere in which the United States has been in a position to do so much good at such a relatively low cost as in Haiti. The prestige of the Obama administration among Haitians and its firsthand knowledge of Haiti's evolving political situation could make Washington the main promoter of a virtuous circle that helps Haitians take the earthquake as an opportunity to rebuild their country.

Washington's history of failures in Haiti is hard to overcome, but it also points to what should be done. The first priority, backed fully by Haitians, is to support an integral development plan with a rigorous financial program, deploying technical rigor in investment decisions relying not only on technocratic criteria but also on further development of Haitian state institutions.

In this key moment in Haitian history, U.S.-Haiti cooperation must be based on an understanding that the quality of Haitian politics will be just as important for reconstruction as for financial support. An effort must therefore be made to establish domestic convergence and consensus so as to prudently and legitimately handle the difficulties that an unbalanced social structure aggravated by the earthquake will unavoidably produce. Just as a strong state operating strictly according to rule of law need not pose a threat to the liberty of its citizens, a regulated association between the Haitian state and the international community to promote reconstruction need not pose a threat to Haiti's sovereignty.

Indeed, the implementation of a development plan for Haiti would itself help to reformulate and consolidate Haiti's institutions and thereby improve the quality of its public administration. If a joint national and international effort leads to a national development plan based on new road networks, improvements in education and health, new port services, and an efficient agricultural production and support policy, this would pave the way for Haiti's institutions to become consolidated, to build a capacity for engaging in effective decisionmaking, and to establish functional transparency and accountability mechanisms. This would, indeed, constitute the "refoundation" to which the Haitian authorities aspire.

Notes

1. The death of Gerardo Le Chevallier, a Salvadorean who dedicated an important part of his life to Haiti's political development, was a particularly great loss for the country. He was MINUSTAH electoral chief in 2006 and a key contributor to the successful elections that led to the normalization of the Haitian constitutional process. At the time of the earthquake, he was the political chief of the mission then headed by Hedi Anabi.

2. UN Security Council, Report of the Secretary General on the United Nations Stabilization Mission in Haiti, S/2010/200 (New York, April 2010).

3. On this topic see *Haïti 2010: Scenarios politiques après le séisme* (Haiti 2010: Political scenarios after the earthquake), formulated following the methodology of project PAPEP/PNUD (Port-au-Prince, March 4, 2010).

4. International Crisis Group, "Haiti: Justice Reform and the Security Crisis," Latin America/Caribbean Briefing 14 (January 31, 2007).

5. Action Plan for National Recovery and Development of Haiti, March 2010 (www.ifud.org/wp-content/uploads/2010/04/Haiti_Action_Plan.pdf).

6. Ibid., p. 3.

7. Ibid., p. 5.

8. Ibid., p. 51.

9. Ibid.

10. The study was carried out in Port-au-Prince and its environs and was based on focus groups and in-depth interviews with key Haitian actors from civil society and political organizations. Scenarios in the report were also based on meetings with representatives of the National Identification Organization, the Provisional Electoral Council, Haiti's political parties, the Parliament, and established focus groups composed of people affected by the earthquake. The report also drew on the observations of civil society representatives engaged in the work of the government for the Preliminary Damage and Needs Assessment exercise (PDNA). See: *Haïti 2010.*

11. Ibid., p. 9.

12. See "Rebuilding Haiti: Dreaming beyond the Rubble," *The Economist,* April 17, 2010, p. 41.

ten

The Democracy Agenda in the Americas: The Case for Multilateral Action

Theodore J. Piccone

Since the 1980s U.S. foreign policy, at least rhetorically, has emphasized democracy and human rights in its approach to Latin America. While respect for liberal democracy has improved markedly in the region, countertrends in places like Venezuela, Nicaragua, Guatemala, and Honduras, along with the entrenched status of the Castro regime in Cuba, keep these issues high on the U.S. agenda. The question for the Obama administration is how to pursue a pro-democracy and human rights policy without repeating the mistakes of the past. One key step would be to build coalitions and expand avenues for multilateral cooperation.

After more than a year in office, the Obama administration is striking the right tone of partnership with the region but has not yet delivered any concrete initiatives on this front. As expected, the very fact of Barack Hussein Obama's decisive election as the first African American president as well as early steps to change the style of leadership has had a notably positive effect in the way others view U.S. foreign policy, even on sensitive issues of democracy and human rights. The strategy of pragmatic, principled engagement and support for multilateral approaches, articulated in a pair of speeches in December 2009 by President Obama and Secretary of State Hillary Rodham Clinton, reaffirmed U.S. support for democratic reform around the world while emphasizing flexibility in applying the policy to specific cases.[1]

Of course, much more than an election and inspiring rhetoric is needed to complete the revamping necessary to make U.S. policies in support of democracy and human rights more credible and effective. This is particularly true in the Western Hemisphere, where democratization trends remain fragile and U.S. influence is waning. The Obama administration, with help from Congress, needs to invest serious time and resources into strengthening and, where necessary, creating new multilateral tools for supporting democratization in Latin America and around the world. This will require a significant shift in thinking, away from traditional bilateral channels of diplomatic pressure and assistance and toward greater multilateral cooperation with like-minded partners.

Why Washington Needs to Expand Multilateral Mechanisms

According to a number of polls, democracy is a strongly held aspiration around the world. Most Latin Americans, like the vast majority of people from other regions, believe that democracy is better than any other form of government. But Latin Americans are by and large dissatisfied with the way democracy works in their countries, particularly when it comes to distributing income and providing social protections. Corruption is considered a huge impediment to improved governance. According to a Barómetro Iberoamericano 2009 poll, corruption tied unemployment as the second gravest problem in the region after security.[2] Trust in politicians and political parties ranks particularly low.[3]

As these numbers illustrate, the positive democratic trends that have unfolded in the region over the past thirty years also reflect serious vulnerabilities. To prevent backsliding toward authoritarian rule, Latin democracies need to achieve tangible improvements in their judicial systems, greater accountability of public institutions and politicians, more transparency, and improved public services. And the United States has a vital interest in seeing a hemisphere of prosperous democratic states governed by the rule of law, a point reaffirmed by successive administrations, including the Obama administration.

Washington has backed up this vision with billions of dollars in aid to help strengthen democratic governance in the region, with mixed results so far. Furthermore, its historical legacy in the region and its more recent errors beyond—such as justifying its invasion of Iraq with inflated promises of spreading democracy to the Arab world—reduce its credibility instead of helping to achieve that goal. While public opinion polls around the world show U.S. favorability ratings have recovered from the historic lows seen during the George W. Bush presidency, they also show that expectations of a more multilateral approach to U.S. foreign policy thus far have gone unfulfilled.[4]

Latin America, a region with a complicated history of hot and cold relations with Washington, is generally in sync with the uncertainty reflected in global public opinion trends, despite the early high marks given to President Obama. In marked contrast to President Bush's 4.3 approval rating (out of 10)—a tie with Fidel Castro—President Obama tops the list with a 7. Daniel Ortega, Fidel Castro, and Hugo Chávez rank last with 4.3, 4, and 3.9 respectively.[5] Nonetheless, a mere 43 percent of respondents in a 2009 Barómetro Iberoamericano survey had a positive opinion of the United States, up only modestly from 34 percent in 2007.[6]

These numbers indicate that the Obama administration has a rare window of opportunity to consolidate a more positive U.S. image and increase its influence in the region. But this honeymoon effect may have a limited shelf life if it is not translated quickly into more concrete and permanent changes in U.S. policy. Already, more respondents to an exclusive Latinobarómetro poll conducted for *The Economist* see Brazil as the most influential country in the region, ahead of the United States and Venezuela.[7]

Just as positive perceptions of the United States have increased since 2008, so have those of other international actors. According to the 2009 Barómetro Iberoamericano poll, the United Nations is trusted by 63 percent of respondents, an increase of six points; the Organization of American States (OAS) received 45 percent approval, a five-point increase; and the European Union met with 57 percent approval, a seven-point increase (figure 10-1).[8]

Given these realities, and the inherent sensitivity of providing external support for domestic political activities, it is critical that Washington move in partnership with others. It needs to reboot its image in the region as an ally of democracy by working closely with countries and international organizations that are accepted as credible actors; that share basic assumptions about the positive link between democracy, development, and peace; and that are willing to join in a deliberate though more nuanced effort to strengthen respect for democracy and the rule of law in the region. Washington needs to walk softly, talk quietly, and join hands with others.

Partners are needed as well to help share the financial and diplomatic burdens of this task. U.S. foreign aid, which has weathered the initial storm of the 2009 financial crisis, will likely face significant cuts in the future as a result of ballooning U.S. deficits. A serious reduction in democracy assistance, which demands a long-term and consistent commitment of resources

Figure 10-1. How Positively the Latin American Public Perceives International Organizations

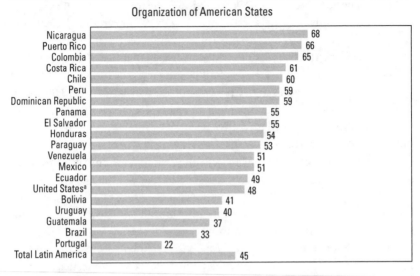

Organization of American States

Nicaragua	68
Puerto Rico	66
Colombia	65
Costa Rica	61
Chile	60
Peru	59
Dominican Republic	59
Panama	55
El Salvador	55
Honduras	54
Paraguay	53
Venezuela	51
Mexico	51
Ecuador	49
United States[a]	48
Bolivia	41
Uruguay	40
Guatemala	37
Brazil	33
Portugal	22
Total Latin America	45

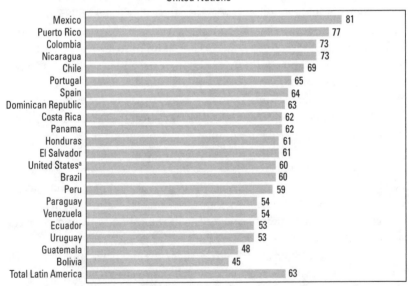

United Nations

Mexico	81
Puerto Rico	77
Colombia	73
Nicaragua	73
Chile	69
Portugal	65
Spain	64
Dominican Republic	63
Costa Rica	62
Panama	62
Honduras	61
El Salvador	61
United States[a]	60
Brazil	60
Peru	59
Paraguay	54
Venezuela	54
Ecuador	53
Uruguay	53
Guatemala	48
Bolivia	45
Total Latin America	63

Source: CIMA, *Barómetro Iberoamericano de Gobernabilidad 2009* (Bogotá), pp. 26–28. For more information, see www.cimaiberoamerica.com.

a. Hispanic respondents.

Figure 10-1. How Positively the Latin American Public Perceives International Organizations (*continued*)

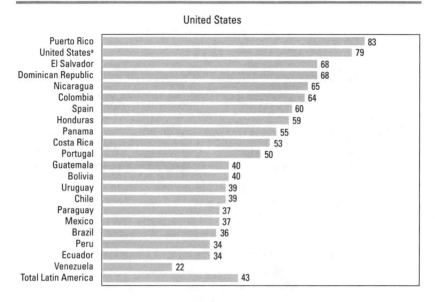

United States

Puerto Rico	83
United States[a]	79
El Salvador	68
Dominican Republic	68
Nicaragua	65
Colombia	64
Spain	60
Honduras	59
Panama	55
Costa Rica	53
Portugal	50
Guatemala	40
Bolivia	40
Uruguay	39
Chile	39
Paraguay	37
Mexico	37
Brazil	36
Peru	34
Ecuador	34
Venezuela	22
Total Latin America	43

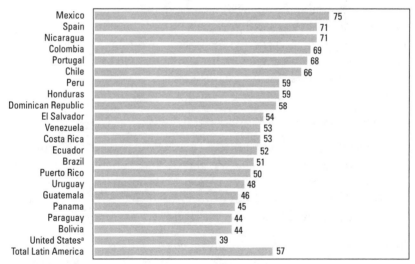

European Union

Mexico	75
Spain	71
Nicaragua	71
Colombia	69
Portugal	68
Chile	66
Peru	59
Honduras	59
Dominican Republic	58
El Salvador	54
Venezuela	53
Costa Rica	53
Ecuador	52
Brazil	51
Puerto Rico	50
Uruguay	48
Guatemala	46
Panama	45
Paraguay	44
Bolivia	44
United States[a]	39
Total Latin America	57

Source: CIMA, *Barómetro Iberoamericano de Gobernabilidad 2009* (Bogotá), pp. 26–28. For more information, see www.cimaiberoamerica.com.

a. Hispanic respondents.

and expertise, would be a mistake and should be resisted: it would undermine America's own interest in making sure that scarce taxpayer dollars go to transparent and accountable governments.

By working in partnership with others, the United States will also be able to offer a more varied menu of democracy assistance to the increasingly diverse set of democracies and political cultures in the hemisphere. The democratic challenges faced by Bolivia, Paraguay, and Guatemala, for example, are different from each other and even more different from those faced by the United States. President Evo Morales of Bolivia, with its large indigenous population, is more interested in learning from South Africa's experience after apartheid than from North America's treatment of its native population. A mechanism is needed, therefore, to bring more diverse actors and experts to the democracy assistance table. Latin American governments should be devoting their own resources and expertise to this joint venture. They should create a unit within their foreign ministries dedicated to democracy and human rights concerns, offer funding and technical assistance on best democratic practices to their neighbors, and provide relevant training and education for their diplomats.[9]

The Obama administration has inherited more than two decades of experience in supporting democracy abroad through both diplomatic and development aid strategies. To fulfill its ambition to implement a more multilateral course, it should build on this experience and consider new avenues for collaboration. A comprehensive strategy anchored in distinct but complementary pillars of diplomatic support and development assistance would serve the United States well in Latin America.

Diplomatic Tools for Democracy Assistance

Building on the lessons learned over the past several years, the United States could employ a number of diplomatic approaches to improve the outcomes of its democracy initiatives in Latin America. However, they require a willingness to yield some control and share the burden with others. Early signs from the Obama administration in this regard are encouraging.

Depersonalize U.S. Relations with the Region's Leaders

Early in its first term, the Bush administration committed a cardinal sin of democracy assistance: it signaled support for an unconstitutional coup against the democratically elected president of Venezuela, Hugo Chávez. An administration ostensibly committed to democratic freedoms abroad chose instead to engage in an old-style game of picking winners and losers, and did so in contravention of both the letter and spirit of important and positive regional norms built up since the 1980s. As a result, the Bush administration lost credibility in the region, just eight months after it had signed the Inter-American Democratic Charter committing all governments in the region to respecting constitutional government, and gave Chávez further ammunition for his anti-U.S. agenda. The U.S. image in the region was further damaged when U.S. officials intervened in national elections in Bolivia, El Salvador, and Nicaragua by endorsing pro-U.S. candidates and threatening to withdraw bilateral benefits if voters supported the leftist candidate.

Advisers to Barack Obama explicitly rejected this kind of approach during his presidential campaign. The Obama administration is now handling similar situations with greater respect for the wishes of Latin American voters. At the April 2009 Summit of the Americas, for example, President Obama proclaimed that "every one of our nations has a right to follow its own path. But we all have a responsibility to see that the people of the Americas have the ability to pursue their own dreams in democratic societies."[10] These words, which suggest that the Obama administration will refrain from interfering in internal elections and will work constructively with whoever wins free and fair elections and respects the fundamental tenets of the Inter-American Democratic Charter, are already being put to the test as new elections unfold around the region.

The two most dramatic cases in 2009 centered not around elections but an old-fashioned coup d'état in Honduras and a long-standing dictatorship in Cuba. The Obama administration's initial response to the forced exile of President Manuel Zelaya of Honduras in June 2009 hewed closely to the predominant and now entrenched rule of the region that extra-legal overthrows of democratically elected governments cannot stand. The successor government in Tegucigalpa, led by president of the National Congress Roberto Micheletti, was quickly rejected as illegitimate and suspended from the OAS. Yet despite repeated efforts to facilitate Zelaya's return, the United States was unable to exercise sufficient pressure directly or through the OAS to force Micheletti to cede control. As a last resort, national elections scheduled long before the coup became Washington's preferred exit strategy, a position at odds with a significant number of other countries, including Brazil, Chile, and Mexico.

Nonetheless, from the standpoint of promoting democracy, it is hard to argue against relying on free and fair elections as the appropriate route out of the crisis, especially when these were legitimately convened and excluded the two main protagonists from the ballot. Indeed, as of January 2010, with the newly elected president Porfirio Lobo sworn into office and Zelaya willingly departing Honduras for the Dominican Republic, most governments in the region were gradually if reluctantly accepting the new facts on the ground. Meanwhile, the United States correctly continued to insist that key terms of the accord between Micheletti and Zelaya be honored in order for Honduras to be fully welcomed back into the inter-American community. In the end, the Honduran experience may have reinforced the hemisphere's anti-coup strictures for obvious cases but still left the region divided on how best to intervene to protect democracy, especially in the period before a coup d'état.

Similarly, in the case of Cuba's readmission to the OAS, the Obama administration was faced with a tricky situation. It signaled early on a willingness to begin a new dialogue with Havana built around cooperation on issues of common concern while maintaining the embargo as leverage toward future normalization. "It is time to pursue direct diplomacy, with friend and foe alike, without preconditions," then candidate Obama told an audience in Miami.[11] But if it accepted the strong consensus of its neighbors and agreed to lift Cuba's decades-old suspension from the body without conditions, it would directly undermine if not violate the core tenets of the Inter-American Democratic Charter, which requires OAS members to uphold core democratic principles that Cuba flagrantly rejects. Through skillful diplomacy and direct intervention by Secretary Clinton at the OAS General Assembly in June 2009, the Obama administration was able to have it both ways: Cuba's suspension was lifted, thereby removing a thorn from the hemispheric agenda, but full readmission was conditioned on Cuba's compliance with the organization's fundamental standards for membership. Thus in both the Honduras and Cuba events it faced in 2009, Washington demonstrated fidelity to core inter-American principles on democracy while retaining some flexibility on their application to mixed effect.

Restore Civilian-Military Balance and Improve Interagency Coordination of U.S. Policy

One worrisome trend in U.S. policy toward the region and globally has been the expanding role of the Defense Department and its regional commands as the face of U.S. foreign policy. This is particularly true in the case of the U.S. Southern Command (SOUTHCOM), headquartered in Florida, which has Latin America and the Caribbean (excluding Mexico) as its area of responsibility.

During the 1990s, as military officers in the region gradually retreated from the presidential palace to the barracks, civilian leaders struggled to assert democratic control of the armed forces. Given the legacy of U.S. support for military regimes in the region, the role of the U.S. military at that time was especially delicate. The Clinton administration sought to ameliorate that situation by elevating civilian defense ministers as the premier interlocutors for defense cooperation and by investing resources in civilian capacity building to train a new generation of civilian leaders in defense management and national security policymaking.[12] In addition, U.S. policymakers in both the Clinton and Bush administrations sought to strengthen anti-coup provisions of the inter-American system as a way to ward off a return to military or authoritarian seizures of power, although the Venezuela debacle noted earlier revived fears of a return to the old ways of U.S. unilateralism.

Despite these efforts, power and resources have demonstrably shifted from U.S. civilian to military agencies over the past decade, starting with the disproportionate emphasis on military aid of Plan Colombia. Between 1997 and 2009, U.S. military and police assistance to the region grew from approximately $325 million to $1.2 billion a year, mostly for counternarcotics assistance to Colombia and its Andean neighbors.[13] The new Mérida Initiative, approved by Congress in the fall of 2008, added $400 million for Mexico and $65 million for Central America, the Dominican Republic, and Haiti in military and police aid for 2008, and another $410 million was appropriated for 2009. For fiscal 2010, the Obama administration requested $550 million in Mérida funding for Mexico and Central America of which Congress approved $210 million for Mexico and $83 million for Central America, including $37 million for a new Caribbean Basin Security Initiative.[14] At the same time, an increasing proportion of U.S. assistance funds was handled directly by the Pentagon—which is subject to less congressional scrutiny and fewer restrictions on how aid is spent—instead of the State Department. During this same period, economic and social aid to the region grew from $594.4 million to $1.7 billion a year, a slightly smaller rate of growth and a reduction in the previous gap between economic and security assistance. From 2005 to 2009 economic and social aid included $578 million channeled through the Millennium Challenge Account (MCA) and another $472 million through the HIV/Aids Initiative.[15] These funds were spent in only six of the poorest countries (El Salvador, Honduras, Nicaragua, and Paraguay for MCA; Guyana and Haiti for HIV/AIDS).

In addition to the shift toward security assistance, SOUTHCOM has sought to emerge as a big player in the projection of U.S. soft power in the region. Over time, it has reengineered its approach to security threats in the hemisphere with a greater emphasis on poverty, crime, and inequality as the primary drivers of instability. Even though these underlying threats cannot be ameliorated through military means, SOUTHCOM has restructured its operations as if they could be. For example, a new SOUTHCOM Partnering Directorate "engages the public and private sector to coordinate and integrate with interagency, non-governmental organizations, and partner nations to facilitate good governance, the strengthening of economies, and a favorable investment climate in order to support economic independence, sustainable development, and prosperity throughout the region."[16] Operationally, this shift in focus also means more attention by the Pentagon to humanitarian assistance and disaster response, areas traditionally handled by civilian agencies. This was most dramatically demonstrated in SOUTHCOM's response to the devastating earthquake in Haiti on January 12, 2010, which included more than 12,000 U.S. military personnel, 17 ships, and more than 40 aircraft.[17] The elevation of SOUTHCOM's naval unit to the status of Fourth Fleet in 2008, which caused a bit of a diplomatic stir in the region, gives SOUTHCOM additional resources to do even more humanitarian work through naval visits to various ports of call. Adding to these concerns was Washington's serious mishandling of the agreement with Bogotá for access to seven Colombian military bases, which prompted angry denunciations throughout South America and annulment by Colombia's Constitutional Court.

This ongoing imbalance in civil-military power and resources, while not a direct challenge to democracy assistance strategies, does present an image of U.S. military power at the expense of civilian capacities. One way to redress this imbalance is to ramp up resources for the State Department and other civilian agencies of the U.S. government. The Obama administration's budget proposals, with the support of Secretary of Defense Robert Gates, adopts just such a course by seeking to expand diplomatic and development resources, even if it means reducing the Defense Department's budget. A much stronger National Security Council is also needed to exert some discipline and pressure on the relevant national security agencies to rebalance the tools of U.S. power in the region so that the main challenges of the hemisphere—poverty, inequality, and crime—are addressed through direct economic, trade, and social aid delivered through civilian, not military, agencies.

Strengthen the OAS and Its Inter-American Democratic Charter

At least on paper, the OAS and the associated Inter-American Court and Commission on Human Rights by and large have what is needed to play a vital role in strengthening democracy and the rule of law in the region. Indeed, member states of the OAS have made some progress over the years toward constructing a set of principles and practices that have made concrete contributions toward stabilizing democratic crises, monitoring elections, and addressing systemic violations of human rights. What is missing from this picture is the political will and financial resources from the member states to give the OAS the capacity to protect democratic norms in the region before and as crises erupt. This was amply demonstrated during the constitutional crisis in Honduras when the OAS proved incapable both of averting the coup and of negotiating a resolution. Instead, the organization has become bogged down in confrontation and stalemate between Venezuela, Bolivia, and Nicaragua, on the one hand, and the United States, on the other.

Brazil has stepped in to the fill the vacuum left by this lack of consensus in the OAS by launching its own initiative to create the Union of South American Nations (UNASUR), a new forum that excludes the United States. UNASUR, which played an important role in defusing an impending civil conflict between opposing sides in Bolivia in October 2008, now has a charter that upholds democracy and human rights as an "essential condition" for the development and integration of the region.[18] Yet it has no mechanism for operationalizing this vague objective.

The future direction of UNASUR is opaque. It could evolve to become a competitor to the OAS with an ascendant Brazil determined to sideline Washington in the affairs of its immediate neighbors. Or it could become a subregional actor working constructively alongside the OAS as it seeks to resolve tensions and mediate conflict. Which course is taken will largely be decided by Brazil's success in bringing other key players along. One could imagine a useful division-of-labor approach in which some localized subregional problems such as migration or other cross-border disputes are handled by the immediate players involved, while issues that affect the entire hemisphere, such as drug control or respect for democracy and human rights, are the lead province of the OAS. On a parallel track, Mexico is breathing new life into an expanded version of the Rio Group as the premier political body encompassing Latin America and the Caribbean (including Cuba) while excluding the United States and Canada. Regardless of UNASUR's and the Rio Group's future trajectory, the ability of the OAS to play a leadership role in the political affairs of the hemisphere depends to a large extent on the Obama administration's relationship with Brazil as well as Brazil's ability and willingness to rein in Venezuela and its allies.

In the wake of the controversy over Honduras, it is even more important that the OAS and its Inter-American Democratic Charter receive an infusion of new commitment and consensus building to function well as diplomatic tools for democracy. Notably, the charter's provisions concerning responses to democratic crises require a member state to initiate a request for assistance, making it less likely to be invoked, as seen in the case of Honduras. In fact, these provisions have never been used, despite abundant opportunity to do so since the charter was adopted in 2001. The charter also limits the secretary general's power to take the initiative to investigate deterioration in democratic standards only to situations involving "an unconstitutional alteration of the constitutional regime." Yet many instances of democratic backsliding do not rise to this level, leaving the OAS member states impotent to act. Compounding this problem is the lack of a more assertive secretary general who could—but chooses not to—play a mediating role. One way to generate momentum for greater activism on the part of OAS states is to support the efforts of the Friends of the Inter-American Democratic Charter, a panel of prominent figures from throughout the hemisphere organized by the Carter Center to serve an unofficial monitoring and advisory role for the secretary general and aimed at preventing tense situations from erupting into conflict.[19]

Support South-South Cooperation through the Community of Democracies

The sheer diversity of democratic systems emerging throughout the region and the world demands a different, more varied approach to supporting democratization, particularly by the new or restored democracies themselves.[20] The Community of Democracies, a multilateral forum created in 2000 by the United States, Poland, Chile, and several other countries, is the only global forum devoted to mutual cooperation to support the consolidation of democratic governance. Under its auspices, the OAS and the African Union have begun working together on joint election observation activities and learning from each other's human rights system. This is the kind of work that should continue and be expanded to other thematic and geographic areas. It creates habits of cooperation on democracy issues at the regional and cross-regional levels and with time will help build an international architecture for like-minded states to reinforce and sustain the democratic wave into the twenty-first century.

A related area that deserves support from the Obama administration is cooperation on human rights issues at the United Nations and its new Human Rights Council, established in 2006. Under the Bush administration, the United States grew increasingly hostile and disengaged from the UN's principal forum for human rights, as evidenced by its vote against creation of the council and its decision not to run for a seat. At the same time, Latin American governments, with the main exception of Cuba, Nicaragua, and Venezuela, have constituted an important bloc of votes in favor of a stronger council. The Obama administration has followed through its commitment to reengage at the United Nations by winning a seat on the council and building cross-regional coalitions in some cases. The State Department should continue this approach and reach out to Chile, Argentina, Brazil, and other council members to find common ground for partnering with them on a positive human rights agenda for the council.

Development Tools for Democracy Assistance

The positive relationship between democratic governance and development is well documented and increasingly incorporated into mainstream development assistance programming at some donor institutions.[21] For example, the UN Development Program gives nearly 40 percent of its development assistance, $1.4 billion annually, to strengthening democratic governance and institution building as a way to improve state capacity to deliver public services and manage revenue effectively.[22] Canada also has made democracy assistance a priority, contributing 16 percent of its total aid budget—$473.7 million U.S. dollars—to democratic governance programs in 2009.[23] The United States, on the other hand, allotted only 9.2 percent ($1.75 billion) of its $18.9 billion 2009 foreign assistance budget to democratic governance programs, the goals of which include rule of law and human rights, good governance, political competition and consensus building, and support to civil society.[24]

The Obama administration, unfortunately, has inherited a fiscal disaster of historical proportions and may have to cut foreign aid programs in the future as part of a government-wide effort to rein in the deficit. In its first budget presentation to Congress, covering fiscal 2011, funding for the Latin America and Caribbean regions was cut more than 10 percent, after a period of increased assistance during the Bush administration. In 2004 it created the MCA, for example, as a special incentives fund to reward low-income states having good governance records with major infusions of grants to support infrastructure and other projects identified by the receiving government.[25] Most of the countries of the Latin America and Caribbean regions, however, are not eligible for the fund because they have graduated out of the low-income category. Those that are eligible—Honduras, El Salvador, and, as of December 2008, Colombia—are at various stages of the complex process of qualifying for the money.[26] In July 2009 the Millennium Challenge Corporation (MCC) terminated funding for Nicaragua in response to flawed municipal elections, described as part of "a pattern of actions by the Government that were inconsistent with the [democracy] criteria used by the MCC to determine eligibility for assistance."[27] Paraguay, Peru, and Guyana must still meet threshold requirements regarding anti-corruption and the rule of law and receive some $107 million in targeted funding to help them become fully eligible.

The MCA program, while theoretically sound, is often criticized for its slow implementation, but it deserves continued support because it requires states to adhere to basic principles of civil and political rights, anti-corruption, sound fiscal policy, and basic social welfare in order to receive funding. MCC's cancellation of Nicaragua's compact is an important demonstration of meaningful enforcement of this conditionality.

Regardless of the levels of funding for democratic governance, the United States needs to ramp up its investment in multilateral mechanisms of democracy assistance. Unfortunately, its tools are inadequate and insufficient as it prefers to conduct most of its democracy assistance bilaterally, through the U.S. Agency for International Development (USAID), the Human Rights Democracy Fund of the State Department, and the National Endowment for Democracy and its four institutes.[28]

Over the past decade, funding for the Human Rights Democracy Fund, administered by the State Department's Bureau for Democracy, Human Rights, and Labor (DRL), has grown significantly, from a mere $7.82 million in 1998 to $79 million in fiscal 2009 (this fund spiked as high as $317 million in fiscal 2007 to support state-building and democracy programs in Iraq).[29] The program's supporters in the State Department say that the increased funding has strengthened the bureau's voice in the department's internal policy debates. Giving the State Department money to run democracy programs runs the risk, however, of politicizing what should be, to the extent possible, a nonpolitical foreign assistance endeavor, because it gives political appointees and diplomats greater power to deploy democracy aid dollars in a way that supports short-term policy goals. For example, DRL funds have been directed quickly to civil society organizations in countries like Venezuela or Bolivia, but this approach has sparked controversy in the region, with critics charging that the United States is funding groups that seek the overthrow of a democratically elected government. This method of delivering democracy assistance further feeds the perception that the United States promotes democracy on its own terms and bankrolls efforts to unseat those it does not like.

At the same time, it is essential that the United States continue to support sectors of civil society and the independent media that are, by their nature, critical of any government in power. These groups are the lifeblood of a well-functioning democracy because they ensure the kind of horizontal accountability needed to check abuses of power between elections and provide voters with independent analysis during an electoral period. Receiving official assistance from the U.S. government, however, particularly under rules that require recipients to display the USAID logo on all their materials, makes them vulnerable to charges of being agents of a foreign government. This approach has been particularly troublesome in closed societies such as Cuba and Iran, in which dissident groups advocating for political reforms have received support via special congressional appropriations. Several advocates genuinely committed to democracy and human rights in those countries have refused Washington's money out of fear of being harassed and imprisoned by a hostile government. This is no way to carry out a democracy assistance strategy.

The answer to this dilemma has two parts. First, the Obama administration should ask Congress to make the National Endowment for Democracy (NED) the primary channel of democracy assistance grants to civil society. An independent nonprofit organization that has enjoyed bipartisan support from its birth in the Reagan era, the NED is a relatively small and nimble grant-making entity whose mission is to sustain large and small civil society groups of democracy and human rights advocates around the world. Its work in building the World Movement for Democracy as a global network of civil society activists to share lessons learned and to build solidarity as a transnational voice for democracy and human rights is also important and should continue. The money currently sitting in the State Department's Democracy and Human Rights fund for direct grants to civil society groups should be moved to NED as a way to help depoliticize U.S. government support for democracy. Democracy funds directed to government and quasi-government entities, on the other hand, should continue to be channeled through official State Department and USAID offices. The DRL bureau can then refocus its energies on the challenging diplomatic work needed to strengthen multilateral mechanisms and coalitions for democracy and human rights.

The second answer is to multilateralize U.S. government funding for democracy assistance wherever possible. President Bush succeeded in doing this when he proposed, in 2004, the creation of a United Nations Democracy Fund (UNDEF). With the early support of India, Australia, and the Community of Democracies, this voluntary fund supports democracy-building initiatives mainly implemented by civil society groups around the world. Since its establishment in 2005, UNDEF has received donations and pledges totaling more than $110 million from a wide range of countries, including India ($20 million), the United States ($33 million), and Japan ($10 million), with smaller donations from countries like Senegal, Romania, Panama, Chile, and Peru. These funds are nearly all dedicated to supporting local and regional nongovernmental organizations, as opposed to government bureaucracies or consulting firms. As noted earlier, the image of the United Nations in Latin America certainly surpasses that of the United States; furthermore, the organization has the legitimacy to be a credible defender of the universal nature of democratic and human rights principles and now has a proven track record that it can spend the money appropriately. Whereas the United States is only one of several voices on the UNDEF governing board (albeit one of great weight), the benefit of working with such a diverse array of partners outweighs the cost of losing some influence in deciding who should receive grant awards. Congress should continue regular and substantial funding for this account.

The UNDEF experience can serve as a model for U.S. democracy assistance funding in Latin America and the Caribbean region. An inter-American democracy fund, housed at the OAS and funded by the United States, Canada, the European Union, its member states, and, most important, some countries from Latin America, would be a regional vehicle to address regional problems. It could focus not only on supporting civil society monitoring and participation in public policy debates but also on development of independent media, legal reform, political party representation, and civic education. It would be a concrete, practical manifestation of the region's commitment to the principles of the Inter-American Democratic Charter and avoid the "regime change" taint associated with past U.S. government funding. It could also provide a source of funds for the Friends of the Inter-American Democratic Charter group, which could be an independent voice in the monitoring of hemispheric standards.

Another way for the United States to multilateralize its democracy assistance is to team up more deliberately with other major donors working in the region. For starters, U.S. diplomatic and foreign aid officials should meet regularly with counterparts from Canada, Europe, and Japan to work out a common needs assessment based on MCC standards, followed by some joint funding projects or vehicles, particularly in countries in greatest need of support. A pooling of funds in one account would save enormous time, especially on the part of recipient countries that spend hours and hours of time fulfilling the myriad and distinct requirements of each donor. What is needed is a complementary multilateral mechanism that will demonstrate to both donor and recipient states the efficiencies and impact of a coordinated approach. This would entail a loosening of the traditional preference for bilateral aid and of the influence that goes with it. A new multilateral window of financing, professionally administered through an intergovernmental or quasi-independent agency, should also be available to handle the more delicate task of political and good governance reforms.

One multilateral tool the United States should consider supporting is the International Institute for Democracy and Electoral Assistance (International IDEA), an intergovernmental organization created in 1995 on the initiative of the Swedish government. International IDEA, which has offices in Costa Rica, Bolivia, Peru, Colombia, and Ecuador, counts among its twenty-five members a diverse range of older and newer democracies worldwide (in this region Barbados, Canada, Chile, Costa Rica, Mexico, Peru, and Uruguay are full members), and Japan is an observer. It provides knowledge resources, offers platforms for debate on democratic development policy issues, and assists in democratic reform processes, drawing on the comparative experience of its members. While U.S. membership in IDEA may not suit the organization's preference for avoiding big-power entanglements, Washington could nonetheless seek to become an observer state or provide direct grants to the organization.

Conclusion

President Obama and his advisers have a special moment of opportunity to advance democracy and human rights in Latin America and the Caribbean region through old and new multilateral mechanisms. Seizing this opportunity will require not only making fullest use of these mechanisms but also bringing a new, more positive attitude toward collaborative partnerships that depart from top-down, unilateral prescriptions. It will also demand a greater willingness on the part of the U.S. Congress and Latin American partners to devote political will and financial resources to the task. As Latin American countries celebrate their bicentennials of independence, the United States should embrace our shared heritage as democratic societies by supporting new multilateral projects for building accountable, transparent, and participatory governance.

Notes

1. Barack Obama, "A Just and Lasting Peace," Nobel Lecture, Oslo, Norway, December 10, 2009 (http://nobelprize.org/nobel_prizes/peace/laureates/2009/obama-lecture_en.html); Hillary Clinton, "Human Rights Agenda for the 21st Century," speech delivered at Georgetown University, December 14, 2009 (www.state.gov/secretary/rm/2009a/12/133544.htm).

2. Consorcio Iberoamericano de Investigaciones de Mercados y Asesoramiento (Iberian American Consortium for Investigating Markets and Consultation, CIMA), *Barómetro Iberoamericano de Gobernabilidad 2009* (Bogotá: Centro Nacional de Consultoría, 2009), p. 11 (www.cimaiberoamerica.com/).

3. Corporación Latinobarómetro, *Informe Latinobarómetro* (Santiago, Chile, 2009), p. 34 (www.latinobarometro.org/docs/INFORME_LATINOBAROMETRO_2008.pdf).

4. Pew Global Attitudes Project, "Confidence in Obama Lifts U.S. Image around the World" (July 23, 2009), p. 36 (http://pewglobal.org/reports/display.php?ReportID=264).

5. Informe Latinobarómetro poll (Santiago: Latinobarómetro Corporation, 2008), p. 108 (see also www.latinobarometro.org).

6. CIMA, *Barómetro Iberoamericano de Gobernabilidad 2008* (Bogotá: Centro Nacional de Consultoría, 2008), p. 29. For more information, see www.cimaiberoamerica.com/.

7. "A Slow Maturing of Democracy," *The Economist*, December 10, 2009. The text states: "More respondents see Brazil as the most influential country in the region, ahead of the United States and Venezuela. But the influence of the United States is ranked higher than Brazil's in the northern part of the region."

8. CIMA, *Barómetro Iberoamericano de Gobernabilidad 2009*, pp. 21–29. For more information, see www.cimaiberoamerica.com/.

9. A useful tool for training diplomats is "A Diplomat's Handbook for Democracy Development Support," a publication launched under the auspices of the Community of Democracies (www.diplomatshandbook.org).

10. President Barack Obama, remarks at the Summit of the Americas Opening Ceremony, Port of Spain, Trinidad and Tobago, April 17, 2009 (www.whitehouse. gov/the_press_office/Remarks-by-the-President-at-the-Summit-of-the-Americas-Opening-Ceremony).

11. Senator Barack Obama, "Renewing U.S. Leadership in the Americas," Miami, Florida, May 23, 2008 (www.barackobama.com/2008/05/23/remarks_of_senator_barack_obama_68.php).

12. Two examples of this approach were the Defense Ministerial of the Americas, launched by Secretary of Defense William Perry in 1995 as a way to make civilian defense ministers the primary policymaking actors in the defense arena, and the Center for Hemispheric Defense Studies, created in 1997 to provide defense management and policy skills mainly to civilian students.

13. Latin American Working Group Educational Fund, Center for International Policy, and the Washington Office on Latin America, "Below the Radar: U.S. Military Programs with Latin America, 1997–2007," March 2007 (http://justf.org/files/pubs/below_the_radar_eng.pdf). In the 1990s U.S. military and police aid was less than half of economic and development assistance to Latin America. For full data on U.S. spending and further information, see http://justf.org/Aid.

14. For more information, see U.S. Department of State, "The Merida Initiative" (www.state.gov/p/inl/rls/fs/122395.htm). For a breakdown of the figures and further explanation, see Congressional Research Service, "Merida Initiative for Mexico and Central America: Funding and Policy Issues," Report R40135 (Washington, January 21, 2010) (http://assets.opencrs.com/rpts/R40135_20100121.pdf).

15. For more information on U.S. spending in Latin America, see: http://justf. org/Aid.

16. For more information on the SOUTHCOM Partnering Directorate, see www. southcom.mil/AppsSC/pages/staff.php?id=32&flag=1.

17. See www.southcom.mil/AppsSC/factFiles.php?id=138.

18. The Constitutive Treaty of UNASUR, signed May 23, 2008, states in its preamble that South American integration and union "are based on the guiding principles of unlimited respect for sovereignty . . . democracy, citizen participation, universal, interdependent, and indivisible human rights," among others (www.mre.gov.br/portugues/imprensa/nota_detalhe3.asp?ID_RELEASE=5466).

19. For further information, see the Carter Center, "Americas Program" (www. cartercenter.org/peace/americas/friends.html).

20. For a study on how democratic governments address democracy and human rights in their foreign policies, see Robert Herman and Theodore Piccone, *Defending Democracy: A Global Survey of Foreign Policy Trends, 1992–2002* (Washington: Democracy Coalition Project, October 2002).

21. See, for example, Morton H. Halperin, Joseph T. Siegle, and Michael M. Weinstein, *The Democracy Advantage: How Democracies Promote Prosperity and Peace* (New York: Routledge, 2005).

22. UN Development Program, *Annual Report 2009* (New York, 2009), p. 6 (www.undp.org/publications/annualreport2009/pdf/EN_FINAL.pdf).

23. Canadian International Development Agency, *Departmental Performance Report 2008–2009* (Ottawa), pp. 38– 39. For more information, see www.tbs-sct.gc.ca/dpr-rmr/2008-2009/inst/ida/ida-eng.pdf.

24. U.S. Agency for International Development, *Fiscal Year 2009 Agency Financial Report*, pp. 18–19 (www.usaid.gov/policy/afr09/USAIDFY2009AFR.pdf).

25. MCC applies a set of seventeen indicators to determine which countries are eligible for assistance. For countries that do not score high enough on these indicators, threshold programs are available to help them improve their performance so that they can become eligible for an MCC grant later on. Paraguay and Guyana were selected as threshold countries in 2005 and Peru in 2007.

26. Bolivia became eligible for an MCA grant in 2004, but its eligibility was canceled in December 2008. El Salvador, Honduras, and Nicaragua have either signed or already implemented their contracts. Millennium Challenge Corporation, "Compact Development Status Report, Bolivia: Update on Progress" (www.mcc.gov/documents/qsr-dev-bolivia.pdf).

27. See www.mcc.gov/mcc/countries/nicaragua/index.shtml.

28. The International Republican Institute, the National Democratic Institute for International Affairs, the AFL-CIO Solidarity Center, and the Center for International Private Enterprise affiliated with the U.S. Chamber of Commerce.

29. See U.S. Department of State, "DRL Programs, Including Human Rights Democracy Fund (HRDF)" (www.state.gov/g/drl/p/index.htm); see also Freedom House, "Making Its Mark: An Analysis of the Obama Administration's FY2010 Budget Request for Democracy and Human Rights," Special Report (Washington, July 1, 2009) (www.freedomhouse.org/uploads/FY2010BudgetAnalysis.pdf).

eleven

Obama and the Americas: Old Hopes, New Risks

Laurence Whitehead

In chapter 1, Abraham Lowenthal provides a judicious overview of the hopes for change in the Americas raised by the advent of the Obama administration in January 2009, despite the complexities of internal bureaucratic politics that hedge in U.S. leadership. He gives four good reasons for keeping alive modest but positive expectations: the importance of Latin America for U.S. policymakers; the existence of a well-grounded set of understandings and agreements among most U.S. analysts, think tanks, and policy experts; an enhanced capacity to discriminate between countries and issues; and a consequent awareness of the need to avoid overreacting to specific local crises.

Old Hopes

As chapter 1 also makes clear, many of those supporting Barack Obama expected that he would act vigorously to repair the damage that his predecessor inflicted on the international standing of the United States. At the time of Obama's inauguration, Latin America offered good opportunities for such demonstrative repositioning. Some fear that the best opportunity for a fresh start may already have been missed, and that the relatively strong continuities observable between late Bush Junior and early Obama foreshadow a deeper inertia. This could generate disappointment and even distrust.

President Obama's initial region-wide popularity put the minority of "anti-Washington" governments of Latin America in a defensive position. They might have liked nothing better than to assert that "nothing has changed," that behind the friendlier façade the United States is still pursuing the same old interests and unilateral practices. The Colombian bases issue and the Honduran constitutional interruption provided grist to that mill. On this view, if there is no overarching policy framework with high visibility executive leadership and support to reshape hemispheric relations, there may be policy fragmentation, a reactive management of crises, and a loss of momentum necessary for cumulative progress. And if U.S. allies develop the impression that Washington lacks a consistent long-term strategy and that they are mostly on their own, it may become difficult to sustain multilateral cooperation and goodwill.

A year and a half into Obama's first term both assessments seem equally plausible: there is still scope for the administration's new team of Latin American officeholders (finally confirmed after a year's delay) to take charge and actively promote the first, more positive, alternative; but it is also possible to detect the early stages of what could grow into a larger estrangement between Washington and its many hemispheric neighbors.

This volume concludes somewhat on the more positive side, in the belief that the Western Hemisphere remains a favorable neighborhood for a repositioned United States and may even provide a relatively "easy" opportunity for it to regain international credibility. But ensuring this requires more innovative thinking, sustained attention, a willingness on the part of the United States to treat its regional partners as equals, and more systematic consultation with them on how best to deal with the challenges the hemisphere faces. This in turn calls for well-prepared and intelligently designed proactive rather than reactive policies, and the ability to differentiate countries and issues, avoiding the old us-versus-them logic that colored the Axis of Evil and War on Terror perspectives.

Early on in the new administration several unforeseen developments created difficulties that—perhaps for very understandable reasons—were not as well handled as they might have been. The Colombia bases agreement and the Honduran constitutional standoff initially caught the administration off balance and highlighted some disconnect between presidential rhetoric and practical performance. One can imagine the ferocity of external and domestic criticisms had the same policy responses been adopted by the Bush administration. This thought puts in focus both the degree of goodwill initially generated by the change of president and the extent to which that fund of goodwill was drawn on during the first eighteen months of Obama's tenure. Other challenging issues foreseeable in the near future include a possible intensification of regional tensions around various "intermestic" issues such as immigration policy and drug trafficking (issues concerning, but by no means confined to, Mexico) and perhaps also frictions with Brazil on various international issues, notably with regard to sanctions against Iran. Five regional snapshots will amply illustrate the diverse challenges involved.

Cuba

The Obama administration inherited long-standing policies ostensibly directed toward promoting a democratic transition in a post-Castro Cuba, which were codified by the U.S. Congress with the 1996 Helms-Burton Law and 2000 Cuban Democracy Act. The prior administration had tightened bilateral sanctions further and appointed a State Department "transition" coordinator. But that was before Fidel Castro's illness, and the smooth transfer of power to his brother.

January 2009 marked the fiftieth anniversary of the Cuban Revolution. It is now generally believed (even among Cuban Americans) that unilateral U.S. sanctions have failed to encourage democratization in Cuba. A multilateral soft-power approach is more likely to help Cubans liberalize and eventually democratize. Listening to the pro-engagement views of Washington's democratic partners (Canada and the European Union, as well as Brazil and Mexico) would also boost U.S. credibility in the region and beyond.

Despite a mildly positive beginning, the ancient standoff between Havana and Washington remains essentially unchanged, as detailed by Dan Erikson in chapter 7. President Obama lifted some Bush-era restrictions on travel and remittances by Cuban Americans, authorized new U.S. investments in telecommunications in Cuba, and began negotiations to restore normal postal communications. But the travel ban on normal U.S. visits to the island remains in place, and licenses for specialized categories of travel continue in short supply. And on the Cuban side, the Castro brothers remain unbending in their commitment to an inflexible and besieged "revolutionary" model. By April 2010 mutual recriminations reached a new peak as the regime clamped down in reaction to economic distress, international censure, and domestic protest by the opposition group known as Damas de Blanco.

From a Latin American perspective, this relapse could be viewed as a missed opportunity. Obama probably did not wish to pay a domestic political price for being more open-handed toward Cuba, and a bipartisan group in Congress has blocked legislation to liberalize trade and travel. But his advisers may have underestimated the external political capital to be gained from making a clean break with Washington's unilateralist past on this front.

Any early bold initiative would have been more likely to produce a worthwhile response in Havana than would comparable gestures toward Moscow and Tehran. And if at the outset the Cuban leadership had failed to respond to a clearly innovative overture, it might have lost its international status as a "David" and faced incomprehension from its own people and regionally.

In the event, the Cuban regime still enjoys a significant degree of legitimacy within the United Nations, where U.S. unilateral sanctions are repeatedly condemned by an overwhelming majority. Even in the Organization of American States (OAS), the June 2009 meeting manifested a united disposition to readmit the Cubans (not that Havana shows any inclination to return). Such supportive international and regional responses are also based on the hope that persuasion may elicit a better response than U.S. intimidation. Furthermore, although the human rights record of the regime is negative, Cuba has a clear record of compliance with its international obligations on migration and narcotics, at least since the end of the cold war.

The U.S.-run detainee camp at the Guantánamo Bay Naval Base, a legal black hole of key concern to the international community, is one recent factor explaining why Washington's long-standing condemnation of the regime has lacked regional and international resonance. The Obama administration stated its intention to close the detention facility, in apparent recognition of the fact that maintaining it undermines Washington's credibility as a defender of the rule of law and promoter of democracy. However, this promise remains disappointingly unfulfilled.

In mid-2010 Cuba certainly still presents Obama with the same old policy dilemma: the Cuban Communist Party seems likely to remain in a dominant position for the indefinite future, and it is not a "reform communist" institution that can evolve into one among various electoral contenders. The harsh treatment meted out to peaceful dissidents was dramatized in February 2010 with the death in custody after a long hunger strike of Orlando Zapata, an Amnesty International prisoner of conscience. This was the worst incident since 1972, and once again it left Washington posturing on the sidelines, while the Vatican and the Catholic Church, for example, proved capable of more constructive mediation.

On a longer view, there remains scope for the new administration to work with allies in the hemisphere and beyond to give Havana further incentives to liberalize. Cooperation with the European Union could be fruitful. EU member states have been divided between punitive action and a "critical dialogue" with Cuba, as supported by Spain in particular, but the European Commission reached a new cooperation agreement with Havana in October

2008. A trilateral dialogue between the United States, the European Union, and Latin America on how to approach the Cuba issue could establish shared responsibility to carefully nurture liberalization and even democratization tendencies within Cuba. But President Obama declined Spain's invitation to the most recent EU-Latin America summit in Madrid. Washington remains unimaginative and unconstructive on this issue. It still enforces unilateral sanctions that aggravate the bad economic situation on the island, not only causing great suffering to ordinary Cubans but also providing the regime with an easy alibi for its failings.

Haiti

In 2004 President Jean-Bertrand Aristide, who had been democratically elected but had lost domestic and international political legitimacy, was forced from office. An interim government invited the United Nations to send a "stabilization mission," which the Security Council charged with demobilizing armed groups, restructuring and reforming the Haitian police, and fostering institutional development, national dialogue, and reconciliation.

Six years after the deployment of multinational forces by the United Nations Stabilization Mission in Haiti (MINUSTAH), there was still no agreed date for its withdrawal, and its mandate was being renewed on a short-term basis. This was apparently a minor priority on the Washington scale of foreign policy concerns, notwithstanding the deep historic U.S. involvement in Haitian affairs. Then in January 2010 the main urban center of the republic was completely devastated by an earthquake of exceptional severity. The death toll has exceeded 230,000, or 2½ percent of the total population, and much of the country's precarious physical infrastructure, the economy, and public administration has virtually collapsed.

This overwhelming natural disaster makes a compelling case for a fresh start. Haiti in 2010 is a laboratory of "state failure" unrelated to conflict or a security threat, if there ever was one: it provides the international community with a unique opportunity to demonstrate how well it can discharge its commitment to humanitarian assistance and reconstruction. If the Obama administration could establish common ground with the rest of the international community to promote reconstruction and economic recovery with a focus on social goals, this would set a significant regional and international example of the new approach it has promised.

In the immediate aftermath of the disaster, all attention focused on the most urgent relief operations, with 13,000 U.S. Marines controlling the airport and port. In practice, this meant they were overseeing the international community's humanitarian response (although in principle this remains a UN-directed responsibility, to be carried out in concordance with what is left of the Haitian government). Secretary of State Hillary Clinton called for the convening of (overdue) congressional elections in order to reestablish a legitimate Haitian counterpart that the international community can work with, but the cost, duration, and mandate of the prospective UN reconstruction effort remain highly opaque.

Failure to cope with the reconstruction challenges would return to haunt the Obama administration, since U.S. involvement is so central. Thus it is a major U.S. interest this time, in contrast to earlier episodes of international suspension of Haitian sovereignty, that a coherent, coordinated, and long-term strategy for national recovery be accomplished. This implies a sustained and effective multilateral commitment (much of the financial support is likely to come from the European Union and the rest of the Americas, including Canada, rather than just the United States). It also requires the participation of a substantial cohort of educated and locally embedded reconstruction workers.

The Haitian diasporas in Canada, the United States, and the Caribbean may well be the best places to provide much of this human response, but tapping their potential calls for a far-reaching reversal of current aid practices that tend to marginalize them. (At the time of writing, Washington is reportedly hesitating over whether to grant temporary protected status to 55,000 Haitian immigrants, many of whom could be helped to contribute financial and human resources to national reconstruction).

If Washington wants to demonstrate that it knows how to help rectify state failure elsewhere, then this is a prime site to show what it can do. Like other failed states, at the very least Haiti needs a generational commitment to reform, the results of which will take years to become visible. Large amounts of resources have already been channeled in this direction, with former president Bill Clinton taking on a personal role as Obama's special envoy, and with the secretary of state providing top-level direction to Washington's Haiti strategy, but a very long-term and multilateral approach will be needed if the legacy of past failures is to be overcome. Beyond immediate disaster relief, the sovereignty of the Haitian nation and the viability of its economy both require the creation of solid institutions, not just courts and police forces, but the kind of educational facilities that will allow Haiti's youngest citizens to develop the capabilities their country needs. This humanitarian tragedy is not easy to fit into any overarching U.S. foreign policy narrative, but there is a lot of moral capital at stake in how well the Obama administration responds to it over the longer run.

The ALBA Challenge

Aggressive high rhetoric and conflict with Hugo Chávez became a staple feature of relations between the United States and Latin America under the Bush administration. The election of President Obama led Chávez at first to tone down his attacks on the United States, but Venezuela's efforts to win over new state allies have persisted, and the persuasive powers of a discourse of "anti-imperialism" and "social justice" are yet to be exhausted.

Many, especially in the United States, have concluded that Venezuela's current populist nationalism presents the gravest threat to democracy in the hemisphere. But in a region where democracy has been accompanied by enduring social and political exclusion and vulnerability to the global financial economy, support for this variant of populism also reflects the failures of the Washington Consensus model. The appeal of the Bolivarian Alternative for the Americas (ALBA) derives not so much from ideological persuasiveness or from the belief that it represents a true "alternative" as it does from its attention to those excluded from enjoying true democratic rights and economic benefits, and from the sense that the United States treats its southern neighbors not as equals but rather with disrespect and double standards.

The best U.S. response to such sentiments is to proffer to the region's governments and citizens a convincing message about Washington's enduring interest in democracy and development, and concerted and coherent policies to match. It is particularly important that the United States assist the smaller, weaker, and more impoverished states that are tempted to join ALBA because of the economic benefits it extends in exchange for a willingness to play the "anti-imperialist" card. It is now generally agreed that the decades-long embargo against Cuba did more to strengthen the Castro regime—providing it with the legitimacy that comes from resisting external hostility—than to weaken it. In much the same way, the ALBA alternative is more likely to become just that—an alternative—to the degree that Washington reacts to crises in the region with a divisive and intrusive unilateral policy.

Alone, ALBA countries can perhaps do little, but as the issues of climate change and Iran sanctions illustrate, they may sometimes secure a broader hearing. Indeed, if the ALBA group concludes that confrontation with Washington is the best card to play, its collective recalcitrance may hamper future negotiations on a variety of issues of vital interest to the United States.

The Copenhagen summit of December 2009 provides one illustration of how neglected regional tensions can stand in the way of Washington's global goals. The summit accord was generally regarded as a disappointment, if not a marked failure for the environment and international cooperation in addressing shared problems, two priorities of the Obama administration. Among the six countries rejecting even the watered-down accord were three ALBA countries—Bolivia, Cuba, and Venezuela—and they did so on the grounds that President Obama had hijacked the negotiations and shifted the burden of adjustment to the developing world.

Climate change is not the only issue on which ALBA could gain a wider hearing within Latin America and beyond. Health care and popular education are also strong suits for them. The Obama administration would be ill advised to continue us-versus-them tactics that mainly serve to cement their solidarity. Each member of that group has its own separate interests and grievances: on some issues they may be implacable and united, but on others they may be divided. Thus a more creative regional strategy might secure their neutrality or even partial cooperation. Washington has begun showing signs of a more sophisticated approach. It should handle this group by seeking common ground where possible and dealing with each challenge on its merits. There is much to be gained by a friendlier approach. These countries could contribute to an effective regional capacity for disaster relief (in the face of episodes such as the Chilean and Haitian earthquakes; Cuba has 1,600 health care workers on the ground in Haiti, for example, many of them of Haitian origin). Other environmental and developmental issues could be productively tackled in the same spirit. Similar considerations might even apply to counternarcotics operations and if so might eventually extend as far as some counterinsurgency issues.

On questions such as international arbitration over investment disputes or guarantees of free speech and media freedom, however, Washington will probably have no choice but to oppose the group's ideas and practices. The Chávez regime, in particular, seems set on a course of both political and economic radicalization that is only likely to produce more conflict and distrust, without much prospect of reaching any stable settlement. In this respect, Venezuela is more problematic than, say, Bolivia or Ecuador. But the hardest and potentially most dangerous sources of disagreement concern ALBA's strong opposition to U.S. "interventionism" in the region and Washington's interpretation of regional security imperatives. This is where clashes between Caracas and Washington are hardest to reconcile.

Jorge Castañeda, Mexico's former foreign secretary, has argued that what Latin American radicals want from Obama is not so much "respect" as "repentance," and he therefore advocates escalation against the pretentions of ALBA. But a cool assessment suggests that outright confrontation is far from inevitable. By working with the grain of opinion in the region, the Obama administration still has scope to shift the profile of the U.S. presence in Haiti, Colombia, Mexico, and elsewhere toward more emphasis on multilateral cooperation and the solution of problems through political agreement, downplaying the unilateral and military features that have figured so prominently in recent years. The rapid drawdown of the U.S. military presence in Haiti is illustrative here. Although Bolivia will never countenance the return of the Drug Enforcement Administration (DEA), that does not preclude different sources of international cooperation to combat illegal narcotics gangs, perhaps led by the UN Office on Drugs and Crime (UNODC). While a sovereign Venezuela has every right to obtain its armaments from whatever legitimate source it deems convenient, its neighbors have the same right to demand its nonintervention in their internal affairs. And finally, even Cuba should be recognized as a state that can be asked to honor its international commitments, and that has provided a considerable margin of stability and even security to the United States in its Caribbean seaways and airspace.

Plan Colombia

The Obama administration seems to have been caught by surprise by the criticism of its decision to negotiate a further ten-year bilateral agreement, which includes U.S. military access to seven Colombian bases to combat drugs and domestic insurgency. Most of the impetus for these negotiations came from the U.S. Defense Department's Southern Command, and it appears that the administration did not prepare an adequate diplomatic strategy to deal with the foreseeable regional backlash.[1]

News of the agreement, in August 2009, provided Venezuela's President Chávez with the perfect explanation for his already agreed program of overseas military procurement. It caused unnecessary embarrassment for Brazil—the Obama administration's best prospect for a reliable South American partnership—which had just taken the lead in creating the Union of South American Nations (UNASUR), a regional alliance of democratically elected governments charged precisely with handling such issues on a multilateral basis. Many South American commentators felt that this highlighted once more Washington's overreliance on bilateralism to the detriment of mutually respectful dialogue with key regional democratic partners. Although Plan Colombia has built up and professionalized the Colombian armed forces over the past decade, it has also destabilized the balance of power in the northern Andes, helping to precipitate an arms race with the Venezuelans and provoking the Ecuadorian military into near confrontation with both Colombia and the United States.

The Dominican-led mediation between Colombia and Ecuador, like the Contadora Group experience in Central America in the 1980s, provides good examples of what more credible multilateral partnerships can achieve. A Contadora-style process would allow for the formulation of principles agreeable to all three states to trigger more specific commitments. Any such mutual support would have needed to build confidence between the competing parties, seeking out common ground on matters of controversy between them, promoting reconciliation, and identifying areas of consensus around the strengthening of democracy and the rule of law in this dangerously divided subregion. But that was not the course chosen by the Obama administration, at least in its first year, even though such an approach would have established a useful precedent for tackling regional tensions in other, more problematic contexts.

The furor surrounding the announcement of the U.S.–Colombian bases agreement and related rhetoric about a possible "arms race" in the northern Andes suggest a shift in a very different direction. It is hard to anticipate how far the current conflict might escalate.[2] But is there an alternative? As with Cuba, the initial hopes raised by Obama's election elicited some resistance from parts of the Latin American left, but the initiative lay with Washington. Now, by contrast, it could prove much easier for ALBA to revive latent anti-U.S. reflexes. A policy forged through consultation that emphasizes the benefits of peace and stability in Grancolombia as a whole would have recognized that whatever the benefits of a decade-long Plan Colombia, it has done little to curb drug trafficking from there, while so much emphasis on one bilateral military relationship has left many damaging humanitarian, socioeconomic, and diplomatic legacies. A more multilateral, broadly based, and democracy/development-oriented relationship with this subregion could have been launched to tackle those issues. Viewed from this perspective, the way Washington actually handled the Colombia bases can be seen as a missed opportunity.

On the brighter side, the issue may have been blown out of proportion and can perhaps be defused now that Obama's team is in office and President Alvaro Uribe has bowed to the ban on any further reelection. The smooth and legitimate process by which Uribe's successor was elected (in a two-round contest) sets a positive example for Colombia's neighbors to follow.

The Obama administration has guaranteed that U.S. military operations will be restricted to Colombian territory, and Secretary Clinton has reassured her South American counterparts that the extended U.S. presence in Colombia will not become a springboard for invasion or infiltration of third states. She has also sought improved relations with Ecuador, although President Rafael Correa remains adamant that any further military incursions into his territory will be met with force. So the setback of 2009 need not prove insurmountable, provided the right lessons are learned and followed. But sporadic or ad hoc responses would be insufficient to address the policy challenges that face Grancolombia, or indeed the Western Hemisphere as a whole.

Honduras

In response to initial criticisms of U.S. policy toward Honduras following the unconstitutional defenestration of elected President Manuel Zelaya, President Barack Obama commented on the "irony that the people that were complaining about the U.S. interfering in Latin America are now complaining that we aren't interfering enough."[3] From a White House standpoint, the sense of being "damned" both ways may seem a fair view of the erratic sequence of Washington's efforts to manage the Honduras crisis between June 2009 and January 2010. Those schooled in the long history of U.S. interventionism in Central America and the Caribbean will recognize the familiarity of this refrain, which also fits a series of earlier Honduran episodes, and indeed does much to explain why the "gunboat diplomacy" of the 1920s gave way to the Good Neighbor Policy of the 1930s. It is important to recognize that the perverse logic of the damned-both-ways interpretation has become entrenched only in a limited subset of small and vulnerable Latin America nations.[4] The United States is not invited by Latin American opinion to intervene anywhere in South America, or in Mexico, or indeed in Cuba or Venezuela.

Honduras constitutes an unusually clear case of a country in which past relations with the United States generate such expectations. It was widely regarded as essentially a platform for President Ronald Reagan's "contra" war against the Sandinistas in Nicaragua in the 1980s, and it came as a shock to Washington when the government of Honduras joined with its neighbors to support the Esquipulas formula to promote a local isthmian solution to that conflict.

Washington policymakers with insufficient time to attend to all the nuances of Latin American history, and with an urgent need to secure results acceptable to domestic U.S. opinion when a crisis blows up, may find the damned-both-ways interpretation a convenient shorthand. But, as Kevin Casas so clearly explains in chapter 8, the local history was crucial, and a better understanding of the background might have helped avert what was far from an inevitable setback. Even when U.S. ascendancy was at its height (as during the Alliance for Progress years), "damned both ways" was a dangerous oversimplification. In current conditions, it applies hardly anywhere in the hemisphere.

Admittedly, Honduras serves as an example of how hard it is to make "democracy-promoting" policy choices. Brazilian President Luiz Inácio Lula da Silva's position was that no quarter should be given to *golpistas*, as this would open an antidemocratic Pandora's Box; but Spain was also right to note that the new elections should be taken into account. In the end, it was a (reasonably) democratic election that brought the confrontation to an end, and a majority of the hemisphere's democratic leaders have since come round to accepting that provisional settlement, although incoming President Porfirio Lobo will remain a contested figure as long as Honduran promises of reconciliation remain unfulfilled. Old hopes that military interruptions would never again be tolerated in the Western Hemisphere have given way to new risks that, one small step at a time, may splinter and erode the region's recent constitutional democratic consensus.

For the United States, the benefits of a democratic neighborhood have been taken for granted and greatly underestimated. Historically, Latin America has not turned to authoritarianism without a corresponding international zeitgeist favoring such political solutions. But the Obama administration will need to work more closely with all its democratic partners, and will need to display more agility than was in evidence in the Honduran case, if it is to regain credibility as an effective friend of democratic stability in the Americas. But there is also scope to improve the functioning of the Organization of American States, and it would be unsatisfactory to try to shift the blame to the OAS for a weakness rooted in U.S. policies.

New Risks

There is broad agreement throughout the subcontinent that local conflicts need to be managed by local actors, and that while international mediation is acceptable, U.S. intervention is either unviable or likely to do more harm than good. Although many policymakers in Washington may view collective regional mediation efforts as ineffective, too slow, or even spineless, the days of "hegemonic presumption" are long since past.[5]

Remember, too, that the Obama administration is in a far less dominant position in the hemisphere than was the Clinton administration only one decade earlier. Even in the 1990s, when the Washington Consensus was at its peak and there seemed to be no alternative political or economic models for Latin America to consider, the regional "convergence" around a unified set of liberal principles was strained and partly artificial.[6] Since 2001 centrifugal forces have clearly outweighed centripetal ones. The Twin Towers atrocity was quickly followed by the Argentine institutional collapse and default of 2001–02, and by the failed coup against President Chávez. By 2003 both Chile and Mexico had declined to join President Bush's "coalition of the willing" in Iraq.

Shortly thereafter, the decade-long Miami Summit process to establish a Free Trade Area of the Americas was dealt a mortal blow with Congress's nonrenewal of the "fast-track" authority necessary for its ratification. With the (clearly democratic) elections of Evo Morales in Bolivia and of Rafael Correa in Ecuador, the Venezuelan-backed Bolivarian Alternative became a multinational initiative. Finally, the financial crisis of 2008 caused the United States to abandon domestic compliance with the core of the macroeconomic prescriptions it had for so long promoted south of the Rio Grande. As remittances from North America plummeted, an increasing range of Latin American elites came to view the emerging economies of Asia as an apparently successful alternative to the lopsided liberalizations they had undergone during the 1990s. At a deeper level, the recent crisis draws attention to an apparent global shift in economic and political power toward Asia.

By the time President Obama took office, the United States seemed to most outside observers to be falling well short of being the attractive model and projecting the confident image it had in the immediate post–cold war period. Some aspects of its leadership, notably the propensity to view international issues through a security lens, were far from attractive to public opinion in most of the region's democracies. Instead of an "end-of-history" Free Trade Area of the Americas (FTAA), it was now building a "fence" controlling illicit movements across its border with Mexico. Its closest partner in Latin America found itself implausibly characterized by the media as an incipiently "failed" state, and the promised reform of U.S. immigration law had been kicked into the long grass. It is worth stressing that if the most important bilateral relationship of the United States went sour, all the other issues that it faces in the hemisphere would be overshadowed. Furthermore, if that troubled bilateral link could be revived and placed on a more equal footing, the Obama administration would establish a precedent that would serve it well in relation to the rest of the region.

Small initial disappointments in Cuba, Haiti, and Honduras will no doubt pass, leaving no more than a modestly bad taste behind. But as the studies in this volume indicate, there are potentially bigger pitfalls ahead if the same approach is applied to future regional challenges that may emerge before the end of Obama's first term. As already noted, the tensions dividing ALBA and even Brazil from the Obama administration have the potential to escalate and could interact with intermestic issues and with other international irritants to damage Washington's more general international diplomacy. Given the severity of the security challenges that Obama now faces in the Middle East and elsewhere, and the still fragile state of the international economy, it could prove very costly for Washington to allow unnecessary frictions in the Western Hemisphere to spiral out of control.

This is not to underplay the positive tendencies discussed by Abe Lowenthal in chapter 1, but to sound a note of concern about the risks confronting the Obama administration in the subcontinent as the cumulative adverse momentum of the past years works through the system. The underlying assumption is that it is in almost everyone's interest (that of the United States and Latin America, even Havana, La Paz, and Caracas) for these risks to be managed prudently. The conditions still exist for intelligent multilateral cooperation to maximize areas of common interest. But to reinforce this potential will require a coherent overarching policy framework and more sustained attention than has been in evidence so far.

Compared with other regions of the world, even Washington's most awkward Latin American neighbors are not, in essence, that intractable. (The European Union has neighbors such as Algeria, Serbia, and Belarus to contend with; China has to live with North Korea and Burma; India abuts Pakistan.) Those who assume that U.S. preferences will ultimately prevail if there is ideological polarization must consider the risk that, on the contrary, in the current climate escalation may rally regional opinion against Washington.

A small straw in the wind was the February 2010 summit in Cancún hosted by the Mexican government. Participants agreed to broaden the Rio Group to thirty-one members but excluded the United States and Canada. So long as the Obama administration works effectively with the Mexican government on bilateral issues and the OAS retains a sufficiently broad base of support in the region (which would mean it could not serve as a mere transmission belt for made-in-Washington priorities), the Cancún initiative may not have much impact. But its existence does underscore the fact that many U.S. allies in the hemisphere share President Lula da Silva's resistance to any variant of Pan-Americanism that seems like a one-sided "coalition of the willing" to serve an essentially unilateral U.S. agenda (even if some also bridle at Brazil's hegemonic ambitions). From a Mexican viewpoint, for instance, such an initiative might serve to avert the danger of being left behind as the rest of Latin America builds regional institutions outside the North American Free Trade Agreement (NAFTA). But it could also reflect some degree of estrangement between the United States and even its closest neighbor. While there is scant likelihood of the ALBA minority taking over such a grouping, it could serve as a sounding board for hostility to the United States. A policy that emphasizes cooperation and shared interests over divergences will produce much more positive results and weaken unnecessarily divisive and provocative alternatives.

The sterile results of hegemonic presumption are apparent in the tensions between Brazil and the United States over Iran. Since Brazil currently holds a seat on the UN Security Council (where the United States favors imposing tighter sanctions on Iran), this divergence is of geopolitical significance. When Iranian President Mahmoud Ahmedinejad was invited to visit Bolivia, Brazil, and Venezuela, Secretary of State Clinton warned South America to "consider the consequences" of deepening regional ties with Iran. Before her arrival on an official visit to Brazil on March 7, 2010, President Lula countered by stating that he was going to visit Iran and did not have to account for his actions to anybody: "Each country exercises democracy as it sees fit. The U.S. does so in its way and not everybody agrees with how their government behaves."[7] This is less a statement of ideological divergence and more about the need for equal respect among the United States and its allies.

There is a risk of escalating provocative rhetoric—Brazilian foreign minister Celso Amorim even compared the Clinton campaign against Iran with pre–Iraq war reports about Iraq's alleged "weapons of mass destruction"— but the administration would be wise to ignore such barbs. Indeed, a better response would be to highlight the fact that under the Treaty of Tlatelolco, Latin America has established a large nuclear-free zone, an achievement to be celebrated given that it required cooperation and leadership from many politically disparate countries. This shows how the region can work together to set an example of good practice to the rest of the world, one that should also chime in with Obama's broader foreign policy agenda.

In the event, Assistant Secretary of State Arturo Valenzuela gave congressional testimony following the remarks of President Lula in which he declared that the U.S. administration intended to be "clear-eyed and proactive" in countering attempts to expand authoritarian or populist rule in the Americas, and by listing the countries whose democratic practices merited

U.S. approval. That list excluded not only Nicaragua and Venezuela but also Bolivia and Ecuador. But this risks inappropriately bracketing diverse cases, some of which may merit severe criticism on democratic grounds, while others arguably perform no worse than some of Washington's favorites. Given Washington's past record of one-sidedness, the Obama administration's lists of the virtuous should be kept to a minimum and based on robust independent criteria: to act otherwise only serves to strengthen "anti-American" populism. On some "red-line issues," the United States is bound to remain unbending whatever its partners think, but, as this chapter has shown, beyond that, at least over the short run, Obama's Washington has too often preferred to take sides in a divided region, rather than to seek reconciliation there.

Not all risks to Washington's standing in the region come from the left, of course. The Honduran episode provided a small illustration of what could happen if larger republics strongly subject to conservative influences (such as Colombia or Peru) become politically divided. The challenges arising from organized crime, drug trafficking, money laundering, and arms trading could also become more acute. Blocking the Mexican access route to the U.S. market is not necessarily a solution, especially if it generates more instability in the Caribbean. There is also a range of other unpredictably contentious issues—the Deepwater Horizon disaster in the Gulf of Mexico, for example, illustrates how the best-laid plans can go unexpectedly awry.

So there are risks in the Americas, and the Obama administration cannot afford to neglect them. But the United States retains a considerable amount of "soft" power in Latin America, and the tradition with regional problem solving and consensus building is strong. If Washington intends to deploy its "smart" power to improve its currently damaged international position, the Western Hemisphere is one place that favors Obama's thoughtful and nuanced "smartness."

There is an obvious coda to this concluding observation, however. Many of the foreign policy challenges reviewed in this chapter, and in this book, concern issues that also impinge on U.S. domestic politics. Often, therefore, an administration's freedom of action is sharply constrained by the inclinations of the U.S. Congress, a body that is in turn often constrained by powerful lobbying interests, the media, and the U.S. electorate. A deep inertia is also built into the policy stances of many government agencies that will continue their understanding of "business as usual" unless actively redirected by their political masters.

But in a democratic Western Hemisphere, it is not sufficient for the U.S. administration to plead inability to act owing to domestic political constraints. These exist in the other republics as well and can cause patience with one-sided U.S. positions to run thin. So if Washington were to prove neither smart nor soft in the region, existing risks in this friendly neighborhood could exact a high price, distracting the United States from more urgent dangers elsewhere and casting doubt over the administration's overall foreign policy competence. If it cannot improve on the legacy it inherited in the Americas, its prospects of making headway in other more difficult arenas may be cast into serious doubt.

Latin America provides the United States with a relatively democratic and amicable regional environment. At the same time, responsible governments there also need to consider the risks that a U.S. setback could pose to their national interests. Even if the Obama team has to focus on priorities elsewhere, and may sometimes lapse into thoughtless hegemonism, it remains a considerably more promising hemispheric partner than the administration that preceded it and could also prove much better than what could come later. So all concerned have a strong interest in avoiding too many unnecessary missed opportunities for regional cooperation. Even a community of good neighbors can fall out if they fail to attend to each other.

Notes

1. The Foreign Assistance Act of 1961 stipulates that it is the State Department, not the Pentagon, that sets policy and makes decisions governing military assistance programs, and establishes a variety of democracy and human rights conditions to foreign assistance.

2. The International Institute for Strategic Studies "Military Balance 2010" report warns against military instability in South America, although it does not endorse the view that a cumulative "arms race" is yet under way. In 2008 Colombia's military manpower totaled 310,567, the second largest in Latin America, behind Brazil with 334,743. Venezuela was fourth—after Mexico—with 163,364, far behind its U.S.-backed neighbor, while little Ecuador had only 37,448 military. *A Comparative Atlas of Defence in Latin America* (Buenos Aires: RESDAL, 2008), p. 98.

3. As quoted by Michael Shifter, "Obama and Latin America: New Beginnings, Old Frictions," *Current History*, February 2010, p. 69.

4. Washington policymakers may have forgotten the coup of October 2, 1963, but Honduran elites surely remembered it when they ousted President Zelaya on June 28, 2009. In 1963, with a presidential election due later that month, the Honduran military ignored warnings from the U.S. embassy and military command in Panama and bundled the democratically elected President Villeda Morales into exile in Costa Rica. Although U.S. ambassador Arthur W. Burrows warned that "President

Kennedy would suspend economic aid if the revolt took place . . . his conservative opponents answered Burrows's threats by arguing that any aid cut-off by Washington would be momentary and that Burrows and company would be back in six months." Dario A. Euraque, *Reinterpreting the Banana Republic: Region and State in Honduras, 1870–1972* (University of North Carolina Press, 1996), p. 113. In the event, this Honduran coup signaled the end of Alliance for Progress–inspired resistance to military interventions.

5. Abraham Lowenthal, "The United States and Latin America: Ending the Hegemonic Presumption," *Foreign Affairs*, October 1976.

6. As I tried to demonstrate in "Navigating in a Fog: Metanarrative in the Americas Today," in *Which Way Latin America? Hemispheric Politics Meets Globalization*, edited by Andrew F. Cooper and Jorge Heine (United Nations University Press, 2009), chap. 1.

7. As quoted in the *Financial Times* (London), March 10, 2010.

Contributors

Kevin Casas-Zamora is a senior fellow at the Brookings Institution.

João Augusto de Castro Neves is a doctoral candidate at the University of São Paulo and founding partner of the CAC Political Consulting Group in Brazil.

Daniel P. Erikson was senior associate for U.S. policy and director of Caribbean programs at the Inter-American Dialogue and is now senior adviser to the assistant secretary of state for Western Hemisphere affairs, U.S. Department of State.

Carlos Heredia is chairman and professor, Department of International Studies, Center for Research and Teaching in Economics (CIDE).

Abraham F. Lowenthal is professor of international relations at the University of Southern California, president emeritus at the Pacific Council on International Policy, and a nonresident senior fellow at the Brookings Institution.

Jennifer McCoy is professor of political science at Georgia State University and director of the Americas program at the Carter Center.

GEORGE GRAY MOLINA is director of the Instituto Alternativo.

THEODORE J. PICCONE is senior fellow and deputy director of foreign policy studies at the Brookings Institution.

ANDRÉS ROZENTAL is a nonresident senior fellow at the Brookings Institution and was founding president of the Consejo Mexicano de Asuntos Internacionales (COMEXI).

MICHAEL SHIFTER is president of the Inter-American Dialogue.

MATIAS SPEKTOR is director of the Center for International Relations at Fundação Getulio Vargas.

JUAN GABRIEL VALDÉS, former minister of foreign affairs of Chile, served as special representative of the United Nations secretary general and head of the Stabilization Mission in Haiti (2003–06).

LAURENCE WHITEHEAD is an official fellow in politics at Nuffield College, University of Oxford, and editor of the Oxford University Press book series Oxford Studies in Democratisation.

Index